SUMMITS & ICEFIELDS 2

Dave Dornian enjoys a great run on McGill Shoulder, near Rogers Pass. Photo Chic Scott

SUMMITS & ICEFIELDS 2

ALPINE SKI TOURS IN THE COLUMBIA MOUNTAINS

CHIC SCOTT & MARK KLASSEN

RMB

Victoria Vancouver Calgary

Gord Rathbone at Bruin's Pass looking toward
Mount Sir Donald. Photo Chic Scott

I know no form of sport which so evenly develops the muscles, which renders the body so strong and elastic, which teaches so well the qualities of dexterity and resource, which in an equal degree calls for decision and resolution, and which gives the same vigour and exhilaration to mind and body alike. Where can one find a healthier and purer delight than when on a brilliant winter day one binds one's 'ski' to one's feet and takes one's way out into the forest? Can there be anything more beautiful than the northern winter landscape, when the snow lies foot-deep, spread as a soft white mantle over field and wood and hill? Where will one find more freedom and excitement than when one glides swiftly down the hillside through the trees, one's cheek brushed by the sharp cold air and frosted pine branches, and one's eye, brain and muscles alert and prepared to meet every unknown obstacle and danger which the next instant may throw in one's path? Civilization is, as it were, washed clean from the mind and left far behind with the city atmosphere and city life; one's whole being is, so to say, wrapped in one's 'ski' and the surrounding nature. There is something in the whole which develops soul and not body alone ...

— Fridtjof Nansen,
from *The First Crossing of Greenland* (1890)

Rocky Mountain Books
www.rmbooks.com

Library and Archives Canada Cataloguing in Publication

Scott, Chic, 1945-
        Summits & icefields 2 : Alpine ski tours in the Columbia Mountains / Chic Scott & Mark Klassen. — 2nd ed.
Previous edition published under title: Summits & icefields : Alpine ski tours in the Rocky and Columbia Mountains of Canada.

Includes bibliographical references and index.
Issued also in electronic formats.
ISBN 978-1-927330-34-0

        1. Downhill skiing—Columbia Mountains (B.C.)—Guidebooks. 2. Columbia Mountains (B.C.)—Guidebooks. I. Klassen, Mark II. Scott, Chic, 1945- . Summits & icefields. III. Title. IV. Title: Summits and icefields two. V. Title: Summits and icefields 2.
GV854.8.C38376 2012   796.93'5097116   C2012-903858-X

Front cover photo: Dustin Eagleston skis the bench below Ymir Peak in the backcountry at Whitewater Ski Resort near Nelson, BC. Photo Kari Medig.
Back cover photo: Starry skies above the Mark Kingsbury Hut in International Basin. Photo Ryan Bavin.

Printed in Canada

Rocky Mountain Books acknowledges the financial support for its publishing program from the Government of Canada through the Canada Book Fund (CBF) and the Canada Council for the Arts, and from the province of British Columbia through the British Columbia Arts Council and the Book Publishing Tax Credit.

This book was produced using FSC®-certified, acid-free paper, processed chlorine free and printed with vegetable-based inks.

Disclaimer
The actions described in this book may be considered inherently dangerous activities. Individuals undertake these activities at their own risk. The information put forth in this guide has been collected from a variety of sources and is not guaranteed to be completely accurate or reliable. Many conditions and some information may change owing to weather and numerous other factors beyond the control of the authors and publishers. Individual climbers and/or hikers must determine the risks, use their own judgment and take full responsibility for their actions. Do not depend on any information found in this book for your own personal safety. Your safety depends on your own good judgment based on your skills, education and experience.

        It is up to the users of this guidebook to acquire the necessary skills for safe experiences and to exercise caution in potentially hazardous areas. The authors and publishers of this guide accept no responsibility for your actions or the results that occur from another's actions, choices or judgments. If you have any doubt as to your safety or your ability to attempt anything described in this guidebook, do not attempt it.

CONTENTS

High above the clouds at Rogers Pass. Photo Roger Laurilla.

PREFACE TO THE THIRD EDITION

This is the third edition of *Summits and Icefields*. For almost twenty years this guidebook has been helping ski mountaineers find some of the best backcountry skiing on the planet. Now, in this enlarged edition, there are even more destinations to choose from.

I would like to thank Mark Klassen, who has played a major part in creating this book, in particular the introductory chapters, the Bugaboos to Rogers Pass Traverse and the section on Rogers Pass. I would also like to thank Will Meinen, who created new maps for this edition. Together the three of us have tried to produce the most up-to-date book possible. I would also like to thank my publisher, Don Gorman, who suggested that we do this edition in colour throughout. This is a wonderful improvement on earlier editions.

The Rocky and Columbia Mountains of western Canada offer, in my opinion, the best backcountry skiing in the world. The combination of large expanses of wilderness and the availability of all the conveniences of the modern world creates a unique experience. We hope that this book helps you to safely enjoy these mountains and that you will return often to our alpine paradise.

—Chic Scott

"In the last resort, it is the beauty of the mountain world in the inmost recesses that holds us spellbound, slaves till life ends."

—*W.H. Murray*

ACKNOWLEDGEMENTS

The authors would like to thank all those who have helped create this new edition of *Summits and Icefields*, in particular Marg Saul, Sandra McGuinness, Ryan Bavin, Robin Tivy, Conor Hurley, Jim Firstbrook, Greg Hill, Stan Wagon, Doug Sproule, The Friends of Mount Revelstoke and Glacier National Parks, Canadian Mountain Holidays, Neills Kristensen, Howard Coneybear, Jacolyn Daniluck, Grant Statham, Aaron Beardmore, Jeff Volp, Jeff Hammerich, Ilya Storm, Karl Klassen, Grant Carnie, Sylvia Forest, Scott Davis, Peter Macpherson, Todd Anthony-Malone, Wayne Sobool, Marc Piché, Conrad Janzen and Chris Gooliaff.

A big thank you to all the staff at the Banff Public Library for providing such a warm and comfortable work space.

We would also like to thank those who have allowed us to use their fabulous images in the book. And we cannot forget the dozens of individuals who contributed to earlier editions of *Summits and Icefields*. Your excellent information and many of your photographs are still included in this new edition.

Major thanks is due to the folks at Rocky Mountain Books who put this beautiful guidebook together – Don Gorman, Joe Wilderson and Chyla Cardinal. It's great to work with professionals.

And finally we must give a special thank you to Will Meinen, who created the new maps in this book. He certainly went the extra mile for this project. If you have any need of Will's expertise, he can be reached at wmcartography@gmail.com.

INTRODUCTION TO THE COLUMBIA MOUNTAINS

The Columbia Mountains offer great opportunity for ski adventure of all kinds. You can spend a few hours making turns on a slope not far from your car or you can head off on one of the Grand Traverses for a two-week wilderness expedition. And there is everything in between – marvellous powder descents, cozy mountain lodges, huts under starlit skies, sun-drenched glaciers and shimmering icefields.

For those of you unfamiliar with this part of the world, you should realize that the distinctive characteristic of the tours described in this book is that they are "wild." This country is wilderness and there is little in the way of man-made amenities. In these mountains you are on your own, so self-reliance is required. You must be prepared to deal with all eventualities yourself. The plus side to this, however, is that you often have the ski descent or perhaps even the mountain range to yourself.

This easy access to wilderness, which can be as little as 100 metres from your doorway, is uniquely combined in Western Canada with ready availability of modern facilities as well, such as hospitals, communication, banking, hotels, restaurants and transportation.

In this book we have collected information on some of the best and most popular tours in the Columbia Mountains. There are, however, many tours and descents that have not been included, as we have chosen only the classics. There should be enough choice to keep you busy for many years. In addition, this area is still being explored and fine new tours are being discovered every winter.

Remember also that this book covers a huge territory. The two volumes of *Summits and Icefields* cover an area larger than the entire European Alps. Consequently this guidebook does not go into as much detail as guides to smaller areas do. All the information needed to open the door is presented here, but to walk through the door you have to be prepared to do some further research on your own.

To venture into these mountains in winter requires a solid background of mountain skills and a considerable depth of experience. If you are new at the game, don't be afraid to take some time to learn the skills. Pay your dues on the less demanding tours before venturing out on the more serious ones. It is also advisable to invest some time and money in a few courses. Finally, there are many good clubs in western Canada where you can meet people of like mind and have the opportunity to share a trip or two with a seasoned veteran.

"But if adventure has a final and all-embracing motive it is surely this: we go out because it is in our nature to go out, to climb the mountains and sail the seas, to fly to the planets and plunge into the depths of the oceans. By doing these things we make touch with something outside or behind, which strangely seems to approve our doing them. We extend our horizon, we expand our being, we revel in a mastery of ourselves which gives an impression, mainly illusory, that we are masters of our world. In a word, we are men, and when man ceases to do these things he is no longer man."

—*Wilfred Noyce*

ALPINE SKI TOURING IN THE COLUMBIA MOUNTAINS by Mark Klassen

This section is meant to help readers understand the unique nature of ski touring in the Columbia Mountains and what resources are available to help them plan their trips. It is assumed that users of this book have previous training and experience in ski touring and ski mountaineering.

A list of resources and contact information can be found beginning on page 338.

HAZARDS

Hazards that may be new to skiers coming from other regions include the following:

Persistent weak layers in the snowpack These are unstable layers that continue to produce avalanches for days, weeks or months after they are buried. In the Columbia Mountains these PWLs are usually made up of surface hoar. In some years a crust and facet combination buried near the ground also causes issues that may last the entire season. When PWLs are in play within the snowpack, skiers in the Columbias must employ more conservative terrain selection than may be required at other times or in other snowpack climates. For many tours, patience is often required to wait for the right conditions or time of year.

Variable snow depths and layer distribution Wind may transport the region's low-density snow and cause windslabs days after a storm, resulting in highly variable avalanche hazard. Care must be taken when moving from one type of terrain to another.

Extreme cold Although temperatures are generally milder than those found farther east in the Rockies, temperatures in the -20° Celsius range are not uncommon. Equipment and clothing strategies must reflect the possibility of encountering very cold temperatures.

Weak crevasse bridges The glaciers in the region are active, and extensively crevassed areas are common. This, combined with a relatively low-density snowpack, means crevasse bridges may be both somewhat weak and hard to distinguish. Carrying and using a rope on the glaciers is common practice here.

Tree wells The low-hanging branches of small and medium-sized coniferous trees may prevent snow from packing in around the trunk of the tree, causing a deep, hidden hole to form. Falling headfirst into one of these holes can be as dangerous as getting buried in an avalanche. Fatal tree-well accidents occur almost every year in the Columbia Mountains. In the trees, ski in control and with a partner.

Short days On the winter solstice at Rogers Pass (about halfway between Nelson and Valemount), the sun rises at 7:53 a.m. and sets at 3:45 p.m. (Pacific Standard Time). On the spring equinox, daylight hours are significantly longer, with sunrise at 5:53 a.m. and sunset at 6:03 p.m. At this latitude, twilight begins and ends about half an hour either side of sunrise and sunset.

Remoteness Although more and more skiers are seen in the backcountry of the Columbias, it is not uncommon to have a tour to yourself where you will not see another party. On some of the multi-day trips you may not see anyone else for days at a time. Ski touring parties should be prepared to take care of themselves if any issues arise, as outside rescue resources can take some time to get to you, especially in bad weather. Carrying a communications device such as a satellite phone or personal locator beacon is recommended.

WHEN TO GO

The ski season in the Columbia Mountains can be long. Dedicated skiers often get their first turns in early November and continue skiing well into May. Some of the icefield tours and ski mountaineering ascents may be done into June if valley bottom travel is not required.

In most years there will be some good skiing available in most zones by late November and the season is normally in full swing by early to mid-December. Higher elevations with a smooth ground surface may have the earliest opportunities for skiing. Lower-elevation alder thickets can be difficult to travel through in many areas before Christmas.

January and February are the best powder skiing months. There is usually widespread good snow coverage by this time and temperatures remain cold, resulting in the blower pow that BC is famous for. The skiing continues to be outstanding through March, although suncrusts can be expected on solar aspects as the season progresses.

For many local skiers the spring is their favourite time to ski. By late March more serious tours may become practical because of longer days and better coverage on the glaciers. A significant warming event usually takes place sometime in mid- to late April, resulting in easier travel and a more stable snowpack. Often there will be a variety of ski options available in late April and early May, with corn snow on the solar aspects and powder on the north-facing slopes. This may be the time to do that committing traverse or ski mountaineering ascent you've had on your list all winter. Late-season touring in the Columbias is exceptional.

In seasons when PWLs are active, late February and March can be the trickiest times of the season. Layers that formed earlier in the winter often become the most reactive at this time, when they have a critical load of snow on them.

Every ski season is different and there are always exceptions to these broad rules. It is important for readers to practise proper pre-trip planning and investigation to find out where the safest and best skiing is at any given time.

GEOGRAPHY

The geography and toponymy of the Columbia Mountains are complicated. The region is actually a group of four separate mountain ranges: the Purcells, Selkirks, Monashees and Cariboos. These ranges are bounded by the Rocky Mountain Trench to the east, the Fraser River to the north, the edge of the Interior Plateau to the west and the US border to the south.

The Purcells lie in the southeast corner of the region, with the Rocky

Mountain Trench (upper Columbia and Kootenay rivers) to the east. The Duncan and Beaver rivers separate the Purcells from the Selkirks to the west and north.

The Selkirks are in the centre of the range, with the Purcells to the east, the lower Columbia River to the west and the Monashees on the west side of the Columbia. The Selkirks' northernmost reaches are surrounded by the Big Bend of the Columbia River.

The Monashees are west of the Selkirks and south of the Cariboos. The Interior Plateau lies to the southwest and the Columbia River to the east. The boundary to the northeast is Kinbasket Lake, and to the northwest it is Highway 5 between Kamloops and Valemount.

The Cariboos are the northernmost range and the only part of the Columbias that do not extend to the US border. They are bounded to the north by the Fraser River, to the east by Highway 5, and on the west and south by the Interior Plateau.

The Kootenays are also often referred to as a distinct range but are more correctly defined as a region within the Columbias, as they incorporate parts of the southern Purcells, Selkirks and Monashees. For this book, the Kootenays are roughly defined as being encompassed on the north by Highway 31 between Galena Bay and Meadow Creek; to the west by the Arrow Lakes and Christina Lake; to the east by Highway 93 south of Canal Flats; and to the south by the US border. Nelson is the focal point for this zone.

This complexity of geography leads to a complexity of weather, snow and avalanche conditions. The region is huge (about 136,000 km²) and has incredibly diverse snow conditions. It is important for skiers to understand where they are within the bigger picture of the Columbia Mountains and which Public Avalanche Bulletins to refer to so they can properly assess what hazards they will encounter on their chosen tour.

WEATHER

The Columbia Mountains lie in a snowpack climate region that is transitional between maritime and continental. Large, sustained storms with mild temperatures, moderate to strong winds and significant amounts of snow are a regular event. However, long spells of clear, dry weather are also to be expected every winter. These are often accompanied by cold temperatures, but rarely last more than two weeks.

The general flow of weather throughout western Canada comes from the west, resulting in westerly winds at ridgetops. In the Columbias this westerly flow brings consistent snowfalls throughout the winter. Western areas of the Cariboos and Monashees receive significantly more snow than areas farther east, with this east–west variation being most pronounced in the central part of the region. Farther south in the Kootenays, the Monashees are lower and do not block precipitation as much, so the southern Selkirks and southern Purcells receive more snowfall than the northern end of those ranges.

The driest ski zones in the Columbias lie in the Purcells and northeastern Cariboos. In the Purcells, the northern end, around Golden, and the east-central section in areas such as McMurdo and International Basin see significantly less snow. This is where both the Monashees and the Selkirks to the west steal much of the precipitation before it has a chance to fall in the Purcells. In the Cariboos, the area just west and northwest of Valemount sees a similar "snow-shadow" effect.

Which areas get the most snow in any given storm depends on the directional variation of the westerly flow. If it is coming from the southwest, then the entire Kootenay region, the central Monashees and central Selkirks often get the most accumulation. If it is coming from the northwest, then the Cariboos and the northern Monashees may receive more snow. A flow straight out of the west may cause a more even distribution of snowfall through the region, with west-facing parts of all the ranges getting larger amounts.

High-pressure systems also affect the Columbias. These may come from the south, causing relatively warm temperatures, or from the northeast (arctic), causing colder temperatures. These systems, especially the arctic variety, are often directly linked to the formation of weak snow (surface hoar and facets) on the snow surface that may eventually be buried, becoming persistent weak layers.

Typical variable mountain weather in the Columbias: a
calm, −15°C March evening with alpenglow highlighting
tracks on the Sunset run at Valkyr Lodge ...

... and a photo taken from the same spot, looking in the other direction.
A stormy February afternoon: −2°C, a rising west wind and a snowfall
rate of over 10 cm accumulation per hour. Photos Mark Klassen

A moist westerly flow contacting an arctic front is also a recipe for good snowfalls. This type of weather may cause the biggest storms of the season, especially in the drier zones of the Purcells and Cariboos.

Temperatures at treeline elevations are fairly mild, averaging perhaps between −8 and −10°c during the day in mid-winter. Colder events with temperatures in the −20s occur a few times each season and extreme events of −30°c or colder may happen once or twice a winter. The northern and eastern Purcells and the Cariboos generally have the coldest average temperatures; the Kootenays usually have the warmest. Above-freezing temperatures may happen at any time but begin to regularly occur in late March in many areas.

SNOWPACK

Mid-winter snow depths at treeline vary widely. In many ski zones the average is usually between 2 and 3 metres. Below treeline, depths can be significantly less than that. In sheltered alpine areas, 4 metres or more may be expected. The northern and eastern Purcells, and the northeastern corner of the Cariboos, often have a snowpack that is 30 per cent less than these averages.

Typical mid-winter snowpack layering consists of low-density surface snow overlying stronger mid- and base layers. Within that stronger snow, thin and hard-to-detect unstable surface hoar layers are often present and may persist for long periods. During some years a melt–freeze crust forms near the ground in the late autumn. The crust often has facets above or below it and it weakens after it gets buried. This can create a problematic pwl that lasts right to the end of the ski season.

An exception to the snowpack described above exists in the drier areas of the Purcells and Cariboos. In those places a faceted layer near the ground will persist for the season in most years. The snowpack in these areas is somewhat similar to the Rocky Mountains, only with more of a load atop the weak base.

The low-density surface of the snowpack is heavily modified by the wind. It is not unusual to see open windward areas scoured down to a significantly thinner snowpack than that found a short distance away on lee slopes. The wind effect causes significant variability in snowpack layering and loads on weak layers.

The wind effect means windslabs and cornices on lee slopes are often a major avalanche problem. These windslabs may load on top of weak snow, including facets or surface hoar that formed on the top of the snowpack during a clear spell. As a result, windslab instability may persist for longer in the Columbias than it might in other snowpack climates.

The surface hoar layers and deep facet–crust combination often found in the Columbias (and the basal facets in the drier regions) are typical of any other PWL. They are quicker to form than they are to disappear; they are usually widespread in their distribution; they may be sensitive to subtle changes in weather and load; and, even for professional avalanche forecasters, it is surprisingly difficult to predict how they will react on any particular slope at any particular time.

Persistent weak layers will sometimes cause concern for skiers from the beginning of the season to the end on nearly all slopes. In other years there are significantly fewer PWL issues. It is imperative for backcountry skiers to understand when PWLs are in play and to track them through their own investigations as well as through the Public Avalanche Bulletins available through the Canadian Avalanche Centre. During periods of persistent instabilities, a distinctly conservative and patient attitude in terms of terrain selection needs to be exercised to tour in the Columbias.

During times when PWLs are not an issue, instabilities will usually be in near-surface layers associated with storm events. These types of storm snow weaknesses often stabilize relatively quickly after the snow and wind stop.

A spring melt–freeze cycle creates firm surface crusts on sunny aspects every year, usually in mid- to late April. These warm temperatures often also cause a more stable snowpack on north slopes. This creates a decision-making environment where it is far easier to determine when and where the snowpack will be unstable. Early morning starts to take advantage of cooler temperatures and stronger crusts are recommended at this time of year. Widespread corn snow on all aspects and elevations is usually not found until May.

AVALANCHE ACTIVITY

Avalanche cycles are a regular occurrence in the Columbias throughout the ski season. Most of the time they are direct-action events associated with storms. When it is snowing and blowing, avalanches can be assumed to be occurring. The more intense the weather, the larger and more widespread the avalanches will be. Maximum-event avalanches running from the alpine to the valley bottom may be expected during any large storm throughout the winter. The skiing can still be good, but during storms it is time to stick to lower-angled skiing in dense trees, staying away from runout zones.

Often, several days will be needed for these instabilities to settle before more aggressive terrain may be safely skied, especially at alpine elevations. Cornices and lingering windslabs are often the main concern after a storm event.

Avalanche activity associated with PWLS is harder to predict. They are often triggered during storms, but outside of these periods even subtle changes in terrain and/or weather may be what cause a large avalanche to occur. PWL avalanches are frequently isolated; often a light load such as a skier or a minor wind event is the trigger, and the reason why they occur is not well understood, even by professional avalanche forecasters. The longer a PWL is buried, the more difficult it is to trigger an avalanche on it, resulting in progressively less avalanche activity associated with the layer. However, as the layers become more deeply buried avalanche size tends to increase (size 3 and 4 are common). The consequences, if a rider is caught, increase. It is doubtful that one of these avalanches would be survivable.

The last big avalanche cycle of the ski season usually happens during a thaw instability in late April. Large slab and loose-snow avalanches can be expected, especially during the first period where temperatures remain above freezing overnight.

AVALANCHE DANGER RATINGS

Public avalanche bulletins throughout the area use the North American Public Avalanche Danger Scale, which is consistent with the five-level international danger scale used in alpine nations worldwide. Avalanche Danger Scale definitions can be found in the graphic that begins on page 338.

PUBLIC AVALANCHE BULLETINS

Public Avalanche Bulletins (PABS) are available at the Canadian Avalanche Centre website, www.avalanche.ca. The Columbias are divided into several different PAB regions. Users are encouraged not only to consult the bulletin that relates to the zone they are skiing in, but also to refer to neighbouring bulletins to get a big-picture idea of snowpack and avalanche hazard.

The Glacier National Park bulletin is available on the CAC website as well as at the Discovery Centre at Rogers Pass. Ski hills may post avalanche bulletins that relate to the terrain immediately adjacent to their area.

TERRAIN

The Columbias have extensive glaciation at upper elevations, dense forests in the valleys and every type of mountain landform in between.

In the areas covered in this book there are numerous peaks higher than 3000 m. In general most peaks are too rocky or steep to skin right up to the summit although there are notable exceptions, such as Youngs Peak in Rogers Pass.

There are scores of large icefields and glaciers. Most of these occur north of the Kootenays; in that region there is still glaciation but to a lesser extent. Average elevation of ice features is about 2600 m, with many of the highest peaks being glaciated right to the summit. Large glaciers draining the icefields may push down to 2000 m or lower, but the average glacier toe is in the 2300 m range.

Glaciers are fairly active and crevassed. A relatively low-density snowpack means that crevasse bridges may be weaker than those found in other ranges, such as on the Coast. Skiers in the Columbias may use a glacier rope more often than they would elsewhere, especially in the early season. Using the rope on ascent to investigate crevasse issues for a descent may be worthwhile.

Treeline is found between 1950 m and 2300 m. Generally, the shallower the average snowpack and/or the farther south one is, the higher treeline will be.

The Columbias are host to one of the few inland temperate rainforests in the world, and perhaps the best tree skiing on the planet is found here. Good runs can be found in glades and open forest at treeline elevations, but the real British Columbia tree skiing experience is found in isolated stands of old-growth forest. It is a remarkable experience to float down a deep powder run amongst the huge, perfectly spaced cedars, hemlocks and firs. These stands are found at lower elevations, often around 1500 m.

In the Kootenays and southern Monashees, lower elevations and older first-order glaciation have created a landscape heavily modified by erosional forces. This causes the terrain to be convoluted, and route finding may be difficult. For skiers unfamiliar with this region it can be tricky to find continuous ski lines, especially in the trees. It is also easy to become disoriented. I must admit that more than once in a Kootenay forest, even when skiing fall line, I have ended up a long ways from where I wanted to be because I followed a small, unobvious drainage that cut across the grain of the mountain!

The rest of the range has more classic alpine topography of broad icefields, glacier-filled bowls, moraines and well-defined incised drainages and valleys. The terrain is larger with longer, uninterrupted fall lines.

The geology of the Columbia Mountains is as complex as its geography. There are granitic intrusions, multiple accretion zones and areas of intensive metamorphism and deformed sedimentary rock. Extensive glaciation past and present adds to the complicated geomorphology and terrain features. Many variations in geology will be encountered in the Columbias, but skiers only need concern themselves with two broad rock types: intrusive and stratified.

Areas with intrusive rock, typically granitic plutons and associated metamorphics, include the Bugaboos and Olive Hut area in the Purcells; Fairy Meadows (Adamants) in the northern Selkirks; the Albert and Battle groups in the central Selkirks; much of the southern Selkirks in the Kootenay region; and a good part of the Monashee Range along its highest crest. These groups often have steep-walled granite summits with glaciers cascading down their flanks; expansive, smooth slabs of rock directly below retreating glacier tongues; and steep talus slopes and associated moraines made up of large blocks.

All other zones are generally made up of layered meta-sedimentary rocks such as limestone and quartzite, which are also heavily glaciated. In these areas intensive faulting and glacial erosion have generally caused north and east aspects to be steeper, with ledges and benches that develop along with prominent cliffs. While on these aspects, skiers must often work their way through the steeper terrain by utilizing gullies and discontinuous ramps. Since they are of a lower angle and often uncluttered by cliffs, travel on the south and west aspects may be easier. This mountain architecture also promotes more diverse wind effect, with the southwest aspects being stripped and the northeast slopes getting loaded. Greater snowpack and avalanche hazard variability is the result.

TERRAIN RATINGS

In this book, terrain is rated according to the Avalanche Terrain Exposure Scale (ATES). This scale was formulated by Parks Canada and is in wide use throughout the Canadian mountains.

Most of the trips in this book are rated as "Challenging" or "Complex." The main difference between the Challenging and Complex ratings is that in the former the terrain will contain more route-finding options that may reduce risk.

ATES ratings are defined on page 340.

MAPPING RESOURCES

Maps commonly used in the Columbia Mountains come from several sources. For a list of where to obtain maps see the Resources section at page 343.

National Topographic System (NTS)

Scale 1:250,000 (200 m contours); 1:50,000 (40 m contours)
Map Datum NAD 83 (NAD 27 for older maps in feet)

Produced by the Government of Canada, these maps have been the standard in the past and cover all the tours in this book. The 1:50,000 series used to have 100 ft. contours but as they were switched to metric the interval went to 40 m, a 30 per cent loss of definition. Some of these maps actually have 20 m contours for lower elevations and 40 m contours at upper elevations, which can be confusing. Those of us with the old 100 ft. maps guard them zealously!

NTS maps are available at park information centres and some of the gear shops. Mountain Equipment Co-op (Calgary and Vancouver), MapTown (Calgary) and International Travel Maps & Books (Vancouver) have the largest selection. Digital versions are available as a set on a CD.

Free downloads are also available from the Mapping Services Branch of Natural Resources Canada. The downloads are large files and do not have a UTM grid on them.

The Adventure Map

Scale 1:50,000 (25 m contours)
Map Datum NAD 83

There is only one map from this company that is relevant for this book. Their Rogers Pass map is the best resource of its kind for that area.

Summit Series

Scale 1:25,000 (20 m contours)
Map Datum NAD 83

The Summit Series Bugaboos map is the best map for that area.

CanadaMapStore.com

Scale 1:20,000 (20 m contours)
Map Datum NAD 83

These are probably the most detailed commercially available maps, based on the Terrain Resource Information Management (TRIM) data provided by the BC government. They are more expensive, however, and do not come on waterproof paper.

These maps are only available online from CanadaMapStore.com.

Selkirk College – Selkirk Geospatial Research Centre

Scale Various
Map Datum NAD 83

The SGRC has all the BC TRIM data needed to easily create your own maps of various scales and print them for free. A variety of overlays are available, such as contour lines laid atop aerial photographs. Unfortunately, the grid on the printed maps is latitude/longitude rather than UTM. There is a tutorial available on the site.

The BC government has a similar site called iMap BC. Mac users will need their Windows emulator at iMap BC.

Google Earth

Scale various
Map Datum WGS 84

Google Earth has good imagery for most trips described in this book.

Backroad Mapbooks

Scale various
Map Datum NAD 83

These books are a good resource for finding your way along the logging roads. The "Thompson Okanagan" and "Kootenay Rockies" books cover the Columbia Mountains.

GRID REFERENCES AND MAP DATUMS

The grid references used in this book are Universal Transverse Mercator (UTM) coordinates based on the NAD 83 map datum. UTM has been used in this edition, as that grid is common to most of the mapping resources outlined above. The UTM coordinates given in this book are estimates and accurate only to 100 m. Users must double check all listed coordinates to ensure accuracy.

Some users may be more familiar with the Military Grid Reference System (MGRS). Conversion from UTM to MGRS is straightforward. Simply drop the last two digits of each of the UTM coordinates; the MGRS coordinates are now the last three digits of the remaining numbers. In this book the MGRS coordinates are in **bold** font within the UTM.

Example: UTM 52**830**0 E 57**243**00 N becomes MGRS 283 243.

The NTS and Summit Series maps have the UTM numbers on the corners of the map and MGRS on the edges. The Rogers Pass Adventure Map has MGRS along the edges, and Canada Map Store maps have UTM along the edges.

All paper maps commonly used in this area are based on the NAD 83 map datum. Google Earth uses the WGS 84 datum but it is virtually the same as NAD 83.

On the older series of NTS maps (no longer available), NAD 27 is used. There is a significant difference between this datum and NAD 83, so grid references used in this book will not translate well to the old NTS maps.

HELICOPTER ACCESS

Helicopter access is available to many areas mentioned in this book. Glacier National Park does not allow helicopter use. Bugaboo and Wells Gray provincial parks allow limited helicopter access.

Trips that are regularly accessed and/or supported by helicopter include many of the hut- and tent-based backcountry centres and the Grand Traverses. The commercial backcountry lodges and huts also utilize helicopters.

For a list of helicopter companies see the Resources section at page 345.

Don McTighe, who retired in 2012, flew skiers safely to their destinations for several decades and is regarded as one of the best helicopter pilots in the area. Photo Chic Scott

SNOWMOBILE ACCESS

Many skiers use snowmobiles to access backcountry zones. Snowmobiles are not allowed in national or provincial parks.

Trips that may be entirely or partially accessed by snowmobile include the McMurdo, Kingsbury, Jumbo, Olive and White huts as well as some of the tent-based backcountry centres and longer traverses.

TRIP PLANNING RESOURCES

The Canadian Avalanche Centre, Parks Canada and the Association of Canadian Mountain Guides all have resources available that can help you plan trips. The most up-to-date information about conditions can be found on the CAC forums and the ACMG Mountain Conditions Report. See the Resources section at page 344 for more information.

SAFETY REGISTRATIONS

Ideally you should leave a written itinerary with a reliable person.

In Glacier National Park there is a voluntary registration system. To do this it is necessary to register in person at a park information centre, and by law you must report back once the trip has finished. If you forget to report back and a search is initiated you may be required to pay for it. If you do not have a vehicle, you will be required to leave a passport or other form of identification.

COMMUNICATING FROM THE FIELD

Mobile phone coverage is very limited throughout the Columbia Mountains. If you can see a major highway from where you are skiing you may have cell coverage. If you are skiing anywhere else, you will not be able to call out on your phone.

That leaves satellite phones or a personal locator beacon (PLB) as the likely choices for getting a message out from the field. If using a PLB that allows for custom emergency messaging (such as a SPOT unit), remember to enter the pertinent mountain rescue contact information in the message. Note that 911 does not work on satellite phones; you must call a rescue service directly.

MOUNTAIN RESCUE

For immediate emergencies, self-rescue is usually faster than calling in an organized rescue service. However, for serious extrications from the backcountry you will probably need to call in outside resources.

Glacier National Park provides an excellent mountain rescue service. It employs certified guides on dedicated, full-time professional rescue teams. Emergency response is rapid, and in good weather a helicopter can be expected to arrive on site of an accident in a short time. However, parties in the backcountry should be prepared to keep themselves sheltered and warm until help can arrive. Helicopter rescue is impossible at night or in poor visibility, and any rescue is much more time-consuming in stormy weather or darkness.

Outside this park, rescue services are provided through the BC Provincial Emergency Program (PEP), dispatched by the local detachment of the RCMP. PEP teams are locally based volunteers. They often consist of knowledgeable local skiers and certified guides, but due to the volunteer nature of the program and the multi-layered call-out process, response times can be significantly longer than inside Glacier National Park. PEP has the ability to call out other rescue teams for assistance such as Parks Canada, ski area personnel, guide companies or military search and rescue units.

Calling local ski area staff or guiding operations directly may also be an option. However, their first priority is the safety of their guests, so rescue may not be immediate. You may also be asked to pay for expenses incurred in such a rescue.

If you go through the proper channels, mountain rescue is free in all land management areas. For Glacier National Park you must have a valid park entry permit (and wilderness permit for overnight stays) to be eligible for free rescue services. If you do not have these permits you may be asked to pay for a rescue. For PEP rescues you must go through the RCMP to have your rescue covered by the BC government.

If you are outside the parks and just need to be extricated from a location where a helicopter can easily land, it is possible to call a helicopter company directly to get picked up. If you choose this option you will be required to pay for the flight yourself.

CALLING FOR A RESCUE

If calling for a rescue, be ready to relay the following information:

- your exact location (both the name of the tour and a GPS coordinate is best)
- what type of emergency it is and the number of victims
- your name and phone number, including area code
- the time the accident occurred

Emergency phone numbers, 911 and texting

- Glacier National Park: 1-877-852-3100 or 911
- All other areas: 911 and ask for the RCMP detachment nearest to your location

Calling 911 In Glacier National Park it is best to call the local emergency number. But if you do call 911 it is important to tell the operator that you need a mountain rescue for Glacier National Park. This ensures you will be relayed to the correct rescue service.

When outside Glacier National Park, you need the 911 dispatcher to transfer your call to the nearest RCMP detachment. When talking to the RCMP, state clearly that you need a mountain rescue and ask them to call the local PEP team.

Dialling 911 does not work on satellite phones. It is best to call the local rescue service or RCMP detachment directly.

If a helicopter flies by you, use the signals pictured on page 32 to indicate whether you need a rescue or not.

In some areas you may be able to send a text message on a cell or satellite phone but not dial out due to lack of signal strength. Texting to 911 will not work, so your only option there is to text a responsible person who can call in a rescue for you. Be sure to indicate in your

NEED HELP?

YES   **NO**

text your location as well as type of injury so that this information can be passed on to emergency response staff.

"To those who have struggled with them, the mountains reveal beauties they will not disclose to those who make no effort. And it is because they have so much to give and give it so lavishly to those who will wrestle with them that men love the mountains and go back to them again and again."

— *Sir Francis Younghusband*

TRAVEL INFORMATION, REGULATIONS AND FEES

REACHING THE COLUMBIA MOUNTAINS

Edmonton, Calgary and Vancouver all have international airports. It is possible to fly direct to these cities from within North America and from Europe and Asia. Kelowna also receives flights from the USA. Castlegar has connections to Calgary and Vancouver, and Cranbrook is now an international airport with connections to the USA. The areas described in this book are only a few hours drive, along excellent highways, from these airports. In other words, it is possible to fly from Europe and be skiing in the Canadian wilderness the following day.

TRANSPORTATION ONCE YOU ARE THERE

Public transportation in the Columbia Mountains is poor, particularly in winter. It is almost imperative that you have a vehicle to reach most of the trailheads. Cars can be rented from the major international chains (Hertz, Avis, Budget etc.) in Calgary, Edmonton, Vancouver and Kelowna. Highways are well maintained in winter and driving is normally a reasonable proposition, though the cold can make extreme demands on both car and driver. The Columbia Mountains do not normally experience temperatures as cold as in the Rockies but an arctic front can push into the Columbias bringing frigid temperatures. Be sure your car has antifreeze adequate for –40°c and that it is equipped with snow tires, a block heater and a strong battery. You should carry jumper cables in your car in the event of a dead battery. None of these things are provided in rental cars, of course! If the thermometer plunges, it is advisable to plug your car in if at all possible. Propane and diesel vehicles can be hard to start on cold winter mornings. It is best to avoid parking along the roadside if possible, as high-speed snow plows regularly maintain highways and can damage your vehicle.

There are regularly scheduled buses along the Trans-Canada Highway (Highway 1). These buses stop at the major centres between Calgary and Vancouver such as Golden and Revelstoke. Greyhound also stops at the summit of Rogers Pass. There are also regularly scheduled buses from Calgary that stop at Radium, Cranbrook and Nelson. Buses from Edmonton travel to Valemount via Jasper. Phone Greyhound Bus Lines (1-800-661-8747) or visit their web site at www.greyhound.ca.

TELEPHONE AREA CODES

The area code for the interior of British Columbia is 250. Numbers in the lower mainland, near Vancouver, have the prefix 604. Southern Alberta, including Calgary, has the area code 403, and northern Alberta, including Edmonton, has a code of 780.

TIME ZONES

The areas covered in this book are in two different time zones. The regions lying to the west (Revelstoke, Rossland, Rogers Pass, Nelson, Valemount) are on Pacific Time and are one hour earlier than those to the east (Golden, Radium, Invermere, Kimberley, Cranbrook and the summit of Kootenay Pass), which are on Mountain Time. When you are travelling the Trans-Canada Highway the time changes just east of Rogers Pass. When you are driving Highway 3 the time changes at Kootenay Pass between Creston and Salmo. All the ski tours described in this book that are located in the Purcells will be on Mountain Time. All skiers coming from the east should use Mountain Time in Rogers Pass to stay ahead of the Revelstoke skiers!

WHERE TO STAY

When you get off the plane in Calgary, Edmonton or Vancouver you are in a major city with a population in excess of one million. The population of Kelowna is about 100,000. There is an endless variety of accommodation, from five-star hotels to hostels. The major towns in the Columbia Mountains – Golden, Revelstoke and Nelson – all have a variety of hotels, bed & breakfasts and hostels. An Internet search will be the fastest way to find accommodation.

The Alpine Club of Canada

The ACC operates a clubhouse on the outskirts of Canmore, Alberta, in the Rocky Mountains that can make a good base for your trip. The clubhouse has beds for 50, a fully equipped kitchen, comfortable reading room and a sauna. For bookings phone 403-678-3200.

The club also operates a number of backcountry huts. These tend to be rustic and lean toward a philosophy of self-reliance. Some of the huts are secured with a combination lock. Making a booking is a simple matter of exchanging your Visa or Mastercard number for the lock combination. The huts located in the Columbia Mountains that are either owned or operated by the ACC and are found in this book are Wheeler, Asulkan, Sapphire Col, Glacier Circle, Fairy Meadow and Great Cairn plus Kokanee Glacier Cabin. The Conrad Kain Hut in the Bugaboos is closed during the winter but opens May 1. Late-season parties could use it. Bookings for these huts can be made through the ACC office, 403-678-3200. For more information, visit www.alpineclubofcanada.ca.

Backcountry lodges

The Columbia Mountains are blessed with a large number of very comfortable backcountry lodges. They are described in this book starting at page 309. These lodges can provide a truly memorable ski experience and are highly recommended.

Backcountry huts

This guidebook also provides information on a large number of backcountry huts. They offer a tremendous opportunity to have a rustic but memorable ski experience in the Columbia Mountains. See the section beginning at page 118 for more information.

FOOD, GEAR AND OTHER SUPPLIES

The mountain communities of Golden, Revelstoke and Nelson have a wide selection of grocery stores and other shops to serve your needs. White gas and butane are readily available for your stoves. Note that the service station at Rogers Pass was closed in 2012 and it is uncertain whether it will reopen in the future. See the Resources section at page 342 for contact information.

LAND MANAGERS

This book describes tours that lie within three different land management zones. Regulations and rescue response will be different for each of these areas. See the Alpine Ski Touring in the Columbia Mountains chapter at page 30 for more information on mountain rescue in the various land management areas.

National park Many of the tours in this book lie within Glacier National Park. More information on park regulations can be found in the chapter on Rogers Pass.

BC provincial parks Many tours in this book lie within British Columbia provincial parks such as Stagleap, Kokanee Glacier, Wells Gray, Valhalla, Bugaboo, St. Mary's Alpine and West Arm. Note that the Conrad Kain Hut in Bugaboo Provincial Park is closed during the winter, until May 1. If you want to camp near here, the only designated site is the Applebee area. For further information on these parks please check the BC Parks website, www.bcparks.ca.

BC Crown lands These include any lands in BC outside national and provincial parks. Fairy Meadow, Great Cairn, McMurdo Creek, International Basin, Forster Basin, Catamount Glacier, Jumbo Pass, Whitewater tours, Mount Brennan, Commonwealth Mountain, Goat Range Traverse, Gold Range Traverse, Nakusp Range Traverse, Bonnington Range Traverse and most of the Grand Traverses are on BC Crown Lands.

REGULATIONS

Tours in the Rogers Pass area lie within Glacier National Park, where there are regulations and permits you should be aware of. For more detailed and specific information see page 46.

NATIONAL PARK ENTRANCE FEES

Anyone stopping in a national park must pay an entry fee. Day passes for all the mountain national parks cost $9.80 for one adult or $19.60 for a group of up to seven people arriving in the same vehicle. A one-year pass costs $67.70 for one person or $136.40 for a group of up to seven. Passes for just Glacier and Mount Revelstoke national parks are slightly cheaper at $7.80 for one adult or $19.60 for a group and $39.20 for an annual pass for one or $98.10 for a group. Passes are available at the Rogers Pass Discovery Centre.

STAYING OVERNIGHT IN THE BACKCOUNTRY

In the national parks it is necessary to get a wilderness pass if you will be staying overnight in the backcountry. The cost is $9.80 per night or $68.70 for an annual pass that is good for one year from the date of issue. These passes can be obtained from the Rogers Pass Discovery Centre or, if you are staying at an ACC hut, from the Alpine Club of Canada. Random camping is allowed if there is no designated campground nearby. In Glacier Park, camping is not allowed in restricted or prohibited areas. For more information, see the chapter on Rogers Pass beginning at page 42. If you are just going skiing for a day trip, a wilderness pass is not required.

HOW TO USE
THIS BOOK

Summits and Icefields is written for those who know something about backcountry skiing. It is presumed that you are familiar with trip planning, map reading, whiteout navigation, snow stability evaluation, avalanche hazard evaluation, emergency procedures and appropriate terrain selection that reduces risk. If you are not familiar with these matters, you should be skiing with someone who is.

This book covers a huge geographical area and includes many runs and backcountry tours. These are not described in minute detail. Enough information is given in the form of written text, maps and photographs for an experienced ski mountaineer to form a good idea of what is involved. You must be able to fill in many of the details yourself.

ALL TOURS DESCRIBED IN THIS BOOK ARE SERIOUS. THEY ALL OFFER REAL AVALANCHE POTENTIAL, AND WHAT IS A SAFE AND PLEASANT SKI TOUR ONE DAY CAN BE EXTREMELY DANGEROUS THE NEXT. YOU MUST HAVE THE ABILITY TO MAKE THIS JUDGMENT YOURSELF.

Hazards

As well as avalanche potential, many of these tours present other dangers such as crevasses, icefalls, river crossings and cliffs. Sometimes we have drawn the reader's attention to a particular danger, but just because we have not mentioned a hazard does not mean it is not there – this book covers such a large area that it is impossible to be thoroughly acquainted with all the hazards of every tour.

Durations

No specific durations are given for any of the tours. Although it may be indicated that a tour will take about one or two days or that a few weeks will be required, it is difficult to be specific beyond this. Depending on the depth of snow, the strength of your party and the weight of your pack, the same tour can vary from four hours to two days. You must assess how long your party will take depending on conditions.

Terrain ratings

In this book terrain is rated according to the Avalanche Terrain Exposure Scale (ATES). This scale was formulated by Parks Canada and is in wide use throughout the Canadian mountains.

Almost all the trips in this book are rated as "Challenging" or "Complex." The main difference between the Challenging and Complex ratings is that in the former the terrain will contain more route-finding options that may reduce risk.

ATES ratings are defined on page 340.

Maps

The maps in this book are meant to be a rough guide to the routes. Details such as which side of a stream to follow, where to cross the stream or how to work your way through the crevasses on a glacier are not illustrated on the maps. You must work these things out for yourself. The maps in this book are not meant to be used in the field for navigational purposes. For all tours you must obtain and use suitable topographical maps.

UTM grid references given in this book are accurate only to within 100 m. This should be adequate for ski touring purposes.

Distances

All distances are given in metres or kilometres and refer to horizontal distance.

Elevations

Elevation gain and loss are referred to as "vertical metres."

Directions

All directions such as "turn left" or "turn right" are relative to the direction of travel. "Ski along the left bank of the stream" means ski along the bank that is to the left of your direction of travel. This will not necessarily be the same as what is known as "true left bank," which is relative to the direction the stream is flowing.

"Skier's left" and "skier's right" refer to the direction when facing downhill. "Climber's left" and climber's right" refer to the direction when facing uphill.

> *"I learned this, at least, by my experiment; that if one advances confidently in the direction of his dreams, and endeavors to live the life which he has imagined, he will meet with a success unexpected in common hours."*
>
> *—Henry David Thoreau*

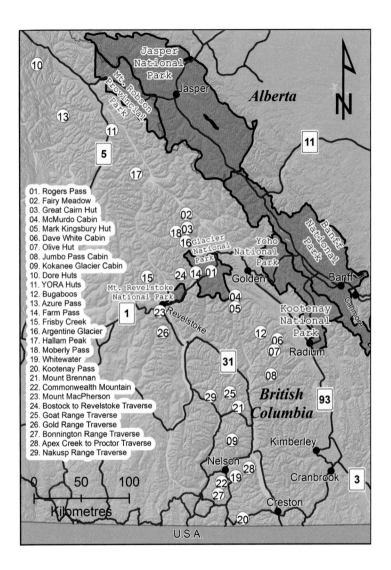

01. Rogers Pass
02. Fairy Meadow
03. Great Cairn Hut
04. McMurdo Cabin
05. Mark Kingsbury Hut
06. Dave White Cabin
07. Olive Hut
08. Jumbo Pass Cabin
09. Kokanee Glacier Cabin
10. Dore Huts
11. YORA Huts
12. Bugaboos
13. Azure Pass
14. Farm Pass
15. Frisby Creek
16. Argentine Glacier
17. Hallam Peak
18. Moberly Pass
19. Whitewater
20. Kootenay Pass
21. Mount Brennan
22. Commonwealth Mountain
23. Mount MacPherson
24. Bostock to Revelstoke Traverse
25. Goat Range Traverse
26. Gold Range Traverse
27. Bonnington Range Traverse
28. Apex Creek to Proctor Traverse
29. Nakusp Range Traverse

ROGERS PASS by Mark Klassen

Rogers Pass is one of the world's premiere roadside ski touring destinations. From the summit of the pass it is a short drive to a variety of valleys and peaks that contain every kind of terrain. Glaciers and trees, couloirs and faces, mellow and steep: it's all here and covered in a big helping of deep Selkirk powder.

A LITTLE HISTORY

Rogers Pass has a long and interesting history. Major A.B. Rogers discovered it in 1881 while searching for a route for the transcontinental railroad then under construction. In 1885 the Canadian Pacific Railway was completed, linking eastern cities with the Pacific coast. For a number of years, with great expense and difficulty, the railway through the pass was kept open during the winter. Often avalanches from surrounding peaks would bury the line, and in 1910 a massive slide swept down and killed 62 workers who were digging out the tracks from a previous avalanche. In 1916 the CPR was forced to reroute the line through an 8-km-long tunnel under the mountains.

In the 1880s Rogers Pass was the birthplace of Canadian mountaineering, and for the next 30 years climbers from around the world gathered at a luxury hotel called Glacier House built near the entrance to the Illecillewaet and Asulkan valleys. In 1899 the CPR began importing Swiss guides to lead guests up the mountains. Glacier House was a bustling mountaineering hub for many years but was eventually closed at the end of the 1925 season due to the rerouting of the railway through the Connaught Tunnel. The building was torn down in 1929 but the concrete foundations are still visible along the Illecillewaet–Asulkan trail.

There was little ski activity in the pass until 1946 when the Alpine Club of Canada built a log hut not far from the site of Glacier House. The hut was named for one of the founders of the club, A.O. Wheeler. During the late 1940s and 1950s keen skiers would take the train to a small stop, called Glacier Station, just west of the pass, then ski up to the hut.

In 1962 the Trans-Canada Highway was officially opened through Rogers Pass and this really opened the area for skiers. Over the years the fame and popularity of "the pass" has grown around the world.

SKIING IN ROGERS PASS

The pass is situated at 1314 m in Glacier National Park, equidistant between the towns of Golden and Revelstoke, on the Trans-Canada Highway. Most skiers begin their day at the Rogers Pass Discovery Centre right at the pass itself, where a variety of information and permits are available.

The highway and the CPR railway line run through the pass. This creates a very busy transportation corridor that passes through significant avalanche terrain, and Parks Canada operates the world's largest mobile avalanche control program to protect it. This control work mostly consists of artillery rounds shot from a howitzer operated by Canadian Army units under the direction of Parks Canada avalanche forecasters. **This avalanche control work is done to protect the highway, not skiers.** Just because control has been completed and restricted areas opened for skiing does not mean the area is safe from avalanches.

This transportation corridor can interfere with the skiing here. To keep all users safe, a complex system of prohibited areas, restricted areas, designated access routes and permits has been put in place. It can be daunting to negotiate it all, but hopefully this book will help. The staff at the Rogers Pass Discovery Centre will also be able to lend a hand. You can consider yourself an experienced Rogers Pass skier once you have an annual Winter Permit, check the closures via your smartphone on your way to the pass, and have planned your ski day around the closures you have already anticipated!

Rogers Pass is perhaps the busiest ski touring venue in Canada. On a busy long weekend in mid-winter over 1,000 skiers can be spread out over the different zones. An average day is far less hectic, though, and there is enough room that scores of skiers can be absorbed quite easily.

On most of the popular tours you will probably see another party, but it is also possible to have an entire day to yourself if you pick your time and place.

The tours described in this book are generally regarded as the classics and should give a broad overview of what the area has to offer. There are dozens more tours and lines to do, though, and once you have familiarized yourself a bit with the trips in this book we encourage you to explore this outstanding touring venue by venturing off the beaten path.

SPECIAL HAZARDS

There are a few hazards that are unique to this area:

- *It's almost all big terrain.* With higher avalanche hazard there are few safe options to ski in the pass, especially when restricted areas are closed. Some less exposed skiing might be found on tree runs in Connaught Creek, Napoleon Spur, Loop Brook, Flat Creek and Bostock Creek. Even those areas may be difficult to work safely, especially when surface hoar instabilities exist or avalanches are big enough to hit the valley bottom. Some situations may require a tactical retreat to the ski areas or tours near Revelstoke, Golden or in the Rockies.
- *Groups above and below.* With the number of skiers in the area it is easy to get into a situation where there are other groups in avalanche terrain above you or where you are skiing above other people. Either position can put you or others in danger if an avalanche is triggered.
- *Tracks leading you on.* Some skiers here choose aggressive lines, and there is nothing wrong with that if conditions are right. But tracks both up and down can lead into some very serious terrain even when conditions are less than optimal. Just because someone else got away with it does not mean you will.
- *Unroped glacier travel.* Many skiers here choose to travel without a rope on the glacier. They may have good reasons for doing

so, but if you do the same, make sure you have good reasoning as well.

- *Closure areas.* There are some areas that are permanently or temporarily closed for avalanche research and control. A fine of up to $200,000 and/or permit cancellation is assessed if you are caught in these areas.
- *Artillery shells.* Undetonated shells are a hazard but they are more commonly found in the summer. In the winter it is the ones flying through the air that are more hazardous to your health. Shrapnel can travel up to 1000 m from the impact point and sympathetic avalanche releases can occur on adjacent slopes. STAY OUT OF CLOSURE AREAS.
- *Avalanche control is for the road, not for skiers.* Just because avalanche control is done in this area does not mean the slopes are stable for skiing. All the normal precautions must always be taken while touring here.
- *Road closures.* During storm periods the road may be closed on short notice for avalanche control. Closures can last for hours or days at a time. Keep track of the weather and ask at the Discovery Centre to see if control operations are planned.
- *Dangerous driving conditions.* Although the road crew does an amazing job of keeping the highway clear, storm events and high traffic volumes can make the roads particularly dangerous here. This is coupled with a few of the parking areas being difficult to turn in to, depending on which direction you are coming from. The Avalanche–Illecillewaet–Asulkan and Loop Brook parking lots can be scary to get into if you are coming from the east.

A NOTE ON TRACKSETTING

Since this is such a popular ski touring area, many people are going to end up following the trail you are breaking. After a few folks have walked up your track it will get hard and slick. If the trail is steep it makes for an unpleasant experience for those behind you. The most serious injury I have ever dealt with in the mountains occurred when someone fell off a steep and slippery uptrack on Grizzly Shoulder!

It is best that you don't go as steeply as possible when breaking a new trail but rather adjust your angle to a lesser grade. Keep looking ahead and use the terrain to lift you up rather than fighting your way steeply uphill. This will help eliminate the myriad uptracks that are often found on the more popular tours, which often interfere with the skiing.

MAP RESOURCES

The Adventure Map for Rogers Pass is highly recommended. It is quite accurate, has trails and trailheads marked, and all the major glade lines are shown. The winter version of this map is heavily marked up; I prefer the summer version.

Google Earth is also detailed for this area and is an invaluable resource.

ROGERS PASS DISCOVERY CENTRE

This park information centre is located at the summit of the pass and is where most ski tourers will start their day. It is a treat to put your boots on in front of the fireplace while the staff give you some pointers on where to go. Avalanche and weather information is posted here. An excellent catalogue of terrain photos helps with your route finding and show the closure boundaries. This is also the place to see what closures are in place and to get permits for entering the restricted areas.

PROHIBITED AREAS, RESTRICTED AREAS AND UNRESTRICTED AREAS

The park is divided into three types of areas to accommodate the avalanche research and control program:

- *prohibited areas* that are permanently closed to all recreational users;
- *restricted areas* that are open to skiers when avalanche control is not planned; and

Rogers Pass Overview

01. Shaughnessy Restricted Area
02. Tupper Restricted Area
03. Macdonald Restricted Area
04. Hermit Restricted Area
05. Grizzly Shoulder Restricted Area
06. Cheops North Restricted Area
07. Cheops Restricted Area
08. Avalanche Restricted Area
09. Loop Restricted Area
10. Ross Restricted Area
11. Camp West Restricted Area
12. Smart Restricted Area
13. McGill Restricted Area
14. Fortitude Restricted Area
15. Heather Hill Prohibited Area
16. Macdonald West Prohibited Area
17. Abbott Prohibited Area
18. Cougar Prohibited Area
19. Fidelity Prohibited Area

Prohibited/Restricted Areas
Prohibited Area
Restricted Area

0   5   10
Kilometres

47

- *unrestricted areas* that are not affected by the avalanche control program.

A permit is required to enter opened restricted areas.

In addition to these areas, there is the Bostock Parking Restricted Area, which also requires a permit.

Prohibited areas

A prohibited area is a zone to which access for recreationists is forbidden all winter. They are closed for snow study or explosives testing or because there is a high risk of triggering avalanches directly onto the highway. There are five prohibited areas in the park, three of which are relevant to the tours described in this book:

- *Macdonald West.* This area lies on the west side of Mount Macdonald, above the Parks compound and adjacent to the Macdonald West Shoulder/NRC Gully tours.
- *Abbott.* The eastern and northern slopes of Mount Abbott in the Asulkan Valley.
- *Fidelity.* The southern, eastern and northern slopes of Mount Fidelity as well as upper Christiana Ridge, in the Bostock Valley.

Restricted areas

A restricted area is where avalanche control is taking place; or where shrapnel from explosive control work may affect the area; or where an avalanche sympathetically triggered by nearby avalanche control may occur. When no avalanche control is planned, restricted areas are opened for winter recreational users.

A valid Winter Permit is required to park a vehicle at trailheads and/or to travel in restricted areas. Permit holders may only enter these areas when they are posted as open.

Restricted areas are posted as "open" or "closed" at 7 a.m. PST each day. The restricted areas are automatically closed again at midnight.

Restricted area status can be obtained at the Rogers Pass Discovery Centre at the summit of the pass or through links from the Glacier

National Park Avalanche Bulletin, available at www.avalanche.ca/cac. A Twitter feed is also available for restricted area status. Follow @GlacierNP.

There are 14 restricted areas in the park, eight of which are relevant to tours covered in this book:

- *Grizzly Shoulder* affects the Grizzly Shoulder, Puff Daddy and Little Sifton Traverse tours.
- *Cheops North* affects tours to the Hourglass.
- *Hermit* affects the Little Sifton Traverse, Tupper Traverse and all tours listed in the Hermit section.
- *Tupper* affects the Tupper Traverse.
- *Avalanche* affects the Macdonald West Shoulder, NRC Gully and Avalanche Crest tours.
- *Cheops* affects the Napoleon Spur tour.
- *Loop* affects tours to Bonney Trees and the Lily Traverse.
- *McGill* affects tours to McGill Shoulder and Christiana Trees.

Bostock parking restricted area

This parking lot is used to access both the Bostock and Flat Creek drainages. Although Flat Creek is an unrestricted area, a permit is required to leave a vehicle at the Bostock parking area.

Unrestricted areas

These areas are open all winter. A Winter Permit is not required but you still need a park pass. The following tours are located in unrestricted areas:

- Balu Pass and all tours on the north side of the Connaught Valley except for Grizzly Shoulder
- All tours in the Illecillewaet Valley
- All tours in the Asulkan Valley

DESIGNATED ACCESS ROUTES

These routes are used to avoid travel on the CPR tracks and are described in the sections dealing with these tours. Travel on the tracks or within 16 m of them is trespassing and violators will be prosecuted. There are three designated access routes, two of which are relevant to tours in this book:

- *Tupper* for exiting the Tupper Traverse
- *Flat Creek* for tours in Flat Creek

PERMITS AND WAIVERS

A National Park Permit is required to leave your vehicle anywhere in Glacier National Park. These are available at the Rogers Pass Discovery Centre, for a fee.

A Winter Permit is required for entering an open restricted area. Every individual in the group is required to get a permit. Winter Permits are free.

Both daily and annual Winter Permits are available. Daily permits are obtained at the Discovery Centre. If you are staying more than a few days it may be worth getting an annual permit. To obtain one of these, attendance at an orientation session is required. These sessions are held regularly at the Discovery Centre. Contact Glacier National Park or talk to the staff at the Discovery Centre to inquire about orientation sessions.

In addition, a waiver must also be signed to obtain any Winter Permit.

PARKING

Parking is allowed in designated areas only and these are described for each tour. Illegally parked vehicles will be towed.

HIGHWAY CLOSURES

If an avalanche control action has started while you are out skiing you may find a card stating this on the windshield of your vehicle. Remain at your vehicle in the designated parking area until you are notified that the highway is open. This may take hours.

If you are able to make it to Glacier Park Lodge, head for the lounge and settle in. Sometimes you may also be able to travel to Golden or Revelstoke from where you are, but not the other direction. This may mean it is time for dinner down the hill until the shelling is finished.

Highway conditions and closures are kept updated on the Drive BC website, www.drivebc.ca.

GLACIER PARK LODGE

NOTE: Glacier Park Lodge went out of business in the autumn of 2012, just before this book went to press. At that time it was uncertain whether the lodge would reopen, but this description is included in case it does.

Glacier Park Lodge. Photo Chic Scott

Glacier Park Lodge is a full-service hotel at the summit of the pass. They may have special rates for tourers, so ask for the "skier's special" and see what happens – this deal varies from year to year. Traditionally, room charges have been reasonable and competitive with the Wheeler Hut, although this seems to fluctuate from year to year.

If you have special dietary requirements it is well worthwhile to talk to hotel staff before your arrival; the menu may be limited. There is no cooking allowed in the rooms but some people bring a cooler with food for a cold breakfast and lunches. There is a coffee maker in each room but no refrigerator.

Roadside amenities

Well, there isn't much! In addition to rooms, Glacier Park Lodge has a lounge, café (which is often closed), dining room, vending machines and a gift shop. The Discovery Centre has a gift shop where you can buy guidebooks, maps and souvenirs.

As of winter 2012 the gas station has been shut down and it is unclear when or if it will reopen.

There is no bank machine at the pass.

OVERNIGHT BACKCOUNTRY USE

Overnight use is not allowed in any restricted area. A Wilderness Pass is required for overnight use in other areas. Contact Glacier National Park or talk to the staff at the Discovery Centre for more information. There is a fee for Wilderness Passes.

HUTS

There are four huts in the area, all operated by the Alpine Club of Canada (ACC). In addition to the hut fee, a Wilderness Pass is required for overnight use. See the section on ACC huts at page 35 for more information.

Wheeler Hut

This is a classic log cabin that sleeps 24. There are two wood stoves for heating, and propane is used for lighting and cooking. The hut is quite easy to access, as it is about a 20-minute flat ski from the road. Trips to Avalanche Crest, Illecillewaet and Asulkan are possible from this base. Other trips require you to ski out to the road and then drive.

The hut is at 1250 m, **4657**00 E 5679300 N. To get to there, park at the Avalanche–Asulkan–Illecillewaet trailhead. Climb up the short, steep hill behind the parking area to the old railway grade. Turn left and follow this trail about 1.3 km to the hut, which is on the left in the trees just after the apex of a major curve in the trail.

Wheeler Hut. Photo Chic Scott

Asulkan Cabin

This may be the most popular hut in the area. A handsome timber-frame structure, it sleeps 12 and has propane heating, lighting and cooking facilities. Tours at the head of the Asulkan valley are possible from here.

Asulkan Cabin. Photo Chic Scott

The hut sits at the top of the Tree Triangle in the Asulkan valley, about 2115 m, 467200 E 5673800 N. To get there, follow the Tree Triangle tour described in the Asulkan section at page 96.

Sapphire Col Hut

This tiny hut is a basic metal shelter that is seldom used in winter and has no amenities other than two sleeping benches. It could be used as part of the Lily Traverse or as a base for some ski mountaineering.

Sapphire Col Hut. Photo Keith Morton

This shelter is located at Sapphire Col, 2581 m, 465200 E 5673300 N. To get there, take the Sapphire Col tour described in the Asulkan section at page 99 or the Sapphire Col Traverse described in the Loop section at page 107.

Glacier Circle Cabin

Glacier Circle Cabin. Photo Mark Klassen

A small, historic log cabin buried deep in the woods far beyond the highway corridor. It sleeps eight and has a wood stove for heat. There is also a cookstove and a lantern, but you need to bring white gas to operate them. None of the tours described in this book are accessible from this cabin and there is not much skiing in the area. It is most often used while completing the Bugaboos to Rogers Pass traverse.

The cabin is located at 1820 m, 0472499 E 5669115 N,

to the south of the Illecillewaet Névé. To get there, begin on the Youngs Peak Traverse, described at page 92 in the Illecillewaet Valley section. Once on the névé, head south across it to about 2400 m, 470700 E 5673000 N and then turn southwest. Descend steeply into Glacier Circle, down a broad gully and moraines below the east face of the Witches Tower. Alternatively a steep descent down a huge draw below the west face of Mount Macoun is also possible. Near the bottom, cut right (west) to avoid steep terrain. Both options involve very big avalanche terrain with significant overhead hazard.

The cabin is notoriously difficult to find and inconveniently surrounded by cabin-sized boulders. Walk south at the edge of the forest below Mount Fox, along a small drainage. Where the creekbed narrows, cut leftward into the forest. You may pass by a large boulder; if so the hut is quite close and it may be almost completely buried in snow.

For more information on accessing and finding the hut, check out the Bugaboos to Rogers Pass Traverse chapter, beginning at page 273.

LINKS

Glacier National Park: www.pc.gc.ca/pn-np/bc/glacier/index_e.asp

Follow these links for additional permit information: *GNP Home Page > Visitor Information > Winter Permit System Information*

Follow these links for daily restricted area status: *GNP Home Page > Winter Restricted Area Status*

Glacier National Park Twitter feed: @GlacierNP

Glacier Park Lodge: www.glacierparklodge.ca, 1-888-567-4477

Alpine Club of Canada: www.alpineclubofcanada.ca, 403-678-3200

Road conditions and closures: www.drivebc.ca.

Go to page 345 in the Resources chapter for more Rogers Pass links.

CONNAUGHT

This valley is directly accessible from the parking area at the Discovery Centre, and most of its tours are in unrestricted areas that do not

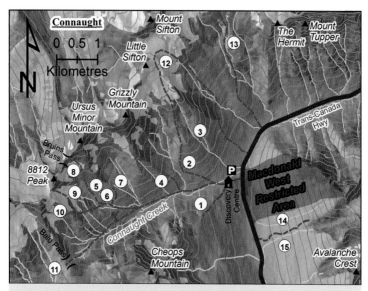

Connaught Creek and MacDonald West Shoulder/NRC Gully area.

Gaining Hermit Meadows on the Tupper Traverse. Photo Mark Klassen

require a permit. As a result it is probably the most popular ski zone at the pass.

That does not mean this is not avalanche country. Large, climax avalanches hit the Balu Pass trail every year. During periods of higher hazard there may be safer places to ski.

There are a variety of terrain options, from steep trees to mellow open bowls. Many of these tours are south-facing and may get a crust after a sunny day. Due to the orientation of the valley this area is also affected by crossloading winds, and many of the spurs on the north side of the valley will get windslabs forming on their lees.

This is the water supply for facilities at the pass, so no dogs are allowed in this valley.

Parking for all tours is at the Rogers Pass Discovery Centre or Glacier Park Lodge. This is 67 km from Revelstoke and 79 km from Golden.

The Balu Pass Trail

The Balu Pass trail runs all the way up the valley, starting at the hotel and finishing at Balu Pass. All tours in Connaught Creek start from some point along this trail.

Start at the sign showing the avalanche areas, at the edge of the parking lot behind the north end of Glacier Park Lodge, at an elevation of 1320 m.

Follow the south side of the creek, crossing a bridge to the north side after a short way. Shortly thereafter you will begin to encounter the massive runout zones of the huge avalanche paths on either side of the valley. Most of these runouts come from Cheops Mountain on the south side of the valley, with the exception of the Grizzly Bowl, Frequent Flyer and 8812 Bowl slide paths, which run down from the Hermit Range peaks to the north. Large avalanches that run out onto the trail do not occur frequently, but if they do you will not want to be anywhere near them.

The first avalanche area you come to is the Grizzly Bowl slide path that runs down from Grizzly Mountain. Grizzly Shoulder is the forest above this point, and Teddy Bear Trees is on the far side of the path, both of them on the north side of the valley. After crossing the Grizzly Bowl run-out the trail usually hugs the trimline along the edge of the forest on the north side of the valley to lessen exposure to Cheops.

Possibly the most exposed section is when you cross the Frequent Flyer avalanche path, about 2 km from the trailhead, **461900** E **568340o** N. This is a smaller but steeper path off Grizzly Mountain that spills avalanche debris onto the trail more regularly than the other paths. With critical inputs of heavy snowfall, rising temperatures or loading winds on the ridges above, this path is a regular performer.

Connaught Creek Overview.
Photo Parks Canada

After Frequent Flyer the trail continues to follow the trimline on the north side, the main concerns being avalanches from Cheops across the valley. This doesn't let up until almost all the way to Balu Pass. Near the pass there is also exposure to 8812 Bowl, the basin to the north on Ursus Major Mountain. The smaller but steep side slopes of the valley the trail traverses, and the final slopes to Balu Pass, may also be a concern in certain conditions.

The Hourglass is described first, then the tours on the north side of the valley in succession as they are encountered along the Balu Pass trail up the Connaught valley.

1 THE HOURGLASS

Permit Cheops North
Length uphill 2 km
Max elevation gain 550 m
Skiing elevation band 1460–1850 m
Aspect north
Avalanche Terrain Rating Challenging

This is a steep, narrow shot through the trees, good for only a couple of skiers. Get there first! It is the only north-facing run in Connaught described in this book. Combine it with a run in Grizzly Shoulder or Teddy Bear Trees.

Start at the same trailhead as the other tours up the valley, but begin ascending almost immediately through the forest up the northeast ridge of Cheops Mountain. As you ascend, the ridge begins to narrow somewhat. At about 1800 m the ridge flattens and the trees open up a little. You can see the opening in the trees of the large Cheops 2 slide path to the south (Cheops permit required to go there).

The top of The Hourglass is an indistinct bowl feature in the trees. There are lines through steep trees and glades in this bowl from either side. The terrain funnels into a narrow gully, and then opens up into a fan that takes you down to the valley bottom. Beware of buried surface hoar causing avalanche conditions, especially at the bottom of the run on the fan.

Be careful of going too far along the ridge past the indistinct bowl. There is skiing into Connaught from higher along the ridge but it is very steep and rugged – there is a reason it is called The Killing Fields. Assess the conditions and terrain carefully before going there.

2 GRIZZLY SHOULDER

Permit Grizzly Shoulder
Length uphill 2 km
Max elevation gain 800 m
Skiing elevation band 1400–2100 m
Aspect southeast
Avalanche Terrain Rating Challenging

This trip is one of the most popular in all of Rogers Pass and deservedly so. Steep trees and open glades after only a short walk! The classic line gets tracked out early but there are other runs to explore. Be careful of buried crusts and/or surface hoar in the glades.

Shortly after the bridge crossing you will enter open terrain along the creek. Many groups will continue on to the edge of the Grizzly slide path a bit farther along and then skin steeply all the way up the thickly treed shoulder above.

I prefer a less steep route. From the open area beyond the bridge, start a rising traverse and switchbacks through the forest above, heading west. Don't get too high too fast or you will get into steeper terrain. There are a variety of glades and open trees above you on this initial traverse; with some exploring you'll find several ski lines there.

If you are going for the classic Grizzly Shoulder run, head for about 1630 m, 462500 E 5683800 N. At that point you should be in a large glade; gain the treed shoulder on its west side. You will often meet another uptrack here. At this point there is nothing for it but to put in some steep, narrow switchbacks through the forest in the next section. This will eventually get you to treeline at about 2050 m on the shoulder beside the open Grizzly slide path to the west.

The main ski run is down the big, steep glade below you, back to the valley. There are also more serious tree lines that lead west from slightly higher up, starting at a boulder field. These lead into Grizzly Bowl, where there will be big avalanche terrain above your head. Once in Grizzly Bowl you have to negotiate a steep, narrow throat with even steeper sidewalls, starting at about 1800 m. Staying high on one side or the other seems to avoid this terrain trap. You could also consider putting skins back on and uptracking through steep trees to get back toward the classic Grizzly Shoulder lines.

3 ROGERS RUN AND PUFF DADDY

Permits Grizzly Shoulder, Hermit
Distance uphill 3 km
Max elevation gain 900 m

Skiing elevation band 1300–2200 m
Aspect southeast
Avalanche Terrain Rating Complex

Puff Daddy is one of my favourite runs in the pass, but it is steep and complex and requires lower avalanche hazard. Rogers Run is also steep but not as open or exposed. Both runs start from the ridge above Grizzly Shoulder and descend to the highway straight below. Beware of suncrusts and cliffs here.

The downhill portion of the tour can be clearly seen from Glacier Park Lodge. It is worth your while to study it carefully and perhaps take a few pictures to refer to later so you can find your way down the run safely.

Take the route to the top of Grizzly Shoulder. From there continue up through the boulder field toward the base of the small cliff below a ridgecrest. You may cut back to the southeast here and work through small trees and rocks to gain the ridge above. Or contour below the base of the cliff until it is possible to make an end run around it a short way to the northwest. Some walking may be required on either route to get through a short but steep rocky section.

For Rogers Run, start at the south end of the ridge, at about 2150 m, 462200 E 5684600 N. Ski a small, steep alpine bowl off the east side of the ridge to open trees. Wrap a bit to the right (south) through these steep trees. There is a narrow gully to skier's left which you should avoid, as there are cliffs in it. There are also small cliffs immediately skier's right of the gully, at about 1800 m. The farther right you are, the lower-angled the terrain is. The skiing is mostly through open trees and glades all the way to the highway.

For Puff Daddy, go up the flattish ridge above Grizzly Shoulder until it is possible to drop into a mellow alpine bowl to the east. Ski down this bowl, traversing to the far skier's left side before it starts dropping off precipitously.

Once things steepen it is best if you are beneath the broad ridge that bounds the east side of the bowl. The least exposed line may be an indistinct, lightly treed ridge that is an extension of the upper ridge, which is between two shallow gully features. Around 1750 m you will get into small cliff bands that you will need to work your way through.

Alternatively, near the top of the steep terrain you can bump left across the easternmost shallow gully into more open terrain. This line is more exposed. You will run into an extension of the cliffs found on the other line and I find that traversing left around them on steep, unsupported slopes has worked the best for me. Once past the cliffs it is more straightforward, and chutes through the trees lead to the highway straight below.

4 TEDDY BEAR TREES

Permit none
Length uphill 2.5 km
Max elevation gain 650 m
Skiing elevation band 1475–1950 m
Aspect southeast
Avalanche Terrain Rating Challenging

This is the narrow, treed shoulder between the Grizzly slide path and the Frequent Flyer slide path. The lines are steeper and less open than Grizzly Shoulder.

From the west side of the Grizzly slide path, switchback through the forest and glades. The higher you go the steeper it gets. If the terrain pushes you to the east you will get into very steep, sparsely treed terrain. It is best to try and stay in the thicker forest on the shoulder itself if you can.

Even steeper and rougher terrain starts where the forest thins and the shoulder turns into a spur at about 1950 m. Most choose to ski down from here, through the forest the same way they came up. There are many lines to explore. It is also possible to continue up to get to serious alpine lines that lead off the ridge above.

Ursus Area

This area has classic tree and open-bowl skiing with many different lines. There is mellow terrain that can be used on days with higher avalanche hazard, although getting there can be exposed. There are also some steep, serious runs.

There are a couple of ways to access this area from the Balu Pass trail. You may start at the west edge of a runout zone where two avalanche paths from the north side of the valley converge just above the main Connaught trail (this is first major avalanche path west of Frequent Flyer), 1620 m, **461**200 E 5683000 N. Work the thickly treed shoulder above into Hospital Bowl at about 1850 m, **460**700 E 5683000 N.

Alternatively, continue up the trail to a slight shoulder at 1730 m, **460**700 E 5682600 N. Cut back hard to the east to traverse and switchback through forest, a gully, then more forest. Eventually a slope covered

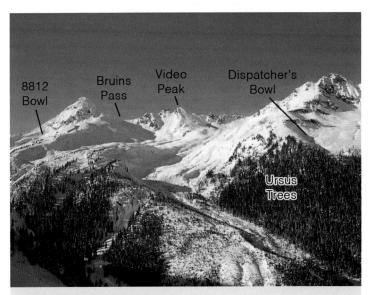

The Ursus area. Photo Parks Canada

in small Christmas trees leads into Hospital Bowl at the same point as noted above. This uptrack is longer but easier.

5 HOSPITAL BOWL

Permit none
Length uphill 5 km
Max elevation gain 900 m
Skiing elevation band 1650-2200 m
Aspect east through southwest
Avalanche Terrain Rating Complex

This is the main, generally low-angled bowl in the Ursus area. The terrain rating is Complex due to the approach up Connaught Creek. The terrain in Hospital Bowl itself could be rated Challenging.

The skiing in Hospital Bowl is obvious, with many lines available in the mostly gentle, open alpine terrain. There are some short, steeper lines off the ridges on either side of the bowl.

6 URSUS TREES

Permit none
Length uphill 5 km
Max elevation gain 800 m
Skiing elevation band 1650-2100 m
Aspect south
Avalanche Terrain Rating Complex

From the base of Hospital Bowl, looking up and to the right, there is an area of open trees. This is called Ursus Trees and it has great skiing when there is not a suncrust. Beware of buried crusts and surface hoar causing avalanche hazards here. The terrain rating is Complex due to the approach up Connaught Creek. The terrain in Ursus Trees itself could be rated Challenging.

To get there, cut across the bottom of the trees to the east, not getting too high too fast to avoid steep and awkward tracksetting. Gain the shoulder on the far side and climb up that to the top of the ski lines at about 2100 m.

7 DISPATCHER'S BOWL

Permit none
Length uphill 5 km
Max elevation gain 900 m
Skiing elevation band 1650–2200 m
Aspect east to southeast
Avalanche Terrain Rating Complex

From the top of Ursus Trees (or from higher along the ridge) you can drop into this bowl, which lies to the east. It is a short run with a steep, possibly windloaded roll at the top that can be avoided somewhat by accessing it from lower on the ridge. The terrain rating is Complex due to the approach up Connaught Creek. The terrain in Dispatcher's Bowl itself could be rated Challenging.

Below the initial slope, fun rolling trees lead to a steep gully. To exit, either ski the steep gully (there may be ice in it), skin back up to the ridge and ski Ursus Trees, or avoid the gully by traversing into the steep forest to the right and skiing into lower Hospital Bowl. It is also possible to stay high on the left and avoid the gully that way.

8 VIDEO PEAK

Permit none
Length uphill 6 km
Max elevation gain 1265 m
Skiing elevation band 1650–2565 m
Aspect east
Avalanche Terrain Rating Complex

This is the unnamed 2565 m peak at the head of Hospital Bowl and to the north of Bruins Pass. It is a serious undertaking up a steep, lee alpine slope. Some Banffites filmed a run down this peak back in the '80s and it was the first amateur ski video many of us had ever seen!

Skin to the head of Hospital Bowl, to below the east face of Video Peak. Gain the face from the climber's right side and work your way up it to the summit. If you don't feel exposed here, you should! A descent may be made down this face. The southeast face has also been skied.

9 BRUINS PASS

Permit none
Length uphill 6 km
Max elevation gain 1200 m
Skiing elevation band 1650–2480 m
Aspect northeast
Avalanche Terrain Rating Complex

Bruins Pass is marked on the maps and is the col to the south of Video Peak. This is another big, steep, lee alpine feature that gives a great run. Leave it for a day with lower avalanche hazard and especially when windslabs are not an issue.

From the bottom of Hospital Bowl, ski around Hospital Knob (2020 m, **460**300 E 5682800 N) to the north and west. Traverse west through sparse trees, without gaining much elevation, to the base of an alpine ridge that runs southeast all the way from Bruins Pass. The slope that gains the base of this ridge is short but it is steep, may be windloaded and has an ugly runout.

Cross it if you dare and gain the ridge. Climb up this as it gradually narrows. Some rocks are avoided on the right, and if you go all the way to the pass itself you need to drop a bit into the bowl to the west (8812 Bowl) to make the final ascent. The pass is at 2480 m.

The actual Bruins Pass run goes down the large, steep slopes on the northeast side of the ridge, shortly before you reach the pass. Carefully assess the wind effect before dropping in – it is a committing place.

There is also a run down the fairly gentle glacier to the northwest of the pass, heading toward Ursus Creek. It is a great ski, but if you go down there, understand that it is a long walk back out! Be aware of crevasses.

10 8812 BOWL

Permit none

Length uphill 6 km
Max elevation gain 1200 m
Skiing elevation band 1850–2480 m
Aspect south through southeast
Avalanche Terrain Rating Complex

This is the huge alpine bowl on the southeast side of the unnamed 2660 m peak to the southwest of Bruins Pass. This peak was marked as 8812 ft. on the old maps. The top of the run is steep and may have crusts on the surface or buried, potentially creating different avalanche hazards than on the other runs in the Bruins Pass area. There are also slopes and cornices above that threaten the run.

This basin may be accessed straight down (south) from Bruins Pass. To get there take the same route as described for that tour.

If you commit to this bowl you almost certainly will exit down it to the main Connaught drainage far below rather than via the other routes out of the Ursus area.

The bowl may also be accessed from below. Follow the main Connaught trail until you are below the bowl and put in an uptrack through some moderately steep rolls near the bottom to get into the lower-angled main basin. It would be difficult and exposed to skin up the steep upper terrain to gain Bruins Pass.

Exiting from the Ursus Area

Exits from Dispatcher's Bowl and 8812 Bowl are described in the relevant sections. For the other runs there are a few options:

- Follow the Hospital Bowl drainage down to the valley. This gets into some gullied, steep terrain covered in tight Christmas trees. This is the least steep option and has the easiest route finding.
- From the bottom of Hospital Bowl, gain the low ridge that runs southeast from Hospital Knob (this usually can be done with some shuffling and sidestepping). There is a wide area of

Christmas trees below this ridge. Ski through them to the valley. These trees may feel rather thick with a low snowpack.

- From the southeast ridge of Hospital Knob, Hospital Gully leads down to the right of the Christmas trees (one of the options to get to the Ursus area crosses the bottom of this gully on ascent). The head of the gully is about 1890 m on this ridge but it is quite steep and rocky at the top, so it may be best to access it lower. This exit is more serious than the ones described previously.
- Find the head of a gully (1980 m, 460200 E 5682700 N) to the southwest of Hospital Knob. Some traversing will be required to get into this gully from the Bruins run. The head of this gully is also more serious than the first couple of options described here. There is also a steep narrow gully farther to the west, more in line with the base of the ridge leading down from Bruins Pass.

11 BALU PASS

Permit none
Length uphill 5 km
Max elevation gain 770 m (to the pass)
Skiing elevation band 1900–2070 m
Aspect northeast
Avalanche Terrain Rating Complex

This is the gentlest tour in Connaught and probably in the entire Rogers Pass. It is threatened by significant amounts of avalanche terrain above, though.

Take the main Connaught trail all the way to the pass. There are some moderately angled slopes near the end. Ski back down the way you came or climb higher up the ridges on either side of the pass. Runs can be made back down the ridges or more steeply into the bowls below the ridges.

The terrain rating is Complex due to the approach up Connaught Creek. The terrain in Balu Pass itself could be rated Challenging.

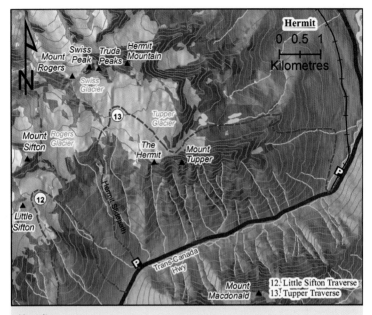

Hermit area.

HERMIT

The Hermit can be seen from the Discovery Centre parking lot. It is the large south-facing zone below Mount Sifton, the Swiss Peaks and Mount Tupper. The rocky peaks provide a dramatic backdrop to the tours here and the views to the north are expansive. It is a good place to go to get an overview of the MacDonald, Illecillewaet and Asulkan areas.

The lower, forested slopes of the basin are complex and offer generally discontinuous, gullied ski lines. The upper portion mostly consists of flattish glaciers and convoluted moraines. As such, the Hermit isn't known for classic Selkirk fall line skiing, but there are two excellent traverses that either begin or end here. Both are highly recommended.

Author Mark Klassen having some great November skiing on the Little Sifton Traverse. Photo Greg Golovach

12 LITTLE SIFTON TRAVERSE

Permits Grizzly Shoulder, Hermit
Length uphill 5.5 km
Max elevation gain 1420 m
Skiing elevation band 1300–2720 m
Aspect mostly southeast with one steep alpine north-facing slope
Avalanche Terrain Rating Complex

This is an outstanding tour. Straight up and straight down, the descent goes through pretty much all the terrain types that Rogers Pass is famous for.

Parking is at the Discovery Centre or Glacier Park Lodge. This is 67 km from Revelstoke and 79 km from Golden.

The trip starts in the Connaught valley. Follow the route description for Puff Daddy (page 60). At its high point, continue up the broad, rolling alpine ridge above. Little Sifton is the unnamed 2720 m peak at

461400 E 5686300 N. Climb toward it, heading for the 2630 m shoulder on its northeast ridge. Be aware of cornices overhanging the north side of the shoulder.

Once at the shoulder, decide whether an ascent of Little Sifton itself is possible. There are some very steep convexities to climb over on a fairly large slope. Windslabs especially are a concern and I often pass on going to the summit. However, if it is safe to ascend the ridge and face to the peak, there is a good but short run back down into the basin you have just climbed up.

Climb back to the shoulder (or cut your run short and traverse back). From here there is a steep north aspect to be skied to the lower-angled glacier below. An entrance beside the cornice on the right is usually easiest. The farther left one skis into this slope, the more windloaded it will be. You may be able to carefully knock a chunk of cornice down to test for slab instability.

Ski down to the glacier, and once you're on it a couple of possibilities present themselves. The farther to skier's right you go, the steeper, larger and more exposed the terrain will be on the run down. If you follow the lowest-angled terrain to the left you will end up in a flat gully between the glacier and moraines that may take a bit of walking to get out of. A centre-left direction may give the best combination of fall line and less-exposed terrain, and this is the route described below.

Ski the short, low-angled glacier to steeper moraine slopes with benches between them. Just as you reach the first trees at about 2000 m you may encounter a steeper section with small rock outcrops. This is the point where, if you do not like any of the options described below, you need to go hard left into the forest and ski down that to the highway. The lower section could be a battle through thick forest.

If continuing down the regular way, either work through the rock outcrops, go right into smoother but bigger terrain or go left onto less steep slopes. All these options lead to open slopes a short way below; ski these until you are above a bowl feature at about 1750 m. There is a massive gully below.

Again a few options present themselves but the best skiing is to keep your elevation and make a long, exposed traverse to the right (large slopes and cornices above you), above the bowl. Head to the top of the trees on a broad ridge down and right, at about 1700 m, **463**200 E **5685**000 N.

Going straight down the bowl and huge gully or staying high on the left of them also work, but the skiing is not great and you wouldn't want to trigger an avalanche in those places.

If you went to the right, you will find yourself at the top of a glade in the forest (clearly shown on The Adventure Map). You can ski down that or traverse farther right into a series of other glades. Ski any of them to the highway below. Think about buried crusts and surface hoar here.

The descent from the glacier may also be reached by ascending up the Hermit basin. From the Hermit parking area, climb through the west side

The Hermit area. Little Sifton Traverse is shown on the left, Tupper Traverse on the right. Photo Mark Klassen

of the thick, steep forest, beside the large slide path on the Sifton side of the Hermit basin. Continue up the moraines to the glacier.

13 TUPPER TRAVERSE

Permits Hermit, Tupper
Length uphill 5.5 km
Max elevation gain 1300 m
Skiing elevation band 1100–2600 m
Aspect southeast through southwest on ascent
  southeast, northeast and east on descent
Avalanche Terrain Rating Complex

This is a magical mystery tour through a variety of terrain. In addition to other avalanche terrain, there is a large, very steep alpine northeast aspect on this trip that deserves respect.

Note: The upper Hermit trail on the summer version of The Adventure Map is marked incorrectly. The trail is actually farther west than marked, and this is the general route described here.

Parking is at the Hermit trailhead, on the north side of the road 1.5 km east of the Discovery Centre, 77 km from Golden. It is worthwhile to park another car at Stone Arch, on the north side of the highway 7.25 km east of the Discovery Centre and 71 km from Golden.

The most direct route into Hermit can be complex and it may be difficult to find a smooth way there the first time. Keep your head up and refer to your map often. This description gives directions that hopefully will keep you on the generally right track on the way up.

Start by switchbacking through the thick forest directly above the parking area. At about 1650 m start trending to the right onto a broad ridge with open trees. Follow that a ways before dropping a bit off the ridge to the right, eventually getting into a forested drainage/gully even farther right. Cross this at about 1725 m, to a ridge between the gully you crossed and another one on the right. This point is about 1750 m, **463**600 E 5**686**100 N. Climb steeply up this ridge to flatter terrain in the moraines.

Once you are in the moraines, head north through rolling terrain to the toe of Swiss Glacier. Ascend that to the flat area between it and Tupper Glacier. This is the start of the first descent.

If at this point you decide you don't want to commit to the big slope on the north side of Tupper, you have a couple of options. You can go back the way you came or ski the Hermit slide path, which is committing in its own right. This path is the large, steep, exposed gully to the west of the south ridge the Hermit, which is a subpeak of Mount Tupper. Warm afternoon temperatures would especially affect it.

To descend the Hermit Path, avoid the prominent but narrow gully on skier's right at the top and instead gain the path from the east side. Once on a bench at about 1950 m it may be easiest to trend left but there is a lot of terrain above you. Ski down big steep slopes into the lower track and runout. Near the bottom, avoid gullied terrain by staying right (west).

To continue on the Tupper Traverse, ski southeast down the low-angled Tupper Glacier to beneath the north face of Mount Tupper. At 2450 m the glacier begins to steepen precipitously. The Venturi effect often causes windslabs or crusts to form on this big, committing slope. If deemed safe, descend it to the flat valley below.

Cruise through the flat moraines, admiring the big quartzite walls above you. Head for a point in the trees beyond at about 1750 m, 467600 E 5688800 N. Slap your skins back on – you didn't think it was over, did you? Climb onto the forested northeast ridge of Tupper to about 1800 m. Either continue up the ridge to the top of an east-facing slide path at about 2000 m or, perhaps less committing, traverse awkwardly through steep forest to a point lower down the slide path. Ski the slide path.

Unfortunately, if you ski all the way down the path you will hit the railway tracks and it is illegal to cross or travel along them to get back to the highway just beyond. Instead, regulations require you to take the following designated route.

You will find an old railway grade at the south edge of the slide path at about 1160 m. Turn right and walk along this about 1 km, travelling through additional avalanche paths. Cross the stone arch bridge on the south side of one of these paths. A well-cleared grade leads downhill to an orange marker on the left; go downhill 100 m through a clearing to an orange marker on the right. Now head right and up into trees following orange markers that lead toward the highway. Avoid the railway here, because it goes into a tunnel. The markers lead back northeast between the tracks and the highway to the Stone Arch parking.

Mount Rogers ascent option

It is possible to ascend Mount Rogers as part of this tour or as an objective of its own. From the high point on the glacier between mounts Tupper and Rogers, climb the steep southeast face of the mountain on

Team Boston reaching the high point on the Tupper Traverse. Photo Mark Klassen

a large, steep snowslope. This is a committing ski mountaineering objective that requires lower avalanche hazard. It is about 585 m elevation gain and 1.5 km travel from the glacier to the summit.

MACDONALD WEST SHOULDER AND NRC GULLY

This is the most obvious skiing at the pass. Looking southeast from the Discovery Centre you will see the broad, open avalanche slopes coming off the west side of Mount MacDonald. Access is quick, route finding is easy and there is plenty of room for a lot of tracks! Road noise from the highway directly below interferes with the wilderness experience somewhat, at least until you are choking on the pow on the way down this long, fall-line run.

Parking for both tours is at the pullout on the east side of the highway, 1.25 km from the Discovery Centre and 67 km from Revelstoke.

14 MACDONALD WEST SHOULDER

Permit Avalanche
Length uphill 2–3.5 km
Max elevation gain 1200 m (significantly shorter trips possible)
Skiing elevation band 1314–2500 m
Aspect west
Avalanche Terrain Rating Challenging

Be aware that there is a lot of real estate over your head on this tour. Large avalanches run down these slopes fairly regularly and have been known to occur even if the area is open. Keep track of weather, especially what the winds are doing up high. Southerly and northerly winds crossload the start zones. Warm temperatures aloft are also something to keep in mind in terms of a possible avalanche trigger.

This tour is pretty much as you see it. From the parking area, clamber over the snowbank and start skinning up the huge avalanche path (see map on page 56). The terrain on the climber's right of the path has the least frequency of avalanches. An uptrack through the forest between the MacDonald slide path and NRC Gully is also possible.

How high you go depends on your motivation and your judgment of conditions. There is a steeper band at about 1800 m with a bench above that. This bench will catch some of the avalanches coming down from above. Higher up, things start feeling more exposed but it is possible to go all the way up to the ridge at 2500 m in stable conditions.

Ski down the avalanche path. Staying close to the trimline on skier's left (south) reduces your exposure.

MacDonald West Shoulder and NRC Gully. Photo Parks Canada

Care must be taken not to cross the boundary into the MacDonald West Shoulder prohibited area. This boundary is not obvious when you are in the field; it pays to have a careful look at the photographs and maps at the Discovery Centre before you go. The boundary lies along the strip of trees on the north side of the southern paths. This strip of trees is the one that runs the highest up the slope. The closed area is the widest avalanche path.

15 NRC GULLY

Permit Avalanche
Length uphill 2 km
Max elevation gain 550 m
Skiing elevation band 1314–1850 m

Aspect west
Avalanche Terrain Rating Challenging

This is the gully draining the hanging valley between MacDonald West Shoulder and Avalanche Mountain.

The route up is the same as for MacDonald West Shoulder. The highest point of the gully can be accessed from the bench above the steep band, at about 1850 m. There is tree skiing on either side of the gully, and the gully itself may be skied partway before it narrows and steepens at about 1720 m. At this point it may be best to ski in the trees on either side of it until it opens up again lower at about 1530 m.

CHEOPS

This is the zone on the southeast side of Cheops Mountain. There are a few runs here but I think the best one is Napoleon Spur. A variety of tree lines are available, with some less-exposed options. This restricted area is sometimes open when other areas are closed, so this run may be a good choice on a stormy day with higher avalanche hazard.

Parking is at the pullout on the east side of the highway, 1.25 km from the Discovery Centre and 67 km from Revelstoke. This is the same as for MacDonald West Shoulder–NRC Gully.

16 NAPOLEON SPUR

Permit Cheops
Length uphill 3.5 km
Max elevation gain 750 m
Skiing elevation band 1150–2075 m
Aspect east and southeast
Avalanche Terrain Rating Challenging

Buried surface hoar is probably the biggest avalanche issue on the upper ski lines. The steep, relatively low-elevation, south-facing glades above the CPR yard will also be more affected by solar radiation and warm temperatures than the other lines described for this area.

From the parking lot, cross the highway and ski south along it to the large avalanche runout that has mound structures in it (these shield the road from avalanches). Go through the mounds to the forest on the other side and make a long, rising traverse to the south. You will probably pass through some glades about 350 m beyond the mounds. It is tempting to work your way up these but if you do you will probably end up in some steep, awkward terrain with small cliffs. It is better to continue on a rising traverse to the south instead.

Work through steepening old growth forest toward the broad shoulder where the terrain changes aspect. Switchback to the other direction and gain a bench in the forest at about 1500 m. Somewhere in here you will probably have to deal with a short steep section.

Work your way up easier terrain. The forest begins to open into nice glades. Once you reach even more open terrain near treeline you can start doing laps in the glades if you want. It is also possible to climb higher and get into open terrain on Napoleon Spur itself, which is the southeast ridge of Cheops. Steeper lines are possible off the east side of the spur below the cliffs of the upper ridge. There are a couple of route options to get up that high. You can either go up a steep, sparsely treed area closer to the shoulder or up a gully feature on climber's right that is more exposed to overhead hazard.

There are a couple of exit options. The safest is to ski to the east through big trees to the highway, through the forest you came up. You will hit the highway a short distance from your vehicle. This can be thick and would not be the best run if tree bombs have hit the area.

A steeper, more open route is to do a hard turn to the right (south) at the bench on the shoulder at about 1550 m. This is perhaps the best skiing to exit this tour but it is significantly more exposed to avalanche hazard. Traverse into a very steep, open avalanche path that leads down to near the CPR yard below. There are other, more densely treed lines just to skier's left of the path that may feel less exposed.

Bigger, steeper lines that also lead south are available from higher on the spur. Be prepared for cliffy terrain in there.

If you take this exit you will need to put your skins on and tour back to the northeast to avoid trespassing on CPR property. The highway is gained a little over 1 km from the parking area.

Napoleon Spur from the Illecillewaet valley. Photo Mark Klassen

AVALANCHE

There is a big, steep, committing, awesome run off Avalanche Crest that is a lot of fun in the right conditions. If you are driving to the pass from the west, this thing stares you right in the face: it is the wide, west-facing avalanche slope above the sharp turn on the highway just before the pass.

This run gets suncrusts on it that can affect skiing quality. These crusts may also get buried and can cause avalanche problems, especially if combined with surface hoar. Sunny days with intense solar radiation may also be a time to give this spot a miss. This place is similar to MacDonald West Shoulder if you were to ski that run from the very top.

Parking is at the Avalanche–Illecillewaet–Asulkan parking lot on the north side of the highway, 4 km west of the Discovery Centre and 64 km from Revelstoke. If you are coming from the summit of the pass, a dangerous U-turn is required to get into the parking area, just past where the twinned highway turns back into two lanes at the big corner. Alternatively you can drive 5.15 km west of the Discovery Centre and pull into a CPR access road on the right, then perhaps more safely re-enter the highway and drive back to the parking lot.

17 AVALANCHE CREST

Permit Avalanche
Length uphill 4.5 km
Max elevation gain 1000 m (more if you do a run in the moraines)
Skiing elevation band 1200–2200 m
Aspect southwest
Avalanche Terrain Rating Complex

The parking area is a good spot to scope the run from before you head up. Mark the steep bands in your mind and try to remember the sequence of lefts and rights you may want to take to avoid the steepest terrain. Taking a picture you can refer to later might be an idea.

From the parking area, climb the short, steep slope through the trees behind the toilet to the old railway grade. Turn left and walk along it past the turnoff to Illecillewaet and Asulkan. Find the Avalanche Crest trailhead on the right (sign), across the railway grade from Wheeler Hut.

Follow the trail as marked on the Adventure Map. It leads up through the steep forest into the basin southwest of Avalanche Mountain and Eagle Peak. The summer trail may be hard to find in the winter but it isn't rocket science here; just work your way up into the basin.

Once in the basin I often make a run in the moraines before going to Avalanche Crest proper. Pick a line; there are plenty.

To get to Avalanche Crest, put in a steep uptrack on the edge of the highest trees on the east side of the ridge that bounds the west side of the basin. Gain the ridge after a short climb and continue up it through scrubby trees.

The farther up the ridge you go, the larger, steeper and more exposed the avalanche terrain you will be in when you ski down. It is a very serious place up there. The skier's left lines through the small trees that start at about 2100 m off the ridge are a bit less severe but it is still a big-time run. Be sure you are making the right decision.

On the way down the skier's left lines a short steep section is encountered at about 1850 m (this is the same band as on MacDonald West Shoulder). Skier's left is less steep. This band is bigger and steeper on the far skier's right lines.

Another steep band, bigger this time, is found starting at about 1600 m. This time an end run to the right avoids the steepest parts. Don't get too low before starting to traverse here or you will end up having to walk or get caught up in the steeper terrain. Following the trim line on the skier's right side of the widest slide path (the

Avalanche Basin from Glacier Crest. Photo Mark Klassen

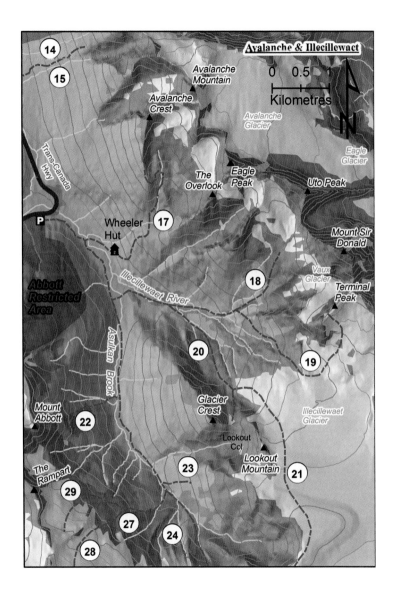

Avalanche & Illecillewaet

0   0.5   1
Kilometres

N

14

15

Avalanche
Mountain

Avalanche
Crest

Avalanche
Glacier

Eagle
Glacier

Trans-Canada Hwy

The
Overlook

Eagle
Peak

Uto Peak

P

Wheeler
Hut

17

Mount Sir
Donald

Illecillewaet River

18

Vaux
Glacier

Terminal
Peak

Abbott
Restricted
Area

Asulkan Brook

20

19

Glacier
Crest

Illecillewaet
Glacier

Mount
Abbott

22

Lookout
Col

Lookout
Mountain

21

The
Rampart

29

23

24

27

28

Avalanche Crest from the highway. Photo Mark Klassen

southernmost one) is the least steep option. Descend beside this all the way to the highway.

ILLECILLEWAET AND ASULKAN

Overview

Mostly north-facing, the runs in this area are very popular. There are a variety of skiing options here, from big loops over cols and summits to steep pillow lines in the trees to mellow alpine bowls. Avalanche paths do not threaten the highway, so permits are not required. As a result, many skiers will congregate in these zones during restricted area closure days.

That does not mean this is not avalanche country. On the contrary, a lot of the terrain here is steep and open. All the tours are exposed to significant avalanche danger. Climax avalanches hit the valley bottom trails most years, especially in the Asulkan. In poor weather and conditions it can be difficult to keep things safe, and during periods of higher hazard there may be better places to ski.

Parking is at the Avalanche–Illecillewaet–Asulkan parking lot on the north side of the highway, 4 km west of the Discovery Centre and 64 km from Revelstoke. If you are coming from the summit of the pass, a dangerous U-turn is required to get into the parking area, just past where the twinned highway turns back into two lanes at the big corner. Alternatively you can drive 5.15 km west of the Discovery Centre and pull into a CPR access road on the right, then perhaps more safely re-enter the highway and drive back to the parking lot.

Approach

The initial trail is the same for both these valleys. From the parking area, climb the short, steep slope through the trees behind the toilet to the old railway grade. Turn left and walk along it to the apex of the big curve on the trail. There is a large clearing on the right; turn into it (the trail sign here may be buried). Continue past the foundations of Glacier House into the forest on the far right side of the clearing.

Follow a trail through the forest. This trail leads up the Asulkan. To get to the Illecillewaet you have to take either of two left turns off the Asulkan trail.

The first turnoff is a connector to the Sir Donald–Perley trail and is about 200 m from the end of the clearing, just before a slight right turn in the trail and a small hill that leads past some large boulders. It will take you across a bridge on the Illecillewaet River, downstream of the Meeting of the Waters (the river's confluence with Asulkan Brook).

The second turnoff (the Great Glacier trail) is about 600 m from the clearing and leads across a bridge on Asulkan Brook above the Meeting of the Waters, before eventually reaching the Illecillewaet River, which is followed upstream.

In the winter the signs for these trails are usually buried in snow and it may be easy to miss both junctions, especially after a snowfall. The Great Glacier trail seems to be more popular among skiers, and that junction will often have a stick and/or flagging tape marking it.

Refer to the relevant sections for further approach details.

ILLECILLEWAET

The Illecillewaet valley is home to four outstanding alpine tours. All of them involve significant amounts of avalanche terrain, but Lookout Col is the least exposed. Windslab and surface hoar instabilities will be the greatest avalanche hazards here. There is no significant tree skiing in the Illecillewaet, so it is not a good place to go in poor visibility or even on flat-light days.

Approach options

To start all the tours, follow the route described in the previous Illecillewaet/Asulkan Overview section. From the Asulkan trail, the different options are described below.

Sir Donald/Perley connector trail

From the bridge over the Illecillewaet, take the left-hand bank of the river upstream over convoluted terrain. Getting off the steep bank and onto a bench in the forest above gives the easiest travel. Eventually you will reach the open avalanche runouts that come down from the north, and the upper valley will open up ahead.

Great Glacier trail

From the bridge across Asulkan Brook, skin through the dense, rolling forest eastward below the toe of the north ridge of Glacier Crest. You may end up in a boulder field here; if so, it is easiest to stay below it. Eventually you should come across the Illecillewaet River (still a stream at this point). Follow the bank until it is easy to get into the streambed itself where it is broad and flat. Continue to the upper valley.

An existing skin track may also take you closer to moraines on the northeast side of Glacier Crest. If so, you may have to drop a bit to gain the flat valley below. Trying to work the sidehill of the moraines doesn't put you in the best position for the rest of the tour.

Another option

Perhaps the least complex way into the Illecillewaet is to walk along the old railway grade to Wheeler Hut and find the trailhead for the

Avalanche Crest trail. This is also the true start to the Sir Donald–Perley trail. Follow the east side of the Illecillewaet River, staying above the steep bank on a forested bench, to the upper valley. This way is a bit longer than the other options but the route finding is easier. It may be the best way to go if you are unfamiliar with the area and there is no trail broken yet.

18 SIR DONALD BASIN

Permit none
Length uphill 6.5 km
Max elevation gain 1325 m (to Sir Donald–Uto Col)
Skiing elevation band 1400-2525 m
Aspect west and southwest
Avalanche Terrain Rating Complex

This is the bowl situated directly beneath the pyramids of Sir Donald and Uto. The massive walls above are a stunning backdrop for the ski down. This is the sunny side of the valley, so it can be a good option on cold days. Suncrusts on the surface can affect the skiing, however, and when buried they can cause avalanche hazards, especially when combined with surface hoar. Wind effect, windslabs and a variable depth snowpack can also be an issue in the moraines.

From the lower, open valley, gain the north bank of the creek that drains the Sir Donald basin. Where the stream splits at about 1620 m, climb up between the two branches on a steep slope with small trees to an open, lower-angled slope. This route is to the climber's left of the summer trail marked on the Adventure Map.

Two options are available here. The first is to climb through more scattered trees on steep slopes above and gain the crest of the moraine below Vaux Glacier. A run can be made down this moraine.

If you want to go higher, stay to climber's left of the moraine and continue through some steep terrain into the upper basin.

Be sure to scope your line while ascending. The terrain offers various options, and most likely you will want to ski down near to where you came up.

The Sir Donald basin from the Lookout Col tour. Photo Mark Klassen

19 PERLEY ROCK AND TERMINAL PEAK

Permit none
Length uphill 6.5 (Perley Rock)
  9 km (Terminal Peak)
Max elevation gain 1100 m (Perley Rock)
  1750 m (Terminal Peak)
Skiing elevation band 1400–2300 m (Perley Rock)
  1400–2950 m (Terminal Peak)
Aspect northwest, west, and south
Avalanche Terrain Rating Complex

Perley Rock is a bluff on the northeast side of Illecillewaet Glacier. Getting there gives a challenging tour up steep slopes and complex moraines. There is also exposure to the large west-facing slopes of Terminal Peak above. The continuation to Terminal Peak gets you to a high peak with great views of the Illecillewaet Névé and Mount Sir Donald. The final, south-aspect slope to get to Terminal is steep and large. Windslabs, buried surface hoar and

Perley Rock

The route to Perley Rock from below. From this perspective it looks like a more direct route is possible, but traversing rightward around the base of the moraine is required. Photo Mark Klassen

perhaps buried crusts on Terminal all affect snow stability here. Both objectives should be attempted only in times of lower hazard. The Terminal Peak option also includes glacier travel.

From the lower valley where it opens up, skin toward a ridge that separates the Sir Donald basin from Illecillewaet Glacier. From near the base of that ridge, about 1675 m, **468000** E **5678100** N, traverse right, below a frozen waterfall, onto a sparsely treed bench between steep slopes. Work into the terrain above the bench, where there is some exposure to the huge slopes of Terminal Peak. Climb up and right on steepening slopes toward the base of the prominent moraine. Round it on the right and continue up lower-angled slopes to Perley Rock.

From here it is a great ski down the way you came up. Don't miss the traverse back right beneath the moraine or you will end up on steeper slopes, cliffs and gullies. It may be possible to go that way, but scope it out on the way up first.

It is also possible to gain Perley Rock from Illecillewaet Glacier. Follow the description for the Youngs Peak Traverse, and once on the glacier, traverse it to Perley Rock. This route is longer and crosses some crevassed terrain.

To continue to Terminal Peak, go around Perley Rock to the south. Travel through moraines to the glacier south of the peak. Climb it to a steep slope which leads to a shoulder of the southwest ridge of the northwest peak of Terminal (not named on the maps). Ascend this very steep slope to the ridge. It is possible to scramble to the northwest peak from there. The main, southeast peak would require significantly more effort and is not normally climbed in the winter.

20 LOOKOUT COL

Permit none
Length uphill 6 km
Max elevation gain 950 m
Skiing elevation band 1400–2150 m
Aspect north (southwest and west for the Asulkan Option)
Avalanche Terrain Rating Complex

This is the shortest tour in the valley and a popular one. It is also the least committing piece of terrain, although care must be taken in the moraines leading to the upper bowl. If conditions are not conducive to ascending the moraines, it is still a good run down to the valley from below them.

From the lower valley, head for the rolling terrain on climber's right of the valley. These are to the left of a prominent moraine and broad gully beneath Glacier Crest. Climb up these slopes, avoiding gullies and dips. Keep a series of small, orangey-brown cliffs to your right while lower down. Once up higher, trending left toward the toe of the glacier may utilize the lowest-angled terrain. There are short, steep slopes throughout this climb and a variety of ways to go. Follow your nose.

The terrain flattens beneath the toe of Illecillewaet Glacier, and the slopes leading to the col will be up and to the right. From here there is often a skin track that goes straight up the steep moraine wall below the final bowl. I prefer a less exposed but slightly unobvious route which goes up a little rib on the right. It is a bit awkward to gain this rib, especially with a low snowpack in the early season, but it leads to smaller and lower-angle terrain that easily brings you up to the crest of the moraine above. Walk along the crest to the left until it is easy to drop into the bowl behind. Continue up the centre of the bowl to the col. While in the bowl there are slopes above on either side of you, so make sure that windloading or intense solar radiation is not going to trigger an avalanche up there.

Route finding in the bowl on descent is easy. The lower, convoluted terrain can be more difficult. It never looks the same on the way down as it does on the way up! Scope it carefully on ascent; there are a variety of lines.

Asulkan option

It is also possible to ski into the Asulkan Valley from Lookout Col. The skiing quality is often not as good as down the north side of the col and it involves significantly steeper and more exposed terrain. However, it is a fun option when conditions are conducive.

From the col, traverse slightly left through scrubby trees and find a ski line down them to open slopes. It is often wind-hammered and/or suncrusted on this steep slope. Once in the basin below, ski down it on gentler terrain to treeline. Avoid going straight down the drainage that leads to valley bottom from here; it is a terrain trap that gives poor skiing.

If you wish, you can put your skins on and climb a bit through the forest to the south to get a longer run down The Ravens, which is the west-facing avalanche path that leads into Asulkan. Otherwise you can make a descending traverse south through the same forest for about 400 m to reach the edge of the path farther down. Ski it to the valley. It may also be possible to ski the trees.

The lower section of the Youngs Peak (left arrow) and Lookout Col tours. Photo Mark Klassen

21 YOUNGS PEAK TRAVERSE

Permit none
Length uphill 10 km
Max elevation gain 1600 m
Skiing elevation band 1550–2815 m
Aspect northeast through northwest
Avalanche Terrain Rating Complex

This is a long, classic ski traverse, one of the best ski ascents in the Selkirks. The initial slopes off the summit into the Asulkan valley are very steep and it would be a drag to turn back from there to ski back down the Illecillewaet. Make sure that windslab or buried surface hoar on alpine north aspects is not a problem before committing to this tour. You will also want a bluebird day to be able to see your way across the névé.

Take the Lookout Col tour to below the toe of Illecillewaet Glacier. From there, climb the steep toe of the glacier to lower-angle slopes and travel south toward the névé. Watch for crevasses, especially lower on the glacier.

Once on the névé, head for the long north ridge of Youngs Peak. Climb up and over the 2650 m bump at **4691**00 E **5674**000 N and continue onto Youngs Peak proper (some bootpacking may be required). There are a few steep rolls on this ridge that feel exposed; if you were to trigger an avalanche you might fall all the way into the Asulkan valley! Near the beginning of the upper ridge, at about 2625 m, **4688**00 E **5673**700 N, you will pass by the Forever Young couloir, a local steep-skiing test piece.

The summit is easily gained. Take a few minutes for a good look around before starting down. This is an excellent viewpoint overlooking the entire central Selkirks.

The descent is the outstanding Steps of Paradise run that leads into the Asulkan Valley. See the description on page 97.

ASULKAN

This place holds some of the most famous runs of Rogers Pass. A long valley walk leads to a massive cirque with tree runs, moraines and glaciers. Asulkan Cabin sits at treeline at the head of the valley and provides a good base for exploring, though most groups will do these tours as day trips.

There is a variety of skiing in the Asulkan valley and some of the runs may be a good place to go in poor visibility or during heightened avalanche hazard. Big slopes cause a lot of overhead hazard, though, so it is not a place to be during a climax avalanche cycle.

The Asulkan Valley Trail

The approach to all the tours is the same: straight up the valley. See the Illecillewaet–Asulkan Overview section at page 84 for initial approach information.

Once past the Illecillewaet junctions, continue up the trail. Asulkan Brook is soon crossed and the rest of the route lies in the forest on the east bank of the stream. The views begin to open up about 3 km up the

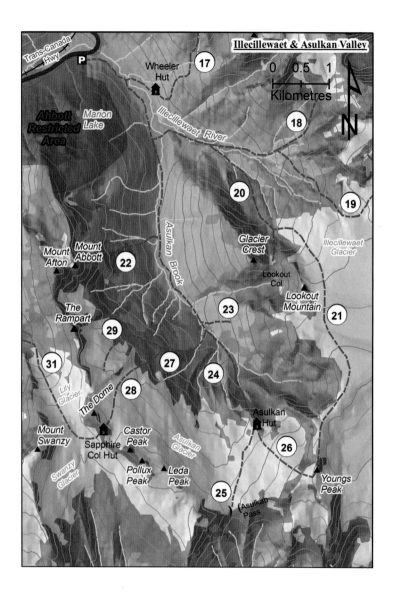

Illecillewaet & Asulkan Valley

0   0.5   1
Kilometres

N

Trans-Canada Hwy
P
Wheeler Hut
17
18
Marion Lake
Abbott Restricted Area
Illecillewaet River
19
20
Asulkan Brook
Glacier Crest
Illecillewaet Glacier
Mount Afton
Mount Abbott
22
Lookout Col
Lookout Mountain
21
The Rampart
29
23
27
24
31
Lily Glacier
The Dome
28
Asulkan Hut
26
Mount Swanzy
Sapphire Col Hut
Castor Peak
Asulkan Glacier
Pollux Peak
Leda Peak
25
Youngs Peak
Swanzy Glacier
Asulkan Pass

trail, with avalanche paths coming down from the west side all the way to the creek bed. Shortly thereafter, the Mushroom People run is passed on the right. Eventually you reach a constriction in the valley, which is called The Mousetrap. Several large avalanche paths converge here from all sides, and huge slides have been known to reach this spot all the way from Leda Peak, almost 4 km away, as well as from Lookout Col and The Ravens to the east.

The valley opens up beyond The Mousetrap. The Tree Triangle lies directly ahead and Triangle Moraine is to the right. The Ravens are the avalanche paths coming down from Lookout Mountain on the left.

When exiting this valley be careful of tourers coming uphill when you are rocketing down the luge run of the lower trail.

22 MUSHROOM PEOPLE AREA

Permit none
Length uphill 5.5 km
Max elevation gain 650 m
Skiing elevation band 1400–1850 m
Aspect east
Avalanche Terrain Rating Complex

These are the first few avalanche paths you come upon while walking up the Asulkan. They lead down from the west side of the valley.

The first couple of paths have skiing in the runout zones. Route finding is fairly straightforward: choose a line and skin up to it. The higher you go, the more you will be exposed to the big terrain above, so pick your day carefully. Be especially aware of high winds aloft which may load the start zones without it being apparent from the valley.

The actual Mushroom People run is a steep pillow line that starts in a boulder field at about 1850 m, 465200 E 5676200 N, below the east ridge of Mount Abbott. The boulders lead to an even steeper avalanche track and a terrain trap in the creek.

It is steep and difficult uptracking to get to the top of this run. Starting in the forest to the north may be the best option, eventually gaining less steep, open ground to the north of the trees at around

1600 m. It is also possible to reach this line from the Dome Glacier descent.

23 THE RAVENS

Permit none
Length uphill 6.5 km
Max elevation gain 700 m
Skiing elevation band 1600–1900 m
Aspect west
Avalanche Terrain Rating Complex

These are the west-facing paths coming down from Lookout Mountain, just beyond The Mousetrap. There is a lot of real estate above your head here, so make sure there isn't wind loading or strong sun effect on the upper slopes.

Skin up the lower path and the trees on climber's left. Most groups don't go higher than 1800 or 1900 m.

This run may also be accessed from the Illecillewaet valley and Lookout Col.

24 TREE TRIANGLE

Permit none
Length uphill 7.5 km
Max elevation gain 900 m
Skiing elevation band 1600–2100 m
Aspect north
Avalanche Terrain Rating Complex

This is the distinctive triangle of trees at the head of the valley. It is a popular run and can get tracked out early. The lower slopes through the trees may be a reasonable place to go on days of heightened avalanche hazard, but you have to walk under a lot of big paths to get there.

From The Mousetrap, gain the moraine to the south and then the forest beyond. Uptrack through the trees, easily at first, then more steeply. The slope narrows to a ridge at about 1900 m and a crux pitch presents itself. The best skiing in the triangle itself is below here, so if conditions are such that you don't want to tackle this crux slope you can still get a good run in. Pick a line down through the forest the same way you came up. You can also ski off the ridge to the east from here, but these lines are steeper and more open.

If continuing toward Asulkan Cabin, the crux slope above is usually ascended on the climber's left side. Then follow the ridge to the cabin at 2100 m, **467200** E **5673800** N.

From the cabin you can ski back down the way you came. Alternatively, take the moraine down and to skier's left (west). Steep slopes lead into a terrain trap at the base of the moraine, so consider conditions carefully before committing to this line.

25 ASULKAN PASS

Permit none
Length uphill 9 km
Max elevation gain 1150 m
Skiing elevation band 1600–2350 m
Aspect north
Avalanche Terrain Rating Complex

Asulkan Pass is the col between Youngs Peak on the east and Leda Peak on the west. It gives a glacier run on lower-angle slopes. Large slopes lie above it to the west.

This is most commonly reached from Asulkan Cabin on a straightforward climb over moraines and glacier. It can also be gained by skinning directly up the valley below the pass. This is also the best descent.

26 THE STEPS OF PARADISE FROM YOUNGS PEAK

Permit none
Length uphill 10 km
Max elevation gain 1600 m
Skiing elevation band 1600–2815 m
Aspect north
Avalanche Terrain Rating Complex

This is one of the classic ski descents in Rogers Pass, best done as part of the Youngs Peak Traverse described in the Illecillewaet section.

From Asulkan Cabin work your way up generally gentle moraines

Labels on image: Tree Triangle, Youngs Peak, Pterodactyl, Asulkan Cabin, Asulkan Pass

Youngs Peak, Asulkan Pass and the Tree Triangle from Triangle Moraine. Photo Mark Klassen

and glacier to the base of the very steep slope of Youngs Peak. Skin up this if you can, or take your skis off and boot hike up it. Usually the climber's right (west) margin is the easiest and least steep way to go. Make sure that windslabs or deeper instabilities on alpine north aspects are not an issue before committing to this slope.

Above this is a bench. Go left (east) along it to a short steep slope and convexity that leads to the summit. There are very large crevasses on the bench, whether you can see them or not!

Descent is back down the face of Youngs to the glacier below. From there a few options present themselves. You can go to the west down Asulkan Glacier below Asulkan Pass; you can ski back to the hut and ski the Tree Triangle; or you can go to the right and ski to the east of the Pterodactyl.

For the Asulkan Glacier and Tree Triangle options, have a look at the descriptions earlier in this chapter.

The Pterodactyl is the small, rocky summit above and to the east of Asulkan Cabin. A steep line leads down on its east side, descending a broad gully. This line is steeper and more exposed than the other Steps of Paradise lines described here.

27 TRIANGLE MORAINE

Permit none
Length uphill 7 km
Max elevation gain 800 m
Skiing elevation band 1600–2000 m
Aspect northeast
Avalanche Terrain Rating Complex

This is the moraine directly west of The Mousetrap.

Start in the trees on the lower moraine, beginning from climber's left. There often is a skin track straight up the open slope of the upper moraine, but a safer route lies along the top of the trees, leading to the right. There are still some steep, open slopes here but they are smaller. Wrap around the end of the moraine to the north before making your way back the other direction on lower-angled terrain above the moraine, scoping your line as you go. The farther up toward the pinnacle of the triangle you go, the steeper and bigger the terrain is.

28 SAPPHIRE COL

Permit none
Length uphill 9.5 km
Max elevation gain 1400 m
Skiing elevation band 1600–2600 m
Aspect northeast
Avalanche Terrain Rating Complex

One of the great glacier runs in Rogers Pass, perhaps best done as part of a traverse from Lily Glacier in Loop Brook. The Sapphire Col run is on a sheltered glacier, and buried surface hoar instabilities are common here.

Take the route to the top of the Triangle Moraine. From there, find a way up the rolling, complex benches above. In flat light this is a difficult place to trackset through. The toe of Asulkan Glacier is at about 2000 m. There is an impressive rock wall on the north side of the glacier here called The Cleaver.

Work your way up the glacier. Whether you can see them or not there are large crevasses on the whole lower section, so many that in the summer it is difficult to find a way through. There is a steeper slope at about 2300 m and more crevasses at the convexity at its top. Once on the lower-angled glacier above, head left toward the col.

The Sapphire Col Hut provides shelter at the summit, but sometimes that little tin can is colder inside than it is out! From the col a descent can be made down Lily Glacier to the west, but the skiing is often better back down the Asulkan side. Skiing back down the way you came up is the usual route. Steeper, more complex lines can be made straight down from the col into the Asulkan Valley. It's best to scope those out well before committing to them, perhaps from Asulkan Cabin.

The northwest ridge of Castor Peak is an easy boot hike from the col.

Triangle Moraine and the routes to Sapphire Col and Dome Glacier, from Glacier Crest. Photo Mark Klassen

Admiring the view from Sapphire Col. Photo Mark Klassen

29 DOME GLACIER

Permit none
Length uphill 9.5 km
Max elevation gain 1200 m
Skiing elevation band 1600–2400 m
Aspect northeast
Avalanche Terrain Rating Complex

This is the pocket glacier on the north side of The Cleaver. Like the Asulkan Glacier run from Sapphire Col, it is a sheltered spot and prone to having buried surface hoar layers.

Start up the Triangle Moraine route but don't go all the way to the top. From the highest trees on the right, continue heading northeast. The trick is not to gain too much elevation, but to contour across and even a bit downhill around the toe of a moraine on some steep slopes at about 1900 m, 465700 E 5675200 N. It is tempting to gain the crest of the moraine and climb that, but if you do you will need to lose elevation

Routes to Sapphire Col, Dome Glacier and Mushroom People as seen from Glacier Crest. Photo Mark Klassen

down a steep sidewall to get to the glacier. You could get a short run if you went that way, though.

Once around the moraine, gain the glacier and climb it. The climber's right side is less steep than the left. Watch for crevasses.

Once you have skied the glacier, the descent to the valley can be a bit complicated. The least steep option is to put your skins on and traverse back to the Triangle Moraine.

It is possible to ski straight down below the glacier, but the terrain is super steep – have a look at it from the valley on your way up in the morning.

A less steep way is to take a bench that slants down to the left (north) from below the main glacier. Work your way down a steep band at about 1775 m (this can be reached more directly from skier's left lines on the glacier) and continue trending north to the edge of the first significant patch of forest that lies to the north of Mushroom People, at

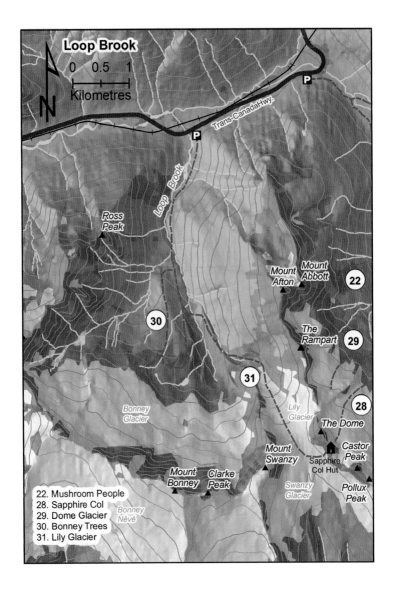

Loop Brook

0   0.5   1
Kilometres

N

Trans-Canada Hwy.

P

P

Ross Peak

Loop Brook

Mount Afton

Mount Abbott

22

30

The Rampart

29

31

Bonney Glacier

Lily Glacier

28

The Dome

Mount Swanzy

Sapphire Col Hut

Castor Peak

Mount Bonney

Clarke Peak

Swanzy Glacier

Pollux Peak

22. Mushroom People
28. Sapphire Col
29. Dome Glacier
30. Bonney Trees
31. Lily Glacier

Bonney Névé

about 1600 m, **465**6400 E 5**676**000 N. Ski down the steep, open slopes below, or find your way through the forest. From this point it is also just a short climb to the top of Mushroom People.

LOOP

Loop Brook is named after the elevated loop that the railway originally made at the mouth of the stream. The stone towers that supported the tracks are still standing near the beginning of the tour.

This feels like one of the more remote areas in Rogers Pass. A walk up the narrow valley immediately isolates you from the highway corridor and eventually opens up into expansive and wild alpine terrain where the foreboding north face of Mount Bonney rises out of the broken glacier below. At the head of the valley, Lily Glacier leads to Sapphire Col, and to the east lies the long Asulkan ridge.

There are two recommended tours here, very different in character. The Bonney area is a wind-sheltered run of moraines and open glades. Lily Glacier is a crevassed tongue of ice that is far more exposed to the elements.

Parking is at the pullout on the north side of the highway, 6.4 km west of the Discovery Centre and 62 km from Revelstoke. This is just before a bridge, and when you are coming from the east it can be a bit of a blind left-hand turn across the eastbound lane of the highway.

30 BONNEY

Permit Loop
Length uphill 5.5 km
Max elevation gain 950 m
Skiing elevation band 1450–2100 m
Aspect north
Avalanche Terrain Rating Complex

This is the area of moraines and trees that lie directly below Bonney Glacier. There is a variety of terrain here, from lower-angled, short runs to longer, steeper and more exposed lines. Since it is a sheltered north aspect, buried surface hoar hazards are especially a concern here.

Getting to the top of the run is a bit of a route-finding exercise. From the parking area, climb over the snowbank by the sign and drop into the creek below. Follow the left bank past avalanche runouts on the east side of the valley. Farther on, the valley narrows and the trail becomes exposed to more avalanche slopes off Ross Peak to the west. These paths catch morning sun, so getting an early start for this tour is recommended, to lessen your exposure.

At about 1280 m, 462200 E 5676900 N, a tributary stream from the west flows through a canyon just before where Loop Brook itself turns into a canyon. From here you need to climb the "Elephant's Trunk" on the left side of the tributary canyon (looked at in just the right way, the feature you climb here looks like – you guessed it – an Elephant's Trunk). To get up the trunk, climb a short but steep sidewall of Loop Brook's west bank just before the side canyon. Turn into the side canyon and cross it almost immediately on a natural bridge. Switchback up the steep slope above to flatter ground. It is always impressive when this canyon gets choked with avalanche debris from Ross Peak high above.

Continue a short way up the south bank of the side canyon until about 1375 m. Now start working your way to the left (south) on convoluted ground, paralleling Loop Brook through forest, contouring and not gaining much elevation.

At this point there may be uptracks leading higher and to the right from this area. That route works but it has thick and steep forest. Still, it may be a better way if surface hoar instabilities are thought to be an issue in the upper moraines, as it gives a less steep track in the upper section. For this option, work through the initially steep, dense trees and a small cliff, heading south until you gain lower-angled, more open forest on a broad ridge. Once in the open terrain of the moraines, take a low-angled gully feature between the two easternmost moraines to get to the crest of them.

For the easier-travelling route, follow a traverse to the south-southeast through the trees, staying below 1450 m. Soon you will break out into the open upper valley. This is where the route to the Lily Glacier breaks off.

To get to the upper moraines, begin gaining elevation on the edge of the forest above before entering it again higher, always trending south. You are aiming for 1600 m, **46230**0 E **5675800** N. This means that once you re-enter the forest at about 1500 m a long traverse with the occasional switchback is made along an indistinct bench. Make sure you don't get too high.

At the waypoint mentioned above you will break out of the forest and into a bit of a depression between the forest on the right and a lateral moraine on the left. From here the route becomes more obvious. Follow the depression easily until you hit a gully eroded into the moraine. Either climb the steep slopes above to the west to gain the crest of a moraine (this accesses the top of the easternmost ski line) or cross the gully across a short, steep slope and skin uphill to the west on low-angle slopes. This brings you to the south of the crests of the moraines. Short slopes lead to the top of the moraines.

The best skiing is off the north sides of the moraines. The shortest run is of a moderate angle and starts from the crest of the easternmost moraine at about 1950 m, **4620**1**00** E **5674900** N. As you go farther west each line gets a bit bigger and steeper. The first few moraines end in the trees. A skier's left line on the farthest-west moraine can lead into a very steep open shot on the edge of the trees and leads down to the stream draining the southeast face of Mount Green. The snow-covered rock slabs to the west of this moraine begin at a moderate angle but end in a steep rollover and small cliffs, and also end up in the Mount Green drainage.

There are also ski lines on the crevassed Bonney Glacier.

Exits

From the easternmost moraine run, continue skiing fall line (which pulls you to the east) through steepening forest. Watch out for small cliffs. Farther down, the trees open up and the steep sidewall of the moraine can be skied toward Loop Brook below. Less steep slopes can be found by traversing skier's left. Alternatively, a long traverse in the region of the uptrack avoids steep terrain altogether. Don't descend all the way to Loop Brook, but stay above 1450 m and traverse back left (north) to gain the uptrack and avoid a canyon.

The exit from the bottom of the steeper western lines goes down the stream below Mount Green. Make sure you stay high on the right (east) bank to avoid a small canyon at about 1500 m. The stream leads to your uptrack.

31 LILY GLACIER AND THE SAPPHIRE COL TRAVERSE

Permit Loop
Length uphill 6.5 km (Lily Glacier)
  8.5 km (Sapphire Col)
Max elevation gain 1325 m (Lily Glacier)
  1750 m (Sapphire Col)
Skiing elevation band 1450–2450 m (Lily Glacier)
  1650–2580 m (Sapphire Col Traverse)
Aspect north and west (Lily Glacier)
  northeast (Sapphire Col Traverse)
Avalanche Terrain Rating Complex

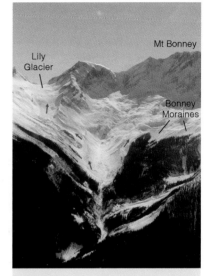

Loop Brook from Cheops Mountain. Photo Parks Canada

Lily Glacier drains down from the pass between Mount Swanzy and The Dome. When not wind affected, Lily Glacier is a great alpine run down a glacier and moraines. The Sapphire Col Traverse is one of the great loop trips in the Selkirks. Both routes have heavily crevassed glaciers.

If doing the Sapphire Col Traverse it is best if you can leave a vehicle at the Avalanche–Illecillewaet–Asulkan parking lot. Otherwise, walking or hitchhiking will be required to get back to your vehicle at Loop Brook.

Begin the trip as for the Bonney tour. Where you enter the open upper valley at about 1450 m, drop back down to Loop Brook. Climb the lateral moraine to the east and gain its crest at the end. Now skin up the ridge of the moraine until it is easy to drop down the moraine's sidewall to the east.

Ascend the steepening morainal bowl to the toe of the glacier and start up it. A crux zone starts at about 2200 m. You are on a big, steep slope; there is overhead hazard; and large crevasses are often thinly bridged here because of downflow wind effect scouring away the snowpack. Carefully assess these multiple hazards.

Above this point the glacier levels off considerably. Go as far as you want before skiing down. Remember those crevasses!

Another option is to ski the smaller glacier on the north side of The Dome into steep moraines below. Watch for cliff bands and a thin, variable snowpack in the moraines. From the top of this glacier a boot hike up a very steep slope leads to a small col at the base of the north ridge of The Dome. You can ski down Dome Glacier on the Asulkan side from here.

To continue on the Sapphire Col Traverse, climb the Lily until below the col. Climb a very steep slope to the col; boot hiking may be required. From the col, ski down Asulkan Glacier as described for the Sapphire Col tour in the Asulkan section.

BOSTOCK

This is a tree skiing area with options for open trees, steep open shots down avalanche chutes, and glade skiing. Both runs are at a bit of a low elevation, so this is not the best place to go when the freezing level is high.

Parking is at the pullout on the north side of the highway, 16.8 km west of the Discovery Centre and 52 km from Revelstoke.

32 MCGILL SHOULDER

Permit McGill, Bostock Parking
Length uphill 4–5 km
Max elevation gain 1200 m (shorter options available)
Skiing elevation band 1200–2200 m

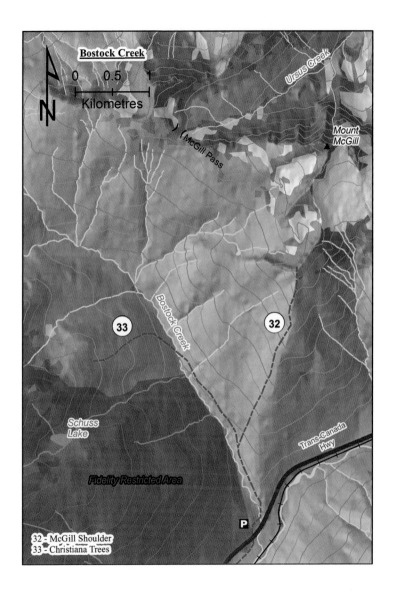

Bostock Creek

Ursus Creek

McGill Pass

Mount McGill

0   0.5   Kilometres

N

33

Bostock Creek

32

Schuss Lake

Trans-Canada Hwy

Fidelity Restricted Area

P

32 – McGill Shoulder
33 – Christiana Trees

109

Aspect southwest
Avalanche Terrain Rating Challenging

There are a variety of lines off the long, forested south ridge of Mount McGill, with options to reduce your exposure to avalanche terrain. This run is southwest-facing and therefore subject to suncrusts. Buried crusts and/or surface hoar are the main avalanche hazards on the tree lines. Wind slabs and overhead hazard are also issues on the avalanche chutes. There is some dense forest to travel through to get to the skiing.

From the parking area drop down a bit and find the trail. Alternatively, ski along the snowbank beside the road to the east and traverse into the trail from there.

Skin up the summer trail through a couple of switchbacks before following it upstream a short way. There is no obvious spot to break off this trail, but what you need to do is follow the broad, densely forested shoulder that points toward the highway. Start uptracking and see where it takes you. At one point you may see an opening in the forest above you while still at a low elevation. This is a blowdown with extensive windfall trees that make travel difficult and needs to be avoided. Stay in the dense forest on climber's right.

Most people follow the shoulder all the way to treeline. Another option is to begin to contour to the bottom of the open terrain visible on the Adventure Map at 1480 m, **453**000 E 5677700 N, and work your way up from there. It is debatable which way is better.

The forest on the shoulder begins to open up at 1675 m and if you want a short, less exposed run you can traverse into ski lines from here. Or continue up to between 1900 and 2000 m on the shoulder, where longer runs through steep open trees are available.

On descent, denser forest begins again at around 1500 m but it is skiable for some way below that. Eventually it gets quite thick and will require a bit of thrashing to regain the trail.

If you are on a skier's right line, you can trend even farther right where the terrain gets less steep low down and catch open lines almost all the way down to the trail.

Continuing up the shoulder to about 2050 m allows a traverse into the Gunbarrel Chutes. These are two steep, narrow shots through the forest that are significantly more serious terrain than the runs lower down. They lead to the lower open lines mentioned above, which you can ski to the trail.

Finally, between 2100 and 2200 m on the shoulder you can drop into the McGill Chutes, which up the ante once more. They are bigger, steeper and more wind-affected than the Gunbarrels. They lead into the same spot as those lines.

From all these lines it is surprisingly easy to miss the trail and ski right over it, especially if no one has broken a track up it yet. Keep a sharp eye out for it at about the 1225 m level. If the trail has been used already, get ready for a fast, thigh-burning luge run back to the road.

There is also lots of skiing to explore farther north, toward McGill Pass.

You may notice some steep skiing off the southeast side of McGill

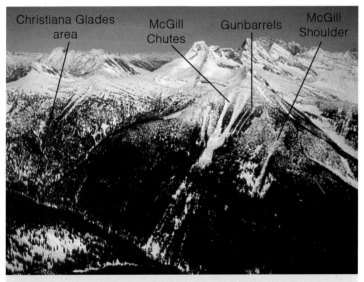

McGill Shoulder area. Photo Parks Canada

Jason Billing on the deepest day of the year, Christiana Glades. Photo Mark Klassen

Shoulder, toward the highway. This leads into a zone called Camp West. Runs here require a Camp West permit.

33 CHRISTIANA GLADES

Permit McGill, Bostock Parking
Length uphill 4 km
Max elevation gain 500 m
Skiing elevation band 1200–1500 m
Aspect northeast
Avalanche Terrain Rating Complex

This is an area with some short, not too steep glade runs on the lower slopes of Christiana Ridge. The glades can be seen on the edge of the Adventure Map, at 45600 E 5677800 N. Even though it is northerly, it is at low elevation and can be affected by warm temperatures. Buried surface hoar layers could also be an issue.

Two ways can be used to access this area. One uses the Bostock Creek trail for about 2.5 km. At this point there will be some steep open slopes to the creek below, and the glades may be seen across the valley. Ski down to the creek.

Alternatively, if there is enough snow, you may ski all the way up the creek itself, to just past the first major drainage that comes into Bostock Creek from the west. At times you are on a steep sidewall with a terrain trap below. The glades are not obvious from the creekbed, so if you have not been here before, it may be worthwhile to take the trail so you can scope the lines.

From the creek, skin up a steep sidewall to get to the lower-angled glades. Work your way to about 1500 m and start doing your hot laps from there.

The drainage to the south of the glades is the boundary of the Fidelity prohibited area, which is closed to skiing.

FLAT CREEK

Flat Creek is not a good descriptive name for this zone. There are some good ski runs here! Like Bostock, this is a tree skiing area with options to reduce your exposure to avalanche terrain. The runs are low-elevation, so beware of high freezing levels. Skiing through the forest with tree bombs falling out of the branches and low ski penetration making the skiing too fast won't be much fun.

Although Flat Creek itself is not a restricted area, the parking at Bostock is and a permit is required for that.

Parking is at the pullout on the north side of the highway, 16.8 km west of the Discovery Centre and 52 km from Revelstoke.

Flat Creek designated route

Starting tours up Flat Creek requires that a designated route be taken to avoid crossing the railway tracks and thus trespassing on CPR property. Start by crossing the highway and walk along it to the west for about 25 m to a tree with an orange marker. Ski down the bank toward Fortitude Ridge and follow orange markers for 150 m to a CPR access road. Cross this unplowed road and travel southwest to a meadow and follow that to its end. Go south, following markers on a trail through

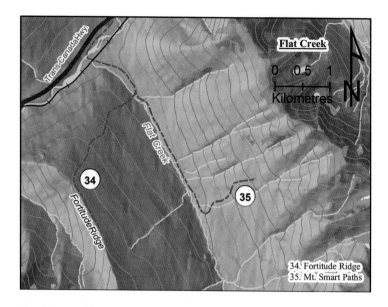

the forest until you reach the railway bridge where Bostock Creek and the Illecillewaet River converge. Go under the bridge.

34 FORTITUDE RIDGE

Permit Bostock Parking
Length uphill 7.5 km
Max elevation gain 950 m
Skiing elevation band 1100–1900 m
Aspect northeast
Avalanche Terrain Rating Challenging

This is the ridgeline on the west side of Flat Creek. It is not actually a ridge of Fortitude Mountain itself, but rather the north ridge of an unnamed 2664 m summit to the north of Fortitude. Getting off the ridge can be steep, and buried surface hoar and windslabs may be an issue. Watch out for tree bombs during warm weather lower down on the run.

Once under the bridge at the end of the designated route past the railway, head south over a low rise in the forest to Flat Creek. Cross the creek (or follow it a ways before crossing) and start ascending through the dense forest toward the ridge, trending south through a beautiful old-growth forest. The largest tree I have ever seen in Rogers Pass is here.

Gain the ridge and follow it up. The forest begins to open up and the most obvious lines through steep, scrubby trees begin to present themselves at about 1900 m. You can ski through the mature forest if you drop off the ridge sooner than that. The farther up the ridge you go, the more open, steeper and bigger the terrain gets.

There is a major avalanche path starting at about 1975 m on the ridge and this is the most committing terrain. Many people will ski the trees to the north of the path and then get into it lower down. A steep, gullied section of the path begins at about 1500 m. It can be a bit of work getting through this section. Avoid it if there are snow instabilities. Skiing the trees on skier's left is steep and a bit cliffy too but perhaps

Fortitude Ridge

Fortitude Ridge. Photo Parks Canada

less prone to avalanches. Lower down, the path flattens a bit before another steep, gullied section is encountered just before the creek.

There is also more skiing on steep, open slopes and in trees farther up the ridge.

Once you have finished your run, follow the creek back to the road. There is a bit of a canyon at the bottom of the run, and getting on the east bank is probably required.

There is more skiing even farther up the ridge, but wind effect may be found on the steep, open slopes there. You will also notice ski lines off the ridge to the west; these are in the Fortitude restricted area and a permit is required.

35 MOUNT SMART PATHS

Permit Bostock Parking
Length uphill 6 km
Max elevation gain 850 m
Skiing elevation band 1100–1800 m
Aspect west
Avalanche Terrain Rating Complex

Directly across from the upper Fortitude Ridge runs are two avalanche paths that run down the west face of Mount Smart. They can be a fun trip all on their own, or may be added to the end of a tour on Fortitude Ridge. Be aware of what the weather is doing in the start zones high above on these paths so that you don't get surprised by an avalanche coming down from above. The sun exposure here may create suncrusts.

If heading straight for these runs, ski up the creek starting on the designated route around the CPR line. Staying higher on the east bank is probably necessary to avoid canyon sections, especially near the bottom of the paths themselves.

Climbing up the southern path is probably easiest, with a detour into the forest between the two paths an option for where it is steeper. Above 1800 m or so the paths become narrower and steeper, and most people will elect to ski down from this elevation or lower. The north path has a major gully in it starting at about 1600 m, and a skier's left line will avoid this.

"Let those who wish have their respectability – I wanted freedom."

—*Richard Halliburton*

Cutting trail toward the Dome Glacier. Photo Mark Klassen

HUT-BASED BACKCOUNTRY CENTRES

The Columbia Mountains are known around the world for their backcountry huts and lodges, located in some of the finest ski terrain in the world. Some are rustic and some are more deluxe but they all offer opportunities for great skiing.

BILL PUTNAM (FAIRY MEADOW) HUT

Fairy Meadow is located in the Adamant Range of the Northern Selkirk Mountains, about 50 km north of Rogers Pass. The Alpine Club of Canada operates a beautiful and well-equipped hut here, named for Bill Putnam, a prominent US mountaineer who played a central role in exploration of the area and construction of the hut. The ski terrain at Fairy Meadow is superb and the snow in this part of the Selkirks is deep, so the area has become a favourite destination with backcountry skiers. Most of the runs are located in high alpine terrain and skiers must be prepared to navigate on glaciers in any weather, perform a crevasse rescue if necessary and deal with any of the other hazards of the high mountains in winter. The NTS maps for the area are Sullivan River 82 N/13 and Mount Sir Sandford 82 N/12, and the CanadaMapStore map is Austerity Mountain 082N071.

Access

In winter all hut users fly in and out. Be prepared for delays due to adverse weather (the chance of being stuck in the hut for an extra day is about 25 per cent; for two or more days about 10 per cent). Please refer to the ACC website (www.alpineclubofcanada.com) for the latest information on hut reservations.

Communication

Contact the ACC for current details on radio communication.

Fairy Meadow Hut. Photo Chic Scott

A little history

The Adamant Range and Fairy Meadow have been a summer climbing destination for many years but only became a ski destination with the construction of the hut in 1965. Americans Bill Putnam and Ben Ferris had often climbed in the area and recommended the site to the Alpine Club of Canada. The club obtained a licence of occupation for the land and paid about half the costs of the hut. Putnam and Ferris, aided by the Harvard Mountaineering Club, paid the other half of the costs and actually undertook the job of constructing the building. Soon people were using the hut as a winter destination because of the outstanding terrain available.

It was quickly realized that the roof was not adequate for the tremendous snow load encountered each winter. Consequently a major rebuilding was done in 1973 – a second floor and new roof were added as well as a custodian wing. The costs were jointly borne by the ACC and Putnam.

The ACC had originally agreed, with serious misgivings, that in return for Putnam's tremendous contribution, he would have certain rights over the hut, and the custodian's quarters in particular. Eventually,

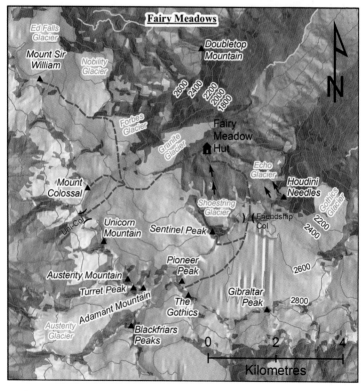

Fairy Meadows

Ed Falls Glacier

Mount Sir William ▲

Nobility Glacier

Doubletop Mountain ▲

2600 2400 2200 2000 1800

Forbes Glacier

Granite Glacier

Fairy Meadow Hut 🏠

Echo Glacier

Houdini Needles ▲

Gothics Glacier

Mount Colossal ▲

Shoestring Glacier

Friendship Col

2200

2400

Uni-Col

Unicorn Mountain ▲

Sentinel Peak ▲

Pioneer Peak ▲

2600

Austerity Mountain ▲

Turret Peak ▲ ▲

Adamant Mountain

The Gothics ▲

Gibraltar Peak ▲

2800

Austerity Glacier

Blackfriars Peaks ▲

0   2   4

Kilometres

N

The Adamants, seen from Mount Sir William, looking across Granite Glacier. Photo Phil Janz

BILL PUTNAM (FAIRY MEADOW) HUT

Location At 2050 m just above the right (south) flank of Granite Glacier (439300 E 5735400 N)

Facilities Two-storey wooden structure with a common sleeping room on the second floor (foam mattresses provided). Propane stoves and lanterns for cooking and lighting. All dishes, cutlery and utensils provided. Wood-burning

however, this arrangement was seen to have created difficulties with the other hut users, and within a few years the deal was terminated, unfortunately with some bitterness and acrimony. Over the years, the situation mellowed and the ACC honoured Putnam with both a Distinguished Service Award and an Honorary Membership for his contribution to the club. In addition, the hut was officially renamed the Bill Putnam (Fairy Meadow) Hut in 2003.

In recent years the hut has received a tremendous amount of attention, and several large work parties have greatly added to its comfort and efficiency. The hut has received a new roof, a new kitchen, an expanded sleeping area and a new rubber floor.

heating stove. This hut has an outstanding sauna!

Capacity 20

Water It is necessary to dig deep down in the snow to a creek south of the hut.

Reservations Alpine Club of Canada (403-678-3200). Due to the popularity of this hut you must phone a year in advance in order to get your name in the lottery.

Ski tours from Bill Putnam (Fairy Meadow) Hut

Some of the more popular tours from the hut are:

• Hut moraines: To the southeast, just outside the door of the hut, there is a large slope that provides excellent skiing. The slope is deceptively big, about 200 vertical metres, and should be treated with respect.

• Tree skiing: One of the short-comings of the Fairy Meadow area is its limited bad-weather tree skiing. There is, however, some good tree skiing a short distance northeast and down the valley from the hut.

• Sentinel Peak (439800 E 5733000 N) makes an excellent tour. Ascend south above the hut to reach Echo Glacier, which is followed to Friendship Col (440500 E 5733500 N). (Note that Friendship Col is between mounts Damon and Pythias, which are mislabelled on most maps. Mount Damon is located immediately northeast of Sentinel Peak, while Mount Pythias is the next peak to the east.) You can stop here and have a great descent back to the hut or carry on south across the ice-field for a short distance before curving around to the right to reach the south ridge of Sentinel Peak and following it to the summit. The last 50

Skiing near Bill Putnam (Fairy Meadow) Hut. Photo Joe Catellani

Climbing to Friendship Col, one of the most popular tours from Bill Putnam (Fairy Meadow) Hut. Photo Roger Laurilla

metres on this ascent are easy but exposed scrambling. This is a good tour for early in your ski week because you get an excellent view of the surrounding area. The ski descent back to the hut is superb and offers generally moderate slopes.

- Pioneer Peak (438700 E 5731800 N) offers another excellent summit although it is not so easy to reach the top. Ascend Echo Glacier to Friendship Col, then cross the icefield in a southerly direction. Ascend a heavily crevassed glacier in a westerly direction to reach the col between Pioneer Peak and Gothics (438800 E 5731700 N). From here climb steep south-facing snow slopes (avalanche hazard) to reach the ridge, where some scrambling leads to the summit. It is about 100 vertical metres from the col to the summit.

- Shoestring Glacier, located south of the hut, above Hut Moraines, offers a steep run and, in stable conditions, excellent skiing.

- Houdini Needles: There are several very steep chutes which descend from Houdini Needles. These are skiable in the right conditions but present serious avalanche risk. Access is either directly up the chutes or via Friendship Col to Gothic Glacier and around the back of Mount Pythias to reach the top of the chutes.
- UniCol is a pass located between Mount Unicorn (436400 E 5732800 N)) and Mount Colossal (436000 E 5734500 N). This is a good destination for moderate skiing. There are serious crevasse problems on this tour and the bergschrund below the pass can present problems in low-snow years. To reach Granite Glacier it is easiest to gain the crest of the moraine west of the hut and follow this along the edge of the glacier to an elevation of about 2400 m, then make your way out onto upper Granite Glacier. Note that the moraine is very steep on its northwest side, near the hut, and a direct descent to the glacier is not recommended.
- Mount Colossal makes an exciting but not too difficult ascent. Ski up Granite Glacier to the bottom of the northeast ridge. Leave your skis behind and kick steps up the ridge to the top. Cornices can often present a problem on this ascent.
- Mount Sir William (434600 E 5737600 N) presents an excellent but long ski tour across Granite, Forbes and Nobility glaciers. It is best done in the springtime when the days are long and glacier travel is easier.
- Enterprise Peak is an excellent ski tour either via the south-facing slopes leading up from Colossal–Enterprise Col or via Forbes Glacier, which provides an excellent northeast-facing ski run (large crevasses must be negotiated carefully).

BEN FERRIS (GREAT CAIRN) HUT

A number of people are now using the Ben Ferris (Great Cairn) Hut as a base for a ski holiday. The cabin is truly a gem and is just the right size for a small group of good friends. The scenery is outstanding, with the massive bulk of Mount Sir Sandford towering above the hut. The skiing opportunities at the hut are not as extensive as at Fairy Meadow but there is some good touring and ski exploration in the area. The NTS map for this area is Mount Sir Sandford 82 N/12, and the CanadaMapStore map is Citadel Mountain 082N061.

Access

Often skiers will make a side trip from the Bill Putnam (Fairy Meadow) Hut to the Ben Ferris (Great Cairn) Hut. This route passes through Friendship Col, Thor Pass and Azimuth Notch and is a serious ski mountaineering trip (see the Northern Selkirks Ski Traverse at page 240). You can also fly directly to the hut by helicopter. Contact Alpine Helicopters in Golden (250-344-7444).

A little history

On a rainy day in August 1953, a group from the Harvard Mountaineering Club, exploring the area near Mount Sir Sandford, passed the day by erecting a giant cairn, six metres high. Ten years later Bill Putnam and Ben Ferris had the idea to construct a hut at the same location. They offered to pay half the costs of the materials if the Alpine Club of Canada would pay the rest. The ACC secured a licence of occupa-

Ben Ferris (Great Cairn) Hut.

BEN FERRIS (GREAT CAIRN) HUT

Location North of Mount Sir Sandford between the toes of Haworth and Sir Sandford glaciers at an elevation of 1800 m (439200 E 5726500 N).

Facilities Wood heating stove, foam mattresses, Coleman lantern and stove. Visitors must bring their own firewood.

Capacity 6

Water Snowmelt

Reservations Alpine Club of Canada (403-678-3200).

tion from the BC government and the following summer, in July 1964, Ben Ferris, assisted by his family and friends, built this beautiful cabin using the stones of the Great Cairn.

COLUMBIA VALLEY HUT SOCIETY HUTS

The Columbia Valley Hut Society owns and operates five huts in the Purcell Mountains – McMurdo Cabin, Mark Kingsbury Hut, Dave White Cabin, Olive Hut and Jumbo Pass Hut. These huts make very comfortable bases for a ski holiday at a very reasonable price. Please respect them and take good care of them, as they are maintained by volunteers.

McMurdo Creek

The Spillimacheen Range, southwest of Golden, is popular with backcountry skiers. The snow is deep, access is not too difficult and McMurdo Cabin makes a comfortable base. Unfortunately this area is also very popular with snowmobilers, so be warned. The NTS map for the area is Mount Wheeler 82 N/3 and the CanadaMapStore map is Spillimacheen Glacier 082N005.

Access

The cabin is accessible by both helicopter and snowmobile. If you choose to fly, contact Alpine Helicopters (250-344-7444). If visibility is poor the pilot can follow the valleys to reach the cabin in almost any weather.

If you choose to go by snowmobile, contact Tembec in Parson (250-348-2211) about the state of the road and whether logging is in progress. The road is usually plowed for a substantial distance, often to km 28. It is another 30 km to the cabin, a trip which takes a couple of hours of being towed behind a snowmobile.

The road up the Spillimacheen River leaves Parson (located on Highway 95, 35 km south of Golden) about 200 m north of the office of Tembec. The road crosses the Columbia River, then after about 2 km starts to climb steeply. It makes four switchbacks, then continues south, climbing up the hillside. The road crosses the crest of the ridge at km 13, then swings west and drops into the drainage of the Spillimacheen River. Continue along this road, ignoring any turnoffs, to a plowed parking area at km 28.

From here the journey continues by snowmobile. For the first 18 km

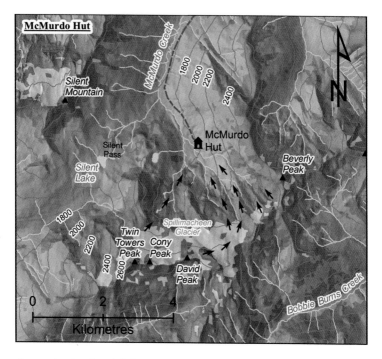

McMurdo Hut

Silent Mountain

Silent Pass

Silent Lake

McMurdo Creek

1800
2000
2200
2400

McMurdo Hut

Beverly Peak

1800
2000
2200
2400
2600

Twin Towers Peak

Cony Peak

Spillimacheen Glacier

David Peak

Bobbie Burns Creek

0   2   4

Kilometres

N

the road is level and follows the north side of the Spillimacheen River. At km 46 take a branch road to the left which is the McMurdo Creek Road. It immediately crosses the river to the south side, then begins to climb more steeply following McMurdo Creek and crossing several bridges. After about 10 km the road swings right at a clear-cut but the way to the cabin climbs straight ahead up a narrow road through the trees. The last kilometre is very steep. When the trees open up into a meadow, the cabin can be found on the left (east), a few metres into the trees.

Other cabin users

This area is very popular with the snowmobile crowd, which means that the road to the cabin will be well packed and offer easy travelling. However, there will likely be a group of these folk and their machines at the cabin on the weekend. This area is also used for heli-skiing, so

McMurdo Cabin. Photo Chic Scott

you may find your peaceful day in the mountains interrupted by the arrival of a load of skiers.

Ski tours from McMurdo Cabin

There are three runs to amuse you during your stay at McMurdo cabin.

- One of the finest runs descends from the shoulder of David Peak. Begin this tour by following an old mining road which starts about 40 m southeast of the cabin. The road climbs the hillside a few metres above the creek. When the road swings off to the right after about 0.5 km, continue directly south up the creek bed toward the east branch of Spillimacheen Glacier. Ascend the creek for several hundred metres (some steep steps) until you come out into a basin with steepish slopes toward the upper end. Ski up into the basin, then work your way up the left flank onto a wooded shoulder. Climb the shoulder until the trees end and you can head up into open terrain. Carry on in a southerly direction over gentle, open terrain toward the pass over into the Bobbie Burns drainage. As you approach this pass, climb

This rustic log cabin is very comfortable. It was once part of a mining camp.

Location On the edge of a meadow on the north slope of the Spillimacheen Range at the head of McMurdo Creek (489500 E 5655600 N) at an elevation of 1760 m.

Facilities Wood cooking stove, wood heating stove and foam sleeping pads. Coleman cooking stove and lantern, axe, pots, dishes and utensils.

Capacity 4

Water Snowmelt (or from a creek not far from the cabin)

Reservations Bookings are now done online at www.cvhsinfo.org.

up the shoulder on the right toward David Peak. Climb as high on this shoulder as you can to reach a point just under the rocks. From here you have a great descent back down to the cabin.

• Another fine run starts high on the shoulder of Twin Towers Peak (487700 E 5652900 N) and descends the west branch of Spillimacheen Glacier. Between 2750 m and 2420 m elevation it is necessary to follow a ramp through steep, broken, glaciated terrain. The last part of the run to the meadow, at about 489300 E 5655000 N, descends a steep drainage through the trees. To reach this descent one can go up the route previously described in the tour to David Peak, then traverse west beneath David Peak and Cony Peak to reach Twin Towers Peak.

• A more advanced run descends from a small subpeak (491900 E 5654000 N) down northwest-facing slopes into a creek bed which leads back to the cabin. Lower down, the run descends some steep chutes which have serious avalanche potential, so only ski this run when you are certain of snow stability.

Ski touring in International Basin near Mark Kingsbury Hut. Photo Ryan Bavin

Mark Kingsbury Hut. Photo Ryan Bavin

MARK KINGSBURY HUT

Location At the head of Bobbie Burns Creek, at an elevation of 2190 m near treeline on the

International Basin

International Basin, at the head of Bobbie Burns Creek, offers many ski opportunities. The new Mark Kingsbury Hut makes a good base for a ski holiday. It is also a good place to spend a night if you are doing the Bugaboos to Rogers Pass Ski Traverse. The NTS maps for the area are Mount Wheeler 82 N/3 and Westfall River 82 K/14. The CanadaMapStore maps are Spillimacheen Glacier 082N005 and Syncline Mountain 082K095. Access is via helicopter from Golden. Phone Alpine Helicopters (250-344-7444).

Ski tours from Mark Kingsbury Hut

The skiing in International Basin can

north side of the valley (4**90**1**60** E 5**649**385 N).
Facilities Foam sleeping pads, wood heating stove, Coleman cooking stoves and lanterns, pots, dishes and utensils.
Capacity 4
Water Snowmelt
Reservations Bookings are now done online at www.cvhsinfo.org.

be good. The south-facing slopes to the west of the hut toward the end of the basin offer open tree skiing, good for those low-visibility days. Across the basin, on the north slopes below Sandilands Peak, more challenging terrain can be found above treeline. One can also ski the east-facing slopes from the end of the basin near the lower lake down to the valley. The slope to the upper lake is short but steep, so good snow stability is required.

Forster Creek Basin

Forster Creek is located directly west of Radium and is the water supply for the town. It is a favourite destination for snowmobilers, with a packed trail along the valley up to Forster Creek Basin. This area is also popular with ski tourers, and Dave White Cabin is an excellent spot for a ski holiday. The NTS map for the area is Howser Creek 82 K/10; the CanadaMapStore map is Welsh Creek 082K068.

Access

The easiest way to get to Forster Creek Basin is by helicopter from Invermere (phone Airspan Helicopters 250-341-3409). This is convenient but expensive.

You can also reach Forster Creek Basin by snowmobile. The map required for the approach is Radium Hot Springs 82 K/9. To reach the trailhead, drive west toward the sawmill at the main four-way stop in Radium. The road descends to the valley bottom and crosses a bridge over the Columbia River. Stay left at a fork in the road (5**623**00 E 5**609**500 N), climb a hill, then continue level for about 4 km to a four-way stop. Go straight through the intersection, continue for about 3.5 km, then take the right-hand branch (5**574**00 E 5**604**700 N) and

Dave White Cabin. Photo Chic Scott

DAVE WHITE CABIN

This lovely cabin was built in 2001 in memory of a local skier who was killed in an avalanche. The hut can be hard to find.

Location The cabin is hidden in the trees about 125 vertical metres above the valley floor, at an elevation of 2190 m on the north side of Forster Basin (532100 E 5612900 N).

Facilities Foam

continue another 5 km to the town's water supply (553900 E 5607600 N). The road is plowed to here but can be slippery, so a four-wheel-drive vehicle is recommended.

From here a packed snowmobile track follows the road along Forster Creek to Forster Basin. If you have your own machine this can be a great way to access the area. If not it may be possible to hitch a ride or a tow from a friendly snowmobiler. But be warned: it is a long way. Being pulled behind a snowmobile on the washboard track can be an exciting and dangerous experience and is very hard on the arms and legs. There is a warming hut owned by the Windermere Valley Snowmobile Society at the end of the road, at the entrance to the basin (533700 E 5611900 N). Dave White Cabin is located about halfway along the basin, in the trees on the north side of the valley, about 125 vertical metres above the creek (532100 E 5612900 N).

Ski tours from Dave White Cabin

There is excellent skiing in Forster Creek Basin – on the south side of the valley toward Olive Hut, at the west end of the basin near Thunderwater Lake and on the treed slopes above Dave White Cabin. The experience can be spoiled, however, by the presence of many snowmobiles.

Catamount Glacier

This is a compact glaciated area with several peaks to climb and some good ski runs. There is no tree skiing, so if the weather is poor there will not be much to do. Because of the adjacent heli-ski operations you may not have the area to yourselves. In addition, snowmobiles sometimes venture up onto the glacier and can spoil the winter silence. The NTS map for the area is Howser Creek 82 K/10 and the CanadaMapStore map is Welsh Creek 082K068.

Access

The best way to get to Olive Hut, located just to the east of Catamount Glacier, is to fly from Invermere with Airspan Helicopters (phone 250-341-3409). If visibility is poor and the helicopter cannot land near the hut, you can be dropped off in the valley and then ski up to the hut.

You can also access the hut by snowmobile up Forster Creek. See Forster Creek Basin (Dave White Cabin) on page 133 for more information on snowmobile access.

From the head of Forster Creek the ascent to reach Catamount

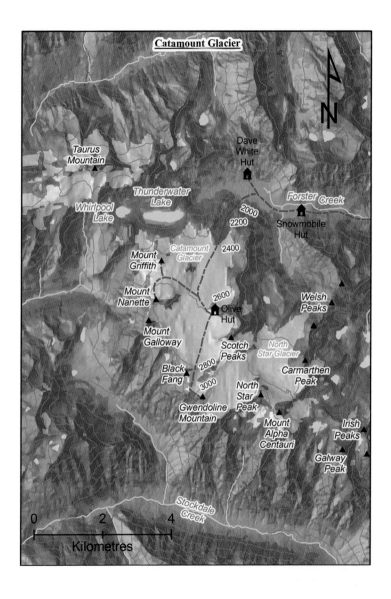

Catamount Glacier

Olive Hut by moonlight. Photo Chic Scott

OLIVE HUT

This delightful stone hut sits on a rocky outcrop at the edge of Catamount Glacier. It was built and named to honour brother and sister Peter and Brenda Olive, who were killed in two separate helicopter accidents.

Location On the west shoulder of the Scotch Peaks, at about 2670 m, 75 metres above the Catamount Glacier (531200 E 5609000 N)

Facilities Wood heating stove, propane cooking stove, Coleman lanterns, foam sleeping pads, pots, pans, dishes and utensils.

Capacity 4

Water Snowmelt

Reservations Bookings are now done online at www.cvhsinfo.org.

Note: It is hard to see the hut from the glacier until you are level with it.

Glacier is moderately steep and does have avalanche potential. The route climbs the big north-facing slope opposite the Dave White Cabin, entering a draw after gaining about 300 vertical metres. Ascend the draw (there is one steep slope where it may be necessary to kick steps) to reach the toe of Catamount Glacier. Ski up onto the glacier, staying right; then, higher up, traverse left toward the Olive Hut. There is some crevasse hazard, so it is recommended that you wear a rope.

At the end of your ski holiday it is possible to ski back to your car down Forster Creek Road. It takes a full day and there is not much downhill. You will not likely have to break trail, as there is lots of snowmobile traffic.

Ski tours from Olive Hut

There are some excellent summits and ski descents near Olive Hut. Here are a few suggestions.

• Gwendoline Mountain makes an excellent ascent if conditions are right. Ski south from the hut across the glacier, then ascend a draw up to the ridge between Gwendoline Mountain and Black Fang (530400 E 5606600 N). To reach the summit, head east up the ridge where there is a steep slope to ascend (use caution). Leave your skis behind, then kick steps and scramble through boulders up the ridge to the top. From here there is an excellent view of the Bugaboos to the northwest and Mount Assiniboine in the Rockies to the east.

- Mount Griffith makes an excellent ascent, and according to one source you can ski right to the top.
- You can ski to the top of an unnamed summit that resembles a giant sand dune (529500 E 5609200 N).
- It is possible to ski to within 75 vertical metres of the top of Mount Harmon, then enjoy a great run back down to Catamount Glacier.
- It is reported that you can ski to the top of Mount Alpha Centauri at the head of North Star Glacier and also to near the top of North Star Peak, though both tours are very steep and require excellent snow stability.
- There is lots of opportunity for ski descents in this area. For short runs near the hut there are the west-facing bowls on the Scotch Peaks. For bigger descents there are runs from Mount Griffith down to Thunderwater Lake, from the col northeast of Gwendoline Mountain (531500 E 5607600 N) down North Star Glacier and from Olive Hut down Catamount Glacier to the Forster Creek valley.

Jumbo Pass

Jumbo Pass in the southern Purcells makes an excellent destination for a ski holiday. There is plenty of good terrain and the hut, though rustic, is very comfortable. The NTS map for the area is Duncan Lake 82 K/7; the CanadaMapStore maps are Volley Mountain 082K037 and Mount Earl Grey 082K038.

Access

You can reach Jumbo Pass on foot or by helicopter. If you choose to fly you should contact RK Heli-skiing (info@rkheliski.com or 250-342-3889). They can usually fly you to the hut at the end of the day.

If you choose to ski in, it is a long day but quite doable. Many people use a snowmobile for the first 15 km along a logging road. To reach the

Jumbo Pass Cabin. Photo Mike Galbraith

trailhead, drive southwest of Invermere along Toby Creek Road to the Panorama Ski Resort. Continue beyond Panorama for about 19 km to a parking lot. Put your skis and pack on and head off along the unplowed road. To begin, the road climbs moderately steeply but then levels off. Continue skiing for 15 km to the turnoff point (528900 E 5579000 N).

From here it is a 600 m climb to Jumbo Pass. Turn left and ascend a road for a short distance to 528700 E 5579100 N. Ascend an old logging road that has been grown over by trees to reach an open space at 528500 E 5579300 N. Climb through the trees to 528300 E 5579200 N, then continue to a clearing where there is a view into an open bowl above (528100 E 5578900 N). Ski left into a subsidiary valley and ascend a trail through the trees (some orange markers on trees). The trail ascends steeply to 528100 E 5578300 N. When the trees start to thin out, climb up and traverse right under the bottom of an avalanche path to reach open trees, then ascend along the right side of the avalanche path to 527700 E 5578200 N. From here you can traverse out to the right, maintaining your elevation, then traverse around the corner on a broad bench to reach the drainage directly below Jumbo Pass. The hut is located along the crest of the ridge about 700 m north of Jumbo Pass Cabin (526700 E 5578900 N).

Ski tours from Jumbo Pass Cabin

There are excellent ski opportunities near Jumbo Pass.

- Just north of the cabin there is a small peak that offers excellent open skiing on its southeast and east flanks.
- Just east of the cabin there is an excellent run down the drainage toward Jumbo Creek. There are steep rolls on this run, so ski with caution.
- Lower-angle tree skiing can be found south and east of the hut, around the corner on the bench. This is an excellent destination on poor-visibility days.
- Good skiing can also be found to the west of the hut toward Glacier Creek.

JUMBO PASS CABIN

Location At an elevation of 2356 m, 700 m north of Jumbo Pass (526700 E 5578900 N)
Facilities Wood heating stove, propane cooking stove, propane and Coleman lanterns, foam sleeping pads, pots, pans, dishes and utensils.
Capacity 6
Water Snowmelt
Reservations Bookings are now done online at www.cvhsinfo.org.

KOKANEE GLACIER PROVINCIAL PARK

Kokanee Glacier Provincial Park is renowned as one of the best destinations in western Canada for powder skiing. There is lots of snow and a great variety of runs to choose from including bad-weather tree

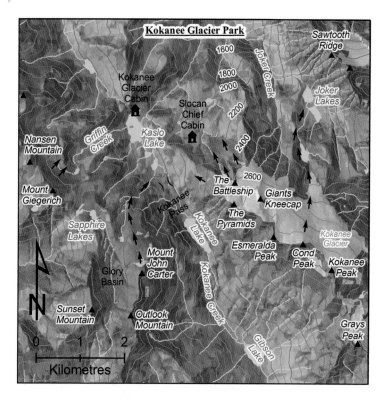

Kokanee Glacier Park

skiing. Now, a new state-of-the-art cabin makes Kokanee even more of an attraction. The NTS maps for the area are Slocan 82 F/14 and Kokanee Peak 82 F/11. The CanadaMapStore maps are Mount Ruppel 082F074 and The Battleship 082F075.

Access

Kokanee Glacier Cabin is reached by helicopter in winter. The weekly hut rate includes the round-trip helicopter fee. During the winter a custodian is stationed at Kokanee Glacier Cabin. He or she is in contact with the outside world and will provide you with Canadian Avalanche Association forecasts and weather forecasts.

A little history

The original Slocan Chief Cabin was built in 1896 for the Smuggler Mining Company, and the mine was in operation as late as 1928. The Kokanee Glacier area was made a provincial park in 1922. In the early years, the cabin was used regularly by local mountaineering groups but it eventually fell into disrepair. By 1962 BC Parks was considering burning the cabin until a group of local mountaineers, headed by Helen Butling, spent much of that summer rehabilitating the structure. In 1964 additional repairs were undertaken and for the next ten years the Kootenay Mountaineering Club took care of the cabin. In 1974 the structure was taken over by BC Parks. A new Kokanee Glacier Cabin was built in 2002 and replaced the Slocan Chief Cabin for overnight accommodation. This new cabin was built as a result of campaign efforts carried out in memory of Michel Trudeau and the many other Canadians who have lost their lives while enjoying Canada's backcountry. The historic Slocan Chief Cabin is now an interpretive centre.

The tremendous ski run below The Battleship and The Giant's Kneecap. Photo Clive Cordery

Skiing to Joker Lakes. Photo Clive Cordery

Bookings

Kokanee Glacier Cabin is now administered by the Alpine Club of Canada. The fee for cabin use is subject to change, so please contact the ACC for the most current rates. The cabin rental also includes helicopter access. There is a lottery system in place to decide which lucky groups get to spend a week skiing in paradise. The ACC can be contacted by phone at 403-678-3200 or by email at info@alpineclubofcanada.com. Their website is www.alpineclubofcanada.com.

Ski tours from Kokanee Glacier Cabin

Here are a few of the more popular ski descents in the Kokanee area:

- The large northwest-facing slope below The Battleship (488200 E 5511800 N) and The Giant's Kneecap (488700 E 5511400 N) down toward the Slocan Chief Cabin gives an excellent run of about 600 vertical metres.
- One of the finest runs is to ski north from the summit of Esmeralda or Cond peak down Kokanee Glacier to an unnamed lake (489700 E 5512400 N), then farther down to Joker Lakes

Kokanee Glacier Cabin. Photo Kevin Giles

KOKANEE GLACIER CABIN

This is a new cabin which uses the latest environmentally friendly technology.

Location In Kokanee Glacier Provincial Park at the north end of Kaslo Lake (485800 E 5513300 N)

Facilities Bunks with foam mattresses; electric and propane heating, cooking and lighting; showers and indoor flush toilets.

(490100 E 5513300 N). This is a long run, about 800 vertical metres.

• Another good run can be had from the north summit of Outlook Mountain (486200 E 5509800 N). Head north, then curve down to the right to reach Kokanee Pass (550 vertical metres). The approach to this peak is up Outlook Creek to Lemon Pass, where the way above is blocked by a short steep section. It is possible to ascend the obstacle by a narrow crest just above Lemon Pass (485100 E 5511300 N).

• Good runs of about 250 vertical metres can be found from the crests of Nansen Mountain and Mount

Capacity 12
Water Running water pumped from the lake.
Reservations Alpine Club of Canada 403-678-3200.

Giegerich into the basin of Griffin Creek.

• If the weather is overcast, a good location for skiing with a few trees to enhance visibility is along the west flank of Smuggler's Ridge and, near the bottom, below the ridge toward Slocan Chief Cabin. Smuggler's Ridge is the crest which descends northwest from The Pyramids (488200 E 5511300 N) to about 486600 E 5512600 N.

• Many summits can be reached at Kokanee Glacier Park. It is possible to ski to the top of the Pyramids, Esmeralda Peak, Cond Peak and Kokanee Peak. You can walk out onto the crest of The Battleship, but reaching the summit of The Giant's Kneecap involves some technical climbing and requires a rope.

DORE HUTS

West of McBride, far up the Dore River, are two huts which offer good ski potential. They are owned by the BC Forest Service but are managed by the Ozalenka Alpine Club. The fee of $10/person/night goes toward maintenance of the huts. To book, phone Glen Stanley at 250-569-2596.

The NTS maps required are Eddy 93 H/1 for Eagle Valley Hut and McBride 93 H/8 for Ozalenka Hut.

Eagle Valley Hut, which sleeps 14, is at the end of a tributary valley of the South Dore River. Ozalenka, which sleeps 10, is along the creek in the valley bottom of a tributary of the West Dore River. Both huts are heated with wood stoves and have propane cooking stoves and Coleman lanterns. There are foam sleeping pads and plenty of pots, pans, dishes and utensils.

The skiing at Eagle Valley Hut is in a big north-facing bowl. All skiing is above treeline on glaciers and the runs are up to 650 vertical metres. The snowpack here is often good. At Ozalenka Hut the runs are generally lower-angled tree skiing, about 350 vertical metres. There is often a shallow snowpack here.

To reach the huts a snowmobile is normally used to begin. Then it is 9 km on skis to Eagle Valley Hut or 7 km to Ozalenka Hut. Another option is to fly in with the Canadian Mountain Holidays helicopter stationed nearby (phone 403-762-7100).

YORA HUTS

The Yellowhead Outdoor Recreation Association maintains two back-country huts in the Valemount Area. These are McKirdy Cabin and Clemina Cabin. Both are noted on the NTS map Valemount 83 D/14.

McKirdy Cabin is about 9 km from where you can drive in winter, of which 5 km is along an unplowed forestry road and the rest is on a relatively steep trail. There is some low-angle skiing above the cabin but the snowpack can be on the shallow side.

Access to Clemina Cabin is about 5 km along a logging road. If active logging is occurring in the area, the cabin is not accessible. The top of a nearby avalanche chute offers some good tree skiing and there is some good ski terrain in the alpine above the chute.

Both cabins have a loft (foamies) that sleeps 4–6 and both are equipped with wood heating stove, pots, pans, dishes and utensils. Each has an axe, saw and firewood. You must bring your own cook stove and candles or lantern.

For more information and to book these cabins, or for information on other backcountry ski opportunities in the Valemount area, call Patricia Thoni at the Caribou Grill 250-566-8244.

TENT-BASED BACKCOUNTRY CENTRES

There are several prime locations for backcountry skiing that do not have huts. However, you can fly in with a large tent, airtight heating stove, Coleman stoves and lanterns, table and chairs, saw and axe, and set up a fine base camp. Then you can explore and ski the surrounding mountains. All of these sites are in the middle of heli-ski tenures, so you will be sharing the slopes and the powder snow. Here are six suggested sites for camps.

BUGABOOS

World famous for heli-skiing, the Bugaboos can also make a great destination for ski touring. Unfortunately the Kain Hut is now closed in winter but it is still possible to camp. The only location where camping is allowed is at the Applebee campsite (515900 E 5621300 N). Care must be taken in managing human waste in this area, and the outhouses must be dug out and used. The NTS map for this area is Howser Creek 82 K/10 and the CanadaMapStore map is Cobalt Lake 082K077.

There is plenty of good skiing in the Bugaboos that is accessible from the campsite. You can do laps below the campsite down to Kain Hut, ascend Anniversary Peak, link cols to Cobalt Lake, tour around Bugaboo Spire via Bugaboo–Crescent Col and Bugaboo–Snowpatch Col or tour around Snowpatch Spire via Bugaboo–Snowpatch Col to the base of the west ridge of Pigeon Spire, then ski down Bugaboo Glacier under the south face of Snowpatch Spire to Kain Hut.

Access to the Bugaboos for most will be by helicopter. To land at Applebee, which is in Bugaboo Provincial Park, the helicopter company must have a Park Use Permit (PUP) and the ski touring party must have a Letter of Permission (LOP). A LOP is reasonably easy to obtain.

The Bugaboos are a spectacular area for ski touring. Photo Marc Piché

Contact BC Parks for information about how this permitting system works and for a list of helicopter companies that have a PUP.

It is also possible to use a snowmobile to reach the Bugaboos and then ski up to the Applebee campsite. For more information on this approach see the section on the Bugaboos to Rogers Pass Traverse on page 273.

AZURE PASS

Azure Pass (309300 E 5839800 N) has been popular for years and has been the site of several ACMG ski guide exams. The skiing is said to be terrific. Take a look at the map and note all the potential ski terrain. Runs are from 500 to 1000 vertical metres on generally moderate terrain. There are good campsites with easy access to water. Azure Pass is in the CMH Cariboo heli-ski area but it sees limited use, as it is at the edge of their tenure. Azure Pass is approached by helicopter

Lunch break near Azure Pass. Photo Leon Kubernus

from Valemount. The NTS map for this area is Azure River 83 D/12. The CanadaMapStore maps are Fred Wells Creek 083D061 and Ella Frye Creek 083D062.

FARM PASS

Locals have long known about Farm Pass (448200 E 5681500 N) and it has been the site of several tent-based ski camps. Fly in by helicopter from Revelstoke. A good spot for a base camp is said to be about 448200 E 5680500 N, where you will find some standing deadfall for firewood. The NTS map for this area is Glacier 82 N/5 and the CanadaMapStore map is Mount McGill 082N022.

The best run is north from the top of Corbin Peak, and there is another good one from the col just south of this peak. You can also traverse through Bostock Pass and climb toward McGill Pass to find lots of skiable terrain. It is possible to ski back to the Trans-Canada Highway via Bostock Creek but it can be tricky to locate the trail.

FRISBY CREEK

This site has been used for Alpine Club of Canada ski camps and also for ACMG ski guide exams. Fly in by helicopter from Revelstoke. A good site for a base camp is at **396900** E **5677400** N. The NTS maps to this area are Mount Revelstoke 82 M/I and Downie Creek 82 M/8. The CanadaMapStore maps are Schrund Peak 082M028 and Frisby Creek 082M029.

There is extensive good skiing in this area. Some areas to check out are the glaciers and bowls to the south of camp, off the ridge dividing Frisby Creek and the Jordan River, and the peaks and cols above the glaciers at the head of Frisby Creek. Loop trips can be made through cols east of Schrund Peak, travelling back and forth between Frisby Creek and Big Eddy Creek, including an ascent of Schrund Peak and descents into Big Eddy Creek from cols east of Schrund Peak. This is big crevasse country. Watch for glide cracks in the spring.

Looking into the head of Frisby Creek. A good campsite can be found at lower left. Photo Mark Klassen

ARGENTINE GLACIER

The ACC has held tent-based ski camps at the edge of treeline below Argentine Glacier. Fly in by helicopter from Golden. A good site for a base camp is 436400 E 5715700 N. The NTS map to this area is Mount Sir Sandford 82 N/12 and the CanadaMapStore map is Argentine Mountain 082N051.

There is opportunity to make several ski ascents in the area, the best one being Argentine Mountain. Ascend Argentine Glacier, climb a steep headwall to the col northeast of the summit (437400 E 5710700 N), then walk to the top. The views are spectacular.

HALLAM PEAK

This is the site of another successful ACC tent-based ski camp. The base camp was located about 6 km southeast of Hallam Peak at the north end of the Monashee Mountains (385500 E 5781300 N). Take care to situate yourself so you are not in a potential avalanche runout zone. The tree skiing is reported to be exceptional – perfectly spaced old-growth timber. The NTS map to this area is Nagle Creek 83 D/2; the CanadaMapStore map is Hallam Peak 083D017. Access by helicopter will be very expensive unless you have friends with Canadian Mountain Holidays.

MOBERLY PASS

Moberly Pass (432000 E 5719000 N) is reported to be an excellent location for a fly-in tent-based ski camp. Not much is known about this area but there appears to be good ski terrain. The NTS map is Mount Sir Sandford 82 N/12 and the CanadaMapStore map is Citadel Mountain 082N061. Let me know if you go skiing here and send me a photo.

NELSON CLASSICS

Nelson is a funky town at the south end of the Columbia Mountains. It is filled with interesting restaurants, organic food stores, friendly bookstores and sports shops. It is a great place to live for those searching for mountain adventure and a little peace and quiet. Nelson is surrounded by excellent ski mountains with famous names like Kokanee and Valhalla. The snow is deep in this part of the world and the temperatures are usually moderate. Here are a few favourites to whet your appetite.

TOURS NEAR WHITEWATER SKI RESORT

Whitewater Ski Resort, about 30 minutes from Nelson, is reached by driving 11 km south on Highway 6 toward Salmo, then turning left up the access road. The resort is another 10 km along this road. The access road is steep, so you should have good snow tires on your vehicle.

The Whitewater Ski Resort is a destination for serious skiers who are looking for steep powder. Although there are a number of tours in the immediate vicinity of the resort, I have included just four of the most popular. Two of them actually begin on lifts from the resort. For more information on this area and a greater selection of tours, see *West Kootenay Touring Guide*, published by Backcountry Skiing Canada (www.backcountryskiingcanada.com). The NTS map to the area is Nelson 82 F/6 and the CanadaMapStore map is Ymir Mountain 082F045.

WHITE QUEEN
Distance 4 km return
Elevation gain 550 m (includes chairlift ride)
Max elevation 2170 m
Avalanche Terrain Rating Challenging

This is a short and pleasant tour, easily accessed from the ski resort.

Begin the tour by taking a ride on the Silver King chairlift to an

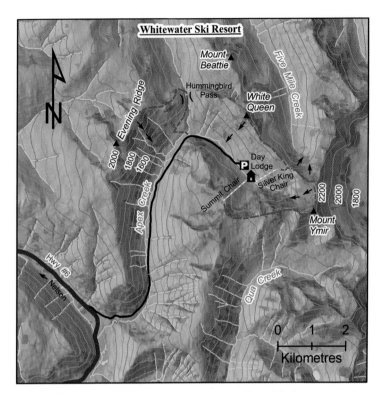

Whitewater Ski Resort

elevation of 1910 m. From the top of the chair, traverse right for a short distance, then turn left, where you should see a SKI AREA BOUNDARY sign. Skin uphill, gaining about 100 vertical metres to reach a saddle on Silver King Ridge between White Queen and Mount Ymir (490700 E 547600 N).

Turn left along the broad ridge crest. The route climbs about 50 vertical metres over a minor peak, then drops about 50 vertical metres into a notch. The final climb along the broad ridge, gaining about 150 vertical metres over 1 km, takes you to the summit of White Queen. From here you have three options:

You can follow your route of ascent back to the ski resort.

You can make your way northwest to Hummingbird Pass (487400 E

5479100 N) by following a shallow draw on the north side of the ridge crest. From Hummingbird Pass, make your way back to the Whitewater access road by reversing the tour to Evening Ridge (see below).

If conditions are stable, a good ski run can be had down the southwest face of White Queen. Ski in the small trees along the margins of two large avalanche paths. Good snow cover is required due to alders at the bottom of the descent. Note that this run is south-facing and can be sun-affected. From the bottom of the run, turn left along the cross-country ski trail (avoiding the set xc tracks) to the Whitewater resort.

EVENING RIDGE

Distance 5 km circuit
Elevation gain 600 m
Max elevation 2075 m
Avalanche Terrain Rating Complex

This is an excellent tour, and the descent of The Whaleback to Apex Creek is outstanding.

The tour to Hummingbird Pass and up Evening Ridge starts from a pullout about 8 km along the Whitewater Ski Resort access road (487500 E 5477800 N). Immediately below the ski resort road, follow an old logging road which heads northeast below the Whitewater road, then curls around and ends up heading west. In the course of this curve it crosses Apex Creek (which descends from the ski resort) and also the small, unnamed creek coming down from Hummingbird Pass. All this happens only a few hundred metres after you've left your car.

The road continues west for several hundred metres without gaining elevation, then turns upward to the right and begins to climb steeply. After gaining about 75 vertical metres, strike out to the right on an indistinct old mining road that could be difficult to find. Follow this through the trees, gradually gaining elevation for about 500 m until the road reaches the unnamed creek draining Hummingbird Pass. From here follow the creek bed for another 500 m up to Hummingbird Pass. There are some large and potentially dangerous slopes above you at one point, so be aware.

Ski through the pass. Then, after about 50 m, just as the angle begins to descend on the other side near a big rock, begin to work your way up onto the left shoulder. Continue working your way up the hillside, heading south. Gain about 150 vertical metres up to the crest of the ridge. Along here you are in open glades which make for excellent, safe skiing. Once you reach the crest of the ridge (487400 E 5478700 N), simply follow it along for another 100 vertical metres to the first summit (487000 E 5478600 N).

Here you should reassess snow stability and decide whether or not to continue. If conditions are unsafe, return the way you came. If conditions are stable, you can continue up Evening Ridge and ski The Whaleback. From the first summit, descend about 75 vertical metres and then continue climbing up to the west, gaining about 150 vertical metres to 486100 E 5478400 N.

From this point a superb 700 vertical metre descent called The Whaleback leads down to Apex Creek. This descent takes you into big country and is surrounded by avalanche terrain. You must find your way carefully and skilfully. The descent follows a broad, rounded shoulder. The upper Whaleback is open and rounded, with only a few trees. To either side are the steep start zones of major avalanche paths. The middle section of The Whaleback offers some tree skiing where you must pick your way through openings and glades for a short distance. At the bottom the terrain opens up again and there is terrific skiing all the way down to Apex Creek. Turn left and ski back to your car.

MOUNT YMIR

Distance 6 km circuit
Elevation gain 720 m
Max elevation 2380 m
Avalanche Terrain Rating Complex

The summit of Mount Ymir makes an excellent ski tour. From the top there are great views followed by a superb descent. There is some avalanche risk on this tour and one must also be mindful of cornices.

Begin the tour by taking a ride up the Summit chairlift. From the top

Looking into Ymir Bowl below Mount Ymir from
Silver King ridge. Photo Kari Medig

of the lift descend the packed run down to the left for about 100 m, then traverse out into Catch Basin. Continue traversing to reach the west ridge of Mount Ymir at 489400 E 5475500 N. Alternatively, you can climb steeply above the chairlift for about 100 vertical metres in a southerly direction to reach the west ridge of Mount Ymir at about 2060 m (488700 E 5475600 N). From here, descend to the east for about 75 vertical metres to reach the point where the Catch Basin traverse reaches the ridge.

The route then follows the west ridge of Mount Ymir to the summit. It climbs fairly easily at first, over treed slopes gaining about 150 vertical metres, then crosses a small bump (490100 E 5475700 N). The route then descends about 50 vertical metres into another notch, where you get a good view out left into Ymir Bowl.

The final climb of about 270 vertical metres to the summit is steep. The route finding is complicated by many steep wind rolls, very dangerous cornices on the left and, toward the top, a large, steep and potentially dangerous slope on the right. Good route-finding skills are required

Steve Ogle in Ymir Bowl. Photo Kari Medig

for ascending this section. After the first 150 vertical metres of steep ascent the angle eases somewhat.

From the summit the best descent is down the north ridge for about 75 vertical metres into a notch (491400 E 5476200 N), then down left into Ymir Bowl. Note that three ridges converge at the summit; you want to descend the north ridge, not the east one. In poor visibility there is potential for a mistake here. The initial descent down the north ridge is done on foot for a short distance until you can put your skis on and continue down to the pass. The 600 vertical metre descent of Ymir Bowl to the ski resort is outstanding. The skiing is open, set at a good angle all the way, and the slope is north-facing. It is potential avalanche terrain, however, so use caution.

FIVE MILE BASIN
Distance 3-4 km return
Elevation gain 500 m from the basin to the broad pass
Max elevation 2200 m at broad pass

Five Mile Basin is a great destination for a day of turns. It is easy to get to and has lots of potential.

From Whitewater Resort take the Silver King chairlift, then head right to access the skin track that leads up to Silver King Ridge (490700 E 5476700 N). The view here gives you a good look northeast at the terrain in Five Mile Basin.

From here there are two options: skin up the ridge to the right and bootpack where necessary until you get to the top of the broad pass (490600 E 5476900 N) of Five Mile Basin. Alternatively, you can ski down sparse trees anywhere off the ridge into the basin. From the bottom you can skin up north-facing trees in the middle of the basin. There are numerous lines in the basin – rocky chutes off the ridge on climber's left, treed fingers down the middle and more open lines on climber's right.

KOOTENAY PASS

The area in and around Stagleap Provincial Park, at the summit of Kootenay Pass, offers excellent ski touring. The area gets heavy snowfall, and deep powder is the norm. The runs are not long but access from the road is quick.

Highway 3 between Salmo and Creston goes directly through the pass and there is an avalanche control program operating to keep the highway open. The road is often closed for short periods while crews do avalanche control work.

Skiing at Kootenay Pass

There is good skiing north of the highway. Two of the finest runs are located on the east flank of what are known locally as Cornice Ridge and Wolf Ridge. These descents are about 400 and 500 vertical metres respectively and the approaches to both runs are reasonably short.

There is also excellent skiing south of the highway. A nice idea is to ski to Ripple Ridge Cabin for the night and do some skiing at

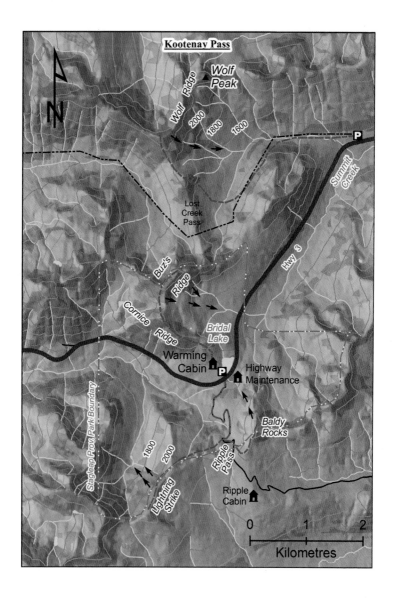

Kootenay Pass

Wolf Peak

Wolf Ridge

2000 · 1800 · 1600

P

Lost Creek Pass

Summit Creek

Hwy 3

Buz's Ridge

Cornice Ridge

Bridal Lake

Warming Cabin

P

Highway Maintenance

Baldy Rocks

Stagleap Prov. Park Boundary

1800 · 2000

Lightning Strike

Ripple Pass

Ripple Cabin

0   1   2
Kilometres

Looking across Kootenay Pass toward Cornice Ridge. Photo Dave Smith

the same time. For more detailed information, refer to *West Kootenay Touring Guide*, published by Backcountry Skiing Canada (www.backcountryskiingcanada.com). The NTS map to the area is Salmo 82 F/3 and the CanadaMapStore map is Ripple Mountain 082F005.

WOLF RIDGE

Distance 10 km return
Elevation gain 700 m
Max elevation 2150 m
Avalanche Terrain Rating Challenging

Park in a plowed parking lot on the north side of the highway about 5 km east of the summit of Kootenay Pass. Note that this is a chain-up area for trucks, so park well out of the way. The approach to Wolf Ridge follows a logging road and power line heading up the unnamed valley to the west. Follow this road for several kilometres, but as you approach Lost Creek Pass do not attempt to climb steeply along the power line route. Instead, take a line more to the north, roughly along the gas transmission line shown on the map. Climb over a small summit (496300 E 5437400 N), then continue north up the crest to the summit of Wolf Ridge (495900 E 5438100 N).

There is an excellent descent down the east flank of Wolf Ridge into the unnamed valley. Return to your car via the road and power line.

CORNICE RIDGE

Distance 3 km return
Elevation gain 360 m
Max elevation 2120 m
Avalanche Terrain Rating Challenging

Park at the Bridal Lake parking area at the summit of Kootenay Pass. Start at the warming hut and work your way up the steep hillside above the lake to reach Cornice Ridge at about 496700 E 5434500 N. Continue climbing along the ridge, passing over a small summit. Be careful of cornices on the east side of the ridge and don't stray too far to the west, as this is an avalanche control area and is closed. Descend to a col and then climb to the crest of Cornice Ridge.

The descent to the southeast from the summit of Cornice Ridge takes you into avalanche terrain. If you want a more mellow descent you can start from the col (495900 E 5435300 N). Both these descents finish straight down the drainage to the highway.

RIPPLE RIDGE CABIN

Distance 3 km one way to cabin
Elevation gain 200 m
Max elevation 1970 m
Avalanche Terrain Rating Simple

Ripple Ridge Cabin is an easy over-night touring destination. The cabin is

Neil Jolly at Ripple Ridge Cabin. Photo Chic Scott

Scott Grady drops in off the back side of Cornice Ridge. Photo Steve Ogle

managed by the Creston Cross Country Ski Club. There is room for four but you could squeeze in six if they were good friends. There is a heating stove and an axe but no foamies, pots, pans, utensils or dishes. Water is from snowmelt.

Park at the Bridal Lake parking area. Then cross the highway and head up the trail to the south. This trail is actually a wide road that climbs steadily in several long switchbacks, reaching Ripple Pass after about 2 km. Ski through the pass and follow the road for another 400 m, descending gradually. Just before the road swings sharply to the left and descends steeply, cut out to the right into the trees and follow the crest of a ridge for about 300 m to the cabin.

BALDY ROCKS

Distance 3 km
Elevation gain 300 m
Max elevation 2075 m
Avalanche Terrain Rating Challenging

Baldy Rocks is the area you see above the highway buildings on the south side of the road. There is great tree skiing, and playful pillows can be found. You can do laps right from the highway.

To get there, walk across the highway from the parking lot and follow the tour to Ripple Pass (see Ripple Ridge Cabin description on page 162). At the pass, turn left (east) and skin up through the forest to reach the ridge. Continue along the ridge to the top of Baldy Rocks. Beware of cornices.

There are numerous options for descent. The north ridge offers the easiest descent. For longer fall line runs, ski down the north ridge a ways, then drop in to the left.

LIGHTNING STRIKE/TWIN LAKES

Distance 5 km
Elevation gain 500 m
Max elevation 2200 m
Avalanche Terrain Rating Challenging

The Kootenay Pass area offers some great tree skiing. Photo Steve Ogle

Lightning Strike offers a longer tour along a beautiful ridgeline and gives you a good look at some of the best terrain that Kootenay Pass has to offer.

Cross the highway from the parking lot and follow the Ripple Ridge Cabin tour to Ripple Pass. From here turn right (west) and gain the ridge. Continue along the ridge, gaining and losing elevation several times. The first high point (496100 E 5432400 N) offers great views into the Twin Lakes Basin to the northwest. From here you can drop into the basin and ski perfectly spaced trees to the lakes. You can also continue skiing to the second high point (495800 E 5431800 N), which is called Lightning Strike.

From here there are numerous options for open and sparsely treed descents northwest into the basin. There is also a classic moderate descent to the low pass (495400 E 5431500 N) southwest of the highpoint from where you can continue down the north-facing drainage to the lakes.

To get back to the highway, ski north along the valley bottom and contour around the toe of the ridge in a northeast direction until you can reach the highway or continue east to reach the Ripple Pass road used on the ascent.

OTHER TOURS NEAR NELSON

The area around Nelson abounds with great ski tours, most of which are known only to locals. Here are a few ideas to get you started.

MOUNT BRENNAN

Distance 14 km return
Elevation gain 1880 m
Max elevation 2280 m
Avalanche Terrain Rating Complex

This is a major ski ascent with a large amount of relief. It is recommended that the trip be done over two days so that you can time your passage through exposed areas for early in the day. Good skiing can be found on the descent, but it is possible, in the springtime, to experience difficult conditions as well. The NTS map for the tour is Roseberry 82 K/3; the CanadaMapStore map is Mount Jardine 082K005.

On Highway 31A, between Kaslo and New Denver, the small settlement of Retallack is marked on the map. This is where the tour begins. A plowed turnout where you can leave your vehicle will be found just east of town on the south side of the highway.

Follow a logging road that begins at 489700 E 5543400 N right in Retallack. Ski behind the old, abandoned mine buildings, then travel west for a short distance before curving around and heading back east. There is quite a maze of logging roads and you should follow the BC Forest Service signs for Lyle Creek that are posted at the junctions. Follow these logging and mining roads to the east, crossing the drainage of Whitewater Creek. Then curve around a shoulder to enter the drainage of Lyle Creek. The first 4 km of this tour follows good roads with posted signs, but at 492300 E 5544900 N the road fades and you will find yourself below a steep headwall. You want to reach this point early in the day so you can climb the headwall while it is safe. The route

ascends a treed ramp up and right to the top of the headwall. The ramp is threatened by avalanche slopes the entire way.

At the top of the headwall there is a lovely campsite overlooking the valley, not far from a small lake (492600 E 5546000 N). This is a good spot to spend the night in order to avoid poor late afternoon snow conditions. Above the campsite the route climbs another short headwall with avalanche hazard. Most skiers ascend a gully (492400 E 5546400 N) for about 150 vertical metres.

From here route choices abound, and a moderate ascent offering no serious difficulties takes you to the summit. Simply work your way northwest over open terrain to the peak.

Mount Brennan offers a terrific ski descent, Lyle Peak in the background. Photo Paul Heikkila

COMMONWEALTH MOUNTAIN

Distance 16 km return
Elevation gain 1545 m
Max elevation 2340 m
Avalanche Terrain Rating Challenging

Commonwealth Mountain is another popular tour in the Nelson area. This is a long trip, so give yourself plenty of time. The NTS map for the tour is Nelson 82 F/6 and the CanadaMapStore map is Commonwealth Mountain 082F034.

Between Nelson and the town of Ymir, along Highway 6, a small settlement called Porto Rico (482400 E 5464200 N) is marked on the map. This is the starting point for a long and interesting tour to Commonwealth Mountain. Park in a plowed turnaround area on the west side of the highway, about 100 m north of the highway bridge over Barrett Creek.

Begin by following a road for 3 km along the north side of Barrett Creek. Then, at 479800 E 5464000 N, turn north on a road along Lost Creek. The Lost Creek Road climbs steeply for about 600

Looking from Upper Barrett Creek toward Commonwealth Mountain. The ascent route follows the right-hand skyline. Photo John Carter

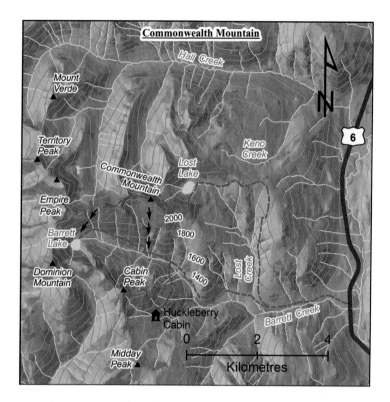

vertical metres up to the ridge crest overlooking Keno Creek (479700 E 5467200). From here the road turns west, climbs up the ridge, then traverses over to Lost Lake (477600 E 5467000 N).

The route now ascends the east ridge of Commonwealth Mountain above Lost Lake. Use caution, as there is avalanche hazard in the lower section of the climb. An ascent of about 370 vertical metres from the lake takes you to the summit of the peak.

You can then traverse the peak to a subpeak (475700 E 5466600 N). From here you can descend southeast down excellent ski slopes for about 250 vertical metres until the terrain begins to get steep. Traverse a short distance to the right to reach slightly gentler terrain, then descend steeply through the trees for another 250 vertical metres to Barrett

Creek Road. As an alternative you can traverse farther along the summit ridge to about 475000 E 5466500 N, then descend somewhat easier terrain to Barrett Lake.

You will most likely find the road along Barrett Creek packed by snowmobile tracks, which makes for a fast trip back to your car.

"The evenings in the tent, when all the party were seated round on their clothes-bags, after having carefully brushed themselves of snow, in order to bring as little of it as possible inside, were without comparison the bright spots in our existence at this particular time. However hard the day had been, however exhausted we were, and however deadly the cold, all was forgotten as we sat around our cooker, gazing at the faint rays of light which shone from the lamp, and waiting patiently for our supper. Indeed I do not know many hours in my life on which I look back with greater pleasure than on these."

— *Fridtjof Nansen*

REVELSTOKE CLASSICS

THE FINGERS OF MOUNT MACPHERSON

Distance 7 km
Elevation gain 900 m
Max elevation 1850 m
Avalanche Terrain Rating Complex

A day at The Fingers is like skiing at Revelstoke's unofficial backcountry ski area. It is a popular place close to town and a real Revelstoke classic. The NTS map for the tour is Revelstoke 82 L/16 and the CanadaMapStore map is Mount MacPherson 082L099.

Drive 7.5 kilometres south on Highway 23 from the intersection with the Trans-Canada Highway just west of Revelstoke and park at the Mount MacPherson Nordic Ski Centre parking lot on the right (west) side of the road. There is a $5 parking fee which goes toward maintenance of the parking lot.

Ski left (south) from the lodge up the hill on the groomed "Main Trail." Follow the trail, gradually climbing and curving to the right for about a kilometre until you see a sign reading MOUNTAIN CLIMB TO THE FINGERS and a trail heading left (south). The trail is also marked by a CAA AVALUATOR sign and a photographic description of Mount MacPherson's avalanche terrain.

Turn left and follow this broad trail for about 300 m to an open area where you cross a creek on a bridge. Follow an old forestry road for about 400 m, climbing steadily and curving to the right. Keep your eyes open for a skin track heading off into the forest on the left (south) side of the road (413100 E 5643900 N).

Follow this skin track for about 100 m through the forest to reach a drainage that trends upward to the right. Follow this drainage for about 500 m to reach an open area at the bottom junction of the middle three fingers. From here, depending on avalanche conditions, you can either uptrack though the trees or centre-punch the fan. There are plenty of options for good skiing.

MOUNT MACPHERSON

Distance 10 km return
Elevation gain 1600 m
Max elevation 2405 m
Avalanche Terrain Rating Complex

Mount MacPherson, showing The Fingers at left and The Womb in the centre. Photo Conor Hurley

Mount MacPherson offers a great ski descent, but getting to the summit is a circuitous affair. The initial approach follows the same route as described previously for The Fingers. As you gain the upper fan of the central three fingers, you will note a gully just to the right of a prominence in the ridge that breaches the ridge crest. Use this steep gully to reach the crest about 412100 E 5642500 N. Sometimes you can ski to the ridge; other times you have to bootpack.

Follow the undulating ridge in a westerly direction to a col (410800 E 5642600 N). Enjoy the view to the north over the precipice and into The Womb. Continue along the ridge to another col (410300 E 5642500 N). You are now standing at the top of The Womb, a big run of about 1300 vertical metres.

From here you can drop into The Womb or continue another 300 m along the southeast face to the summit. It is worth the walk, as there are exceptional views of the Monashees and the Selkirks from the top.

From the summit, reverse your ascent route to the top of The Womb. If you decide to ski this, be warned: it is a committing run, so the stability must be good. At the fan, trend right and bushwhack toward the road. When you reach the road, turn right and ski down toward the Nordic centre.

"There is a kinship among men who have sat by a dying fire and measured the worth of their lives by it."

—*William Golding*

SHORTER TRAVERSES

There are several shorter traverses in the Columbia Mountains that provide a great adventure but are not as long and committing as the Grand Traverses. They take you through spectacular country and are good training for the bigger traverses. Some have them have become classics in their own right.

BOSTOCK CREEK TO REVELSTOKE TRAVERSE

Distance 80 km
Total elevation gain 5300 m
Time 6–8 days

Maps	NTS 1:250,000	Golden 82 N
		Seymour Arm 82 M
	NTS 1:50,000	Illecillewaet 82 N/4
		Glacier 82 N/5
		Mount Revelstoke 82 M/1
	CanadaMapStore	Mount Durrand 082N021
		Mount McGill 082N022
		Mount Moloch 082N031
		Mount Carson 082N032
		Mount Revelstoke 082M010
		Mount St. Cyr 082M020
		Mount La Forme 082M030

Avalanche Terrain Rating Complex

The following information was submitted by Glacier Park warden Eric Dafoe. It looks like a good traverse. The alternative route descriptions, indicated by square brackets, were provided by Ruedi Beglinger.

The route was first completed in April 1999. Much of the terrain lies within the operating area of Selkirk Mountain Experience. Owner and mountain guide Ruedi Beglinger assisted the group with local knowledge and location of a food cache adjacent to his Durrand Lodge. The first party included Eric Dafoe, John Kelly and J.P. Kors of Revelstoke, plus Percy Woods of Lake Louise. Rain and deteriorating conditions

Bostock Creek to Revelstoke

forced this party off the route in the headwaters of La Forme Creek, where they headed west and north to Sale Mountain (420600 E 5669100 N) and descended the west slopes of Sale to Highway 23. Two weeks later Kelly and Dafoe skied up La Forme Creek to the lake at the head of the valley (425800 E 5666800 N) and completed the trip as planned over Mount St. Cyr to Woolsey Glacier, then west to Mount Revelstoke and down to Dafoe's backyard in Revelstoke.

According to the first party, this traverse is a hidden, unknown gem. The terrain varies from steep glaciers to mellow ridges and requires good map reading and route finding skills. One food cache was used, but this is not necessary for most parties. Most days are approximately 10 km long. Rappels were required on Day 2 to drop a steep roll (25 metres) on the south ridge of Grey Fang (439700 E 5683000 N) and to descend a rock wall (45 metres) at the head of the east arm of Dismal Glacier (438100 E 5683500 N). The final day out from Woolsey Glacier to Revelstoke (24 km) could be divided with a stop at Miller Lake. Kelly and Dafoe skied it in one day, as much of the travel is downhill.

Groups that do this traverse should avoid camping in the vicinity of the two Selkirk Mountain Experience lodges – Mount Moloch Chalet and Durrand Glacier Lodge.

The tour begins in Glacier National Park, where fees apply and a safety registration service is available at Rogers Pass, along with weather and detailed snowpack information. Park in the Bostock parking lot (453300 E 5675700 N) and ski up Bostock Trail to Bostock Pass (449700 E 5680700 N). Contour westward into forest and follow the headwaters of Casualty Creek to Farm Pass (448300 E 5681400 N). Descend Farm Creek to the Tangier River through mostly steep, thick forest. Follow the old road southward in the Tangier River valley, looking for a crossing. The first party travelled about 1 km downstream and camped on the east side of the river (444500 E 5682400 N). In the morning Woods tossed the packs across open water and the crew was able to leap the channel and remain generally dry.

Climb up through moderate, forested slopes into the basin draining the northeast corner of Fang Glacier. Trend south below Fang Rock, then ascend north and west to a low pass south of Grey Fang (439700 E 5683000 N). A 25 m rappel over a moderate snow and rock slope was required but may not be necessary under all snow conditions. A block on the east side of the ridge was slung with a 10-metre piece of cord. From the bottom of the rappel, ski down a gentle slope onto a small, flat glacier (Silent Glacier). From here, climb up to a break in the ridge which forms the headwall of Dismal Glacier (438100 E 5683500 N). A steep rock wall drops to Dismal Glacier, requiring a 45-metre rappel. There are bolts at this location but be prepared in case you cannot locate them. Drop down Dismal Glacier.

[Ruedi Beglinger has suggested an alternative route: from Silent Glacier, climb north northwest toward a prominent knife-edge ridge, the Fridding

Peak south ridge. At an elevation of 2500 m you should be able to see a v-shaped notch at the lower end of this ridge. Walk west to reach the notch (438000 E 568390 N). Here you will find a rappel anchor 4 m north of the notch and 1.5 m above a ledge. The anchor might be buried under the snow but you should be able to dig it out. Rappel 30 m to Dismal Glacier.]

Contour the basin westward to the base of a steep north-facing slope on the eastern edge of Dismal Glacier (436200 E 5683300 N). Climb the slope to the highest point on the ridge (435500 E 5682800 N) and enjoy the view. Descend west to a pass between Dismal and Durrand glaciers (433200 E 5682300 N). Follow tracks through the pass and onto Durrand Glacier. Ski past Durrand Lodge and drop into the headwaters of Carnes Creek.

[Ruedi Beglinger describes the route slightly differently: cross Dismal Glacier to Fang Col (436500 E 5683500 N. The climb to the col is across an exposed, shovelled ramp equipped with a fixed rope. From Fang Col, walk along a sharp snow ridge to Juliana Glacier. Ascend Juliana Glacier to an elevation of 2450 m. Aim west, staying west of large crevasses, and ascend the west side of the glacier toward a prominent pinnacle known locally as Point Juliana. From the east side of Point Juliana, climb to the snow ridge above (435400 E 5683000 N). From here, ski southwest, staying east of the Eagle Icefall (434100 E 5682200 N). Ski down a gully to an elevation of 2440 m. Then traverse left (south) for 80 m and ski down to Durrand Glacier. Descend Durrand Glacier to reach Carnes Creek.]

Ascend through easy, rolling terrain to a flat ridge at the top of the drainage. Cross the ridge (430900 E 5676600 N) and contour southwest to about 2200 m in the headwaters of Woolsey Creek. Climb west and through a notch in the ridge (430300 E 5675400 N). Traverse west into a narrow basin. Climb through the head of the basin (429400 E 5675100 N) and continue south over the ridge (429200 E 5674700 N) into a large south-facing bowl above Elm Creek. Descend to Elm Creek. This is serious avalanche country, so be sure of conditions before entering the slope. From the valley bottom ascend the north side of Elm Creek until the heavy timber thins. Cross the creek and climb up to the ridge bounding the south side of the valley. Follow the ridge to a flat bench in the upper basin (427900 E 5671900 N). Continue through rolling terrain to the ridgetop (427100 E 5671100 N).

[Ruedi Beglinger has an alternative route here as well. From the upper Woolsey Bowl, climb west–northwest to a prominent col (430200 E 5675400 N). Traverse steep slopes to the west to a large col south of the prominent La Forme Tower. Continue climbing in a westerly direction to La Forme Glacier (428500 E 5675200 N). From here walk to the summit of Mount La Forme, then ski to the nearest col north of the summit (428300 E 5674900 N). Descend the west side of this col along a ramp to 2400 m, then descend a steep slope west to the bowl below. Now climb in a southerly direction to a prominent col (427400 E 5674100 N). Follow the ridge to the southwest to a summit and then follow the ridgeline south.]

Drop a steep slope to the southwest and climb out of the notch to the next rise in the ridge (426100 E 5670100 N). Follow the ridge around the headwaters of Maunder Creek, crossing the ridge as necessary to follow the most favourable terrain. Continue in a southerly direction to 426400 E 5667200 N and drop down to the small lake at the top of La Forme Creek (425800 E 5666800 N). Options to bail exist via logging roads in La Forme Creek or by dropping down to the junction with the second creek that enters from the southwest (424500 E 5667300 N), then climbing through that drainage to a northwest-trending ridge. Follow the ridge north to the Sale Mountain microwave towers (420700 E 5669000 N) and descend the road to Highway 23. If you are continuing the tour, contour around the lake basin and climb a steep but aesthetic line through the stepped basin west of Mount St. Cyr. Slide through the col at 425300 E 5665200 N. Descend south-facing slopes, trending to skier's right onto gentle slopes and down onto Woolsey Glacier. Continue east on the south side of the glacier and lake to a rock outcrop overlooking West Woolsey Creek. Parks Canada maintains a small A-frame here. The cabin can be booked at the Parks office in Revelstoke and contains two bunks, utensils, a stove and a lantern (427100 E 5664700 N).

Climb west up Woolsey Glacier and over a pass (424300 E 5663300 N), then down onto the remnant Gordon Glacier. Cross this basin southeasterly and climb another low pass (424200 E 5661300 N) into the headwaters of Clachnacudainn Creek. Follow a contour around the steep southeast-facing basin to the convoluted terrain above Lower Jade Lake and descend to the lake (425000 E 5658700 N). Climb the south slopes of Mount Williamson to the pass at 423400 E 5658300 N and descend moderate slopes to Miller Lake. Climb over the rib at the south end of Miller Lake and drop down to the big bend at the top of the southeast fork of Coursier Creek (422000 E 5657500 N). Climb west up and out of this drainage, generally following the summer trail to Heather Lake (419900 E 5655800 N). Descend through the open forest below Balsam Lake (419600 E 5654700 N), following a southerly route toward Bridge Creek and crossing the road several times. At Caribou Cabin (419000 E 5653000) cross Bridge Creek and then trend to skier's right and into open forest. Descend glades to the road at approximately 417800 E 5652400 N. Slide down the road and into Revelstoke.

GOAT RANGE TRAVERSE

Distance 60 km
Total elevation gain 4700 m
Time 5–6 days

Maps	NTS 1:250,000	Lardeau 82 K
	NTS 1:50,000	Roseberry 82 K/3
		Poplar Creek 82 K/6
	CanadaMapStore	Mount Jardine 082K005
		Mount Dolly Varden 082K014
		South Cooper Creek 082K015
		Mount Marion 082K024
		Meadow Mountain 082K025
		Spyglass Mountain 082K034
		Mat Creek 082K035

Avalanche Terrain Rating Complex

From April 13–19, 1999, six young skiers from Rossland traversed the Goat Range, northeast of Slocan Lake. The team was composed of Stewart Spooner, Kirsty Exner, Jordy Hall, Cindy Carrol, Russ Peebles and Sarah Weinberg. There were a number of excellent ski descents on north-facing slopes along the way and at most camps they had running water and firewood. A party that

Goat Range Traverse 1

N

McKian Creek

Rossland Creek

Keen Creek

Mount Cooper

Mount Stubbs

Mount McHardy

Mount Dolly Varden

Marten Mountain

Inverness Mountain

Mount Dryden

Mount Brennan

Whitewater Mountain

Whitewater Creek

Kane Creek

Retallack

Hwy 31A

Seaton Creek

0   3   6

Kilometres

Goat Range Traverse 2

0   3   6
Kilometres

N

31

Mount
Keen

Spyglass
Mountain

Poplar Creek Rd.

Poplar Creek

Cascade Creek

Mount
Emmens

Cascade
Mountain

Wilson Creek

Mount
Marion

McKian
Creek

did the tour in 2011 reported that it was great fun and a good introduction to multi-day ski traverses. The tour is about 40 km in length, followed by a heinous 17 km slog down a logging road. Here is the route as they described it to me (with one variation).

Drop a car off at the base of the logging road at Poplar Creek (on Highway 31 north from Kaslo toward Trout Lake), then return to Retallack (on Highway 31A between New Denver and Kaslo). Begin climbing on the north side of the highway and make your first camp at treeline along Whitewater Creek. Continue up the creek and climb easily to a low saddle (487300 E 5549000 N) northeast of Whitewater Mountain. A long ski run takes you to camp in Kane Creek.

From here it's steep climbing northwest up a treed headwall, then easy going up an exposed valley leading to the lower of two saddles (482900 E 5553000 N). Steep, fun skiing takes you to a small lake. Then easy cruising and pitches of good skiing follow down to Keen Creek. A party in 2011 found an alternative route that rounds Mount McHardy to the west and north, then descends into Keen Creek. Traverse the eastern side of the creek, then climb through an old burn to a camp in Rossland Creek.

Climb north-northeast (crampons may be necessary) to a small lake, then continue on skins to a low saddle (483600 E 5560400 N). A huge cornice on the other side can be avoided by skiing a short, steep pitch at the eastern end of the saddle, then a steep, rolling run that takes you to a camp in McKian Creek. The 2011 party wrote that the cornice could be avoided if you "climb up about 10 m vertically, then take a bench off to the right below some cliffs that block the wind and prevent cornice formation."

Make a long traversing climb across the forested slope (avoiding the avalanche paths) to an obvious low notch in a rocky ridge (481700 E 5565000 N). From here another great descent leads to camp by a lake at 2060 m.

At this point poor snow conditions forced the 2011 group from their intended route. In rotten snow they skied down a narrow gully to Wilson Creek. From there they ascended Wilson Creek to camp in the

The tremendous descent to Kane Creek, looking back up to the col at the head of Whitewater Creek. Photo Jim Firstbrook

Jim Firstbrook crossing avalanche debris on the long slog down Poplar Creek. Photo Aaron Donohue

saddle (480300 E 5571000 N) at the head of the valley. They then found a reasonable route to a high col (483000 E 5567900 N) from where they could descend to upper Wilson Creek.

From the pass at the head of Wilson Creek a long, descending traverse (don't go too far down the creek bed that drains the lake) leads to a branch of the Poplar Creek logging road visible from the pass. Follow the logging road for about 17 km to Poplar Creek. The road crosses many avalanche paths and according to one party is "not for the faint of heart."

GOLD RANGE TRAVERSE

Distance 80 km via route of 2010 party
Total elevation gain 8000 m via route of 2010 party
Time about a week
Maps NTS 1:250,000   Vernon 82 L

NTS 1:50,000	Revelstoke 82 L/16
	Gates Creek 82 L/9
CanadaMapStore.com	Mount Odin 082L060
	Gates Creek 082L069
	Mount Hall 082L070
	Blanket Mountain 082L079
	Cranberry Creek 082L080
	Mount Tilley 082L089
	Mount MacPherson 082L099

Avalanche Terrain Rating Complex

This traverse was attempted and partially completed in April 1979 by Dave Smith, Don Vockeroth, Tim Auger and Bob Sawyer. It travels through spectacular country with serious avalanche considerations and some tricky route finding. Since then a number of parties have completed sections of the traverse in different variations and different directions.

The 1979 party began along Highway 23 just north of Blanket Creek (about 20 km south of Revelstoke). They ascended the shoulder to the north of Blanket Creek, then traversed high above the creek to reach the north fork of it. From here they followed the creek, then climbed a steep headwall to reach gentle terrain above and two lakes. Blanket Glacier Chalet is located near here at 412100 E 562790O N.

The group turned south and ascended lovely alpland toward Blanket Mountain, then crossed the glacier and skied to the col between Armstrong Peak and Blanket Mountain. Here they encountered a difficult cornice overhanging the south side of the pass which necessitated a rope and belay. After negotiating this problem they kicked steps down to lower-angled terrain, then skied to the pass separating Lindmark Creek and the north fork of Cranberry Creek.

Continuing south, they followed a rounded ridge toward Cranberry Mountain. Dave Smith described this section of the tour as follows:

> What a remarkable place! The great bulwarks of the ridge tapered off into rounded undulations that led us ever upward toward the summit of Cranberry. On our left, the north glacier flowed and tumbled into its long canyon in wild contrast

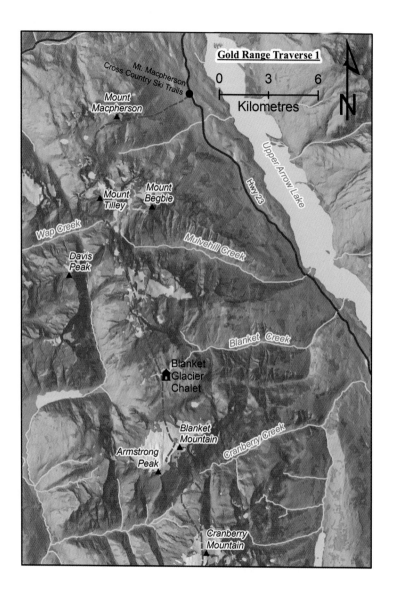

Gold Range Traverse 1

Mt. Macpherson
Cross Country Ski Trails

Mount Macpherson

Kilometres
0   3   6

N

Upper Arrow Lake

Hwy 23

Mount Tilley

Mount Begbie

Wap Creek

Mulvehill Creek

Davis Peak

Blanket Creek

Blanket Glacier Chalet

Blanket Mountain

Cranberry Creek

Armstrong Peak

Cranberry Mountain

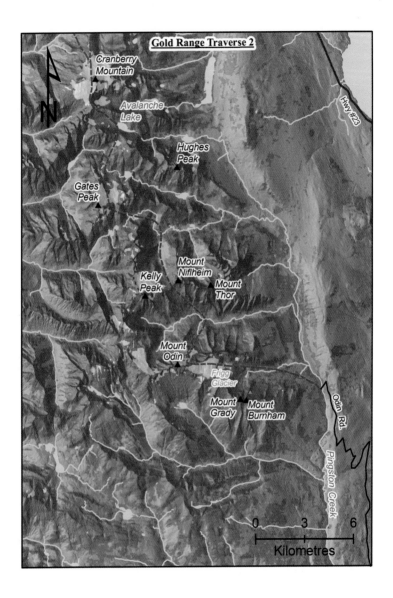

Gold Range Traverse 2

Cranberry Mountain

Avalanche Lake

Hughes Peak

Gates Peak

Mount Niflheim

Kelly Peak

Mount Thor

Mount Odin

Frigg Glacier

Mount Grady

Mount Burnham

Hwy #23

Odin Rd.

Pingston Creek

N

0   3   6
Kilometres

to our ethereal road. Those few hours ascending the ridge were among the finest I have ever enjoyed ski touring.

The team crossed the glacier to Cranberry Mountain, then left their skis behind and scrambled up the north ridge to the summit.

Returning to their skis the team traversed to a small notch just west of the summit, which provided access to the glacier south of Cranberry Mountain. Crossing this glacier, they located a prominent spur leading east. The point where this spur intersects the south ridge of Cranberry Mountain is obscure, and in a whiteout the 1979 party had difficulty locating it. Descending this spur to the east, they continued down a broad gully to the south onto a flat, unnamed glacier. From here they skied east down the glacier to what they named Avalanche Lake.

After five days of marginal weather and severe avalanche conditions the 1979 party bailed at this point, descending the headwall to the east to Pingston Lake, from where they soon reached logging roads. They had intended to continue south past Gates Creek, Kelly Peak and Mount Odin, but that tour would have to wait for a new generation of skiers.

In 2006 Rémy Bernier and James Madden completed this traverse over a period of five days, starting from the south near Mount Odin and continuing north to Mount MacPherson. In 2010 another party – Nev Bugden, C.J. Wright, Audray Ayotte and Conor Hurley – repeated the traverse and provided the following excellent route description.

They made their way up Odin Road West to the Pingston Creek microhydro project and crossed the creek via the bridge below the dam. They then skied northwest around the shoulder of Mount Burnham to a camp at treeline (424400 E 5600000 N) east of Frigg Glacier.

From here the group headed up Frigg Glacier and very nearly reached the summit of Mount Odin. A 1200 m descent starting about 120 m below the summit (420400 E 5600300 N) led to Odin Creek, where they turned west and climbed to a camp at 420000 E 5603800 N.

On frozen snow the group climbed the southeast aspect of Mount Niflheim to a col at 419500 E 5604700 N. From here they descended north to Thor Creek. Following undulating and convoluted terrain,

The 2010 party takes an early-morning lunch break while climbing above Frigg Glacier to Mount Odin. Mount Grady and Mount Burnham are in the background. Photo C.J. Wright

Looking up the descent route on the north side of Mount Niflheim. Photo C.J. Wright

Looking south toward Gates Peak on the right. The 2010 party descended the glacier below the col. Photo C.J. Wright

they continued north, then west, crossed a small lake and ascended mushy south-facing slopes to a camp (416600 E 5609500 N) below a col east of the summit of Gates Peak.

The next day, they crossed the col and skied out onto the Gates Icefield. A mellow run followed by a rambly tour through convoluted terrain took the group to a saddle at 416700 E 5613800 N. Here they waited until the heat of the day had passed, then climbed east a ways and found an excellent 600 m descent to Avalanche Lake. From here they climbed to the south ridge of Cranberry Mountain and continued to a camp at 414700 E 5617200 N.

In the morning, an ascent of Cranberry Mountain and a descent of the northwest face was followed by an inspiring run down its northwest ridge. The group then climbed to a col northeast of Armstrong Peak (412400 E 5622100 N) from where they contoured to the summit of

Neville Bugden skiing with a heavy pack to Avalanche Lake.
The route of ascent up the southeast slopes of Cranberry
Mountain can be seen in the background. Photo C.J. Wright

Blanket Mountain, then descended to Blanket Glacier Chalet (412100 E
562790o N), where they spent the night.

Under clear skies the next day, the group continued north to a col at
410500 E 5632800 N where a few steep turns took them onto Mulvehill
Glacier. A short, steep bootpack took them to camp at 410100 E
5633900 N. From here they continued north to the head of Wap Creek
to camp at 409200 E 5637100 N under the south face of Mount Tilley.

On the last day, the group contoured down Wap Creek, then
climbed to a col west of Mount Tilley (407400 E 5638000 N). From
here a quick run was followed by a climb back up to a col at 407600 E
5638300 N, then a descent to a lake for lunch. From here they contoured
and descended to a small lake southwest of Mount Macpherson, then
climbed the southwest flank to the summit. The final descent of the
trip, an 1800 m ski, walk and bushwhack through alder and avalanche
debris, took them to the Macpherson Cross Country Ski Area parking
lot on Highway 23.

BONNINGTON RANGE TRAVERSE

Distance 45 km
Total elevation gain 2800 m
Time most parties take 4 days

Maps	NTS 1:250,000	Nelson 82 F
	NTS 1:50,000	Rossland/Trail 82 F/4
		Castlegar 82 F/5
		Nelson 82 F/6
	CanadaMapStore.com	Grassy Mountain 082F023
		Siwash Mountain 082F033
		Commonwealth Mountain 082F034

Avalanche Terrain Rating Challenging

This has become a very popular hut-to-hut tour in recent years. The mountains are more rounded and subdued than those in most of the Columbias and the summits are just above treeline. The traverse is in the shape of a horseshoe, and the total distance from Bombi Summit to Porto Rico is about 45 km. Most of the tour keeps to the ridge crests on relatively safe terrain, with the exception of a few narrow spots and the occasional avalanche slope. The tour is usually skied in the direction described here.

There are three huts (plus a possible fourth) along the way, fairly equally spaced and linked by pleasant day tours. These huts are maintained by the Kootenay Mountaineering Club and reservations are required. A fee of $10 per person per night is charged, and reservations can be made on the club website www.kootenaymountaineering.bc.ca. The huts are described on the website as "rustic, wilderness cabins." They have wood heating stoves, Coleman cooking stoves and lanterns and basic cooking and eating utensils. Bring white gas for the stoves and spare mantles for lanterns. There are no foam mattresses in the huts, so bring your own. Grassy, Steed and Copper huts sleep six, while Huckleberry Hut sleeps four.

The following route description is largely courtesy of Sandra McGuinness (search "Bonnington Range Traverse" at www.bivouac.com; subscription required for full report). I have included more accurate grid references for the huts, as I have been advised that the huts are often difficult to find until you are right on top of them.

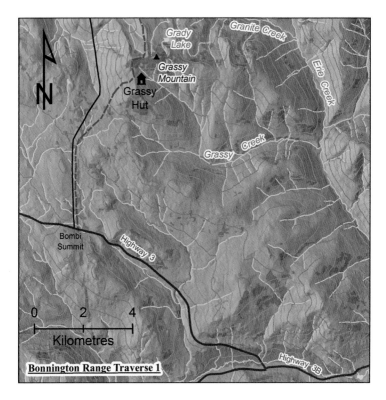

Bonnington Range Traverse 1

Bombi Summit to Grassy Hut (about 9 km)

Start where the power line crosses Highway 3 at Bombi Summit, 17 km east of Castlegar. Follow the power line service road north for about 6.4 km to near tower 154, where you can ascend east to a low pass 1.3 km southwest of Grassy Mountain. From the pass, descend gradually in an easterly direction to the hut at 1900 m (464216 E 5459865). There are some orange markers on the trees showing the route down to the hut but they can be easy to miss. The route from Bombi Summit to the low pass is on private land, so please respect any signs posted by landowners. Since the powerline route goes up and down and can be a bit annoying, an alternative route has been suggested. To reach this, ski north on the main Munson FSR road out of Bombi Summit. Between 3.5 and

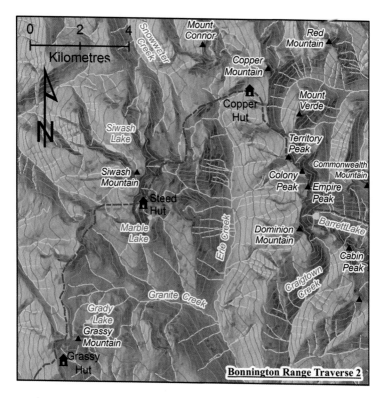

Bonnington Range Traverse 2

4.0 km you will pass two signed forest service roads on your left, the first, at 3.7 km, signed Lower Munson (461500 E 5456700 N); the second, at 3.9 km, signed West Munson (461500 E 5457000 N). Ignore both of these and stay to the right at these junctions. At 5.4 km you will reach another FSR (East Munson) (461900 E 5457600 N), which exits to the right. Stay left at this junction. At 6.3 km there is an old spur to the right. Ski past this spur for another 100 m, then take the next spur (6.4 km) (462800 E 5458200 N), which exits to the right. Follow this for a couple of switchbacks until the road flattens out and it is easy to ski uphill in an easterly direction toward the pass between Grassy and South Grassy.

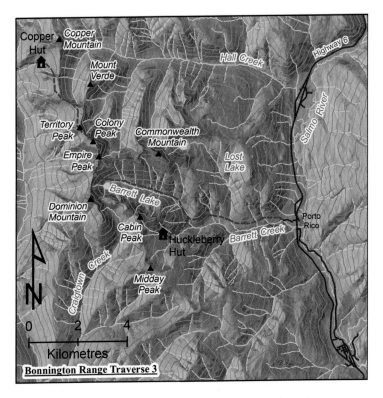

Bonnington Range Traverse 3

**Grassy Hut to Steed
Hut (about 9 km)**

From Grassy Hut ski back up to the pass and continue north to the top of the west ridge of Grassy Mountain. Ski east along this ridge until you can descend the north ridge of Grassy Mountain to a broad pass (4643 00 E 54625 00 N). Continue skiing north over to the top of two minor unnamed peaks, known locally as Twin Peaks.

Helen Sovdat at Grassy Hut. Photo Marg Saul

Sandra McGuinness (left) and Marg Saul on the Bonnington Range Traverse, looking back at Grassy Mountain. Photo Helen Sovdat

From the most northerly of the Twin Peaks, you can either stay on the ridge and ski down to the pass at the height of land between Glade and Granite Creeks or follow the north ridge of North Twin Peak until it is possible to drop off to the east and ski down to a logging road that leads to the height of land between Glade and Granite Creeks. Both routes meet at this pass. From here ski up to the pass on the south ridge of Siwash Mountain at 467100 E 5465900 N. Drop steeply down about 100 vertical metres to Steed Hut (467478 E 5466027) at 2320 m elevation.

Steed Hut to Copper Hut (about 11 km)

From Steed Hut descend about 80 vertical metres and cross over the small ridge (468200 E 5465800 N) north of Marble Lake. Drop down to a small tarn at 468200 E 5466100 N, contour north around Siwash Mountain, then ski up to a small pass at 468400 E 5467600 N. From this pass many parties contour around the headwaters of Erie Creek through a broad pass south of Mount Connor and then climb about

Sandra McGuinness (left) and Helen Sovdat inside Steed Hut. Photo Marg Saul

400 vertical metres to Copper Hut (472016 E 5470525 N) at an elevation of 2000 m. This is a very unpleasant route through forest, cutblocks and a wasteland of snowmobile tracks. A better route is to turn east from the pass at 468400 E 5467600 N and follow this prominent ridge as it travels east, then north. You can follow the ridge right down to Erie Creek. Cross Erie Creek and ski about 400 m up to Copper Hut (472016 E 5470525 N) at 2000 m.

Helen Sovdat at Copper Hut. Photo Marg Saul

Note: There is an escape route from Copper Hut if you get trapped by bad weather. From the broad pass south of Mount Connor, you can escape down a road that contours west across the Snowwater and Midas drainages, then north along Snowwater and Midas Creek to Rover Creek. Note that the roads are not correctly marked on the map.

Copper Hut to Porto Rico (17 km)

From Copper Hut, ski to the pass south of Copper Mountain (472600 E 5470300 N). Follow the ridge generally south to the top of Territory Peak (the final

Marg Saul (left) and Sandra McGuinness on the narrow ridge between Colony Peak and Empire Peak. Photo Helen Sovdat

40 vertical metres is steep but possible on skis). Continue along the ridgetop from Territory Peak to Colony Peak. From Colony, descend the narrow ridge and continue south to Empire Peak. The most difficult part of the route is between Colony and Empire peaks and generally requires a short section or two of bootpacking. From Empire Peak descend south-facing slopes to Barrett Lake, then ski down the forest service road to Porto Rico Road. This section is snowmobile-packed and can be very fast. To avoid a short uphill section from Barrett Lake, descend slightly east as you come down from Empire Peak. If you like, you can overnight at Huckleberry Hut, located at 1600 m on the edge of the road (476800 E 5463600 N). To reach this hut, turn right at the bridge that crosses Barrett Creek and climb for about 2 km and 220 vertical metres back up the road.

APEX CREEK TO PROCTOR TRAVERSE

Distance 34 km
Total elevation gain 3000 m
Time 3 days
Maps NTS 1:250,000 Nelson 82 F
      NTS 1:50,000 Nelson 82 F/6
                        Crawford Bay 82 F/10
                        Kokanee Peak 82 F/11
      CanadaMapStore.com Ymir Mountain 082F045
                        Mount Ferguson 082F055
                        Mount Hartridge 082F056
                        Balfour 082F066
Avalanche Terrain Rating Complex

This traverse follows along the height of land from Apex Creek (Whitewater Ski Resort) to Proctor through the seldom visited West Arm Provincial Park. The area was burned by the fires of 2003 and now provides good skiing through open burnt timber. There is challenging route finding on this traverse, many steep (40 degree) corniced slopes to descend and unavoidable avalanche hazard. Consequently it is recommended that you only undertake this tour when snow stability is good. For more details see "Skiing the Burn: A Three Day Traverse from Apex Creek to Proctor," by Sandra McGuinness, on www.bivouac.com (subscription required for full report).

From Whitewater Ski Resort (see page 153), gain the ridge between Ymir Mountain and White Queen (490600 E 5476900 N), then traverse east into Five Mile Basin and ascend to the col at 491500 E 5476500 N. This is a steep traverse (40 degrees) beneath cliffs but leads to more mellow terrain at the head of Five Mile Creek. In springtime this traverse could be baked hard and ski crampons will be required.

From here, contour around a blunt ridgeline to the north, climb 80 vertical metres over another prominent ridge running southeast (493100 E 5478100 N). A 1-kilometre-long, gradually rising traverse leads to a pass on the next ridgeline north (493900 E 5478300 N). Find a route through the corniced ridge and descend to the valley below. From here another gently climbing traverse leads to a southeast-trending ridge at 2040 m (495500 E 5479500 N). After negotiating another

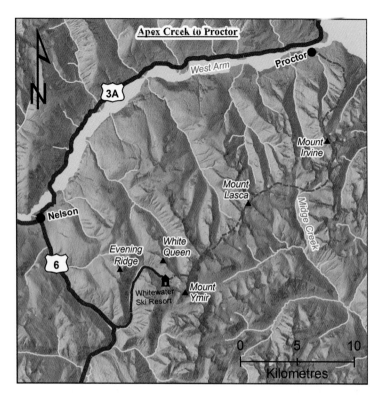

cornice, descend to a tarn (495300 E 5480300 N) in the valley below. Another gentle climb to the height of land leads to a small summit. Continue following the height of land north until you can ski down to a small lake. After you negotiate another cornice, a steep descent leads to a lake at the base of Mount Lasca where a camp can be established (496500 E 5482500 N). From here you can ski to the summit of Mount Lasca (496900 E 5483000 N).

Cross the southeast ridge of Mount Lasca (497400 E 5482800 N). Then, after negotiating another cornice, descend steep slopes to a marshy area below (497800 E 5483300 N). Contour for a kilometre, cross a narrow pass south of Mill Lake (498800 5484200 N), then contour and descend in a northeasterly direction past two tarns to the head of

Skiing along the ridge toward Mount Lasca. Photo Sandra McGuinness

Midge Creek (499800 E 5484900 N). After a steep descent to the forks of Midge Creek (501000 E 5483900 N), ascend for a kilometre following the east fork of Midge Creek. From here a climb of 600 vertical metres leads to the crest of the Wilson–Midge divide (504500 E 5483400 N). From here, ascend a little peak (504400 5483700 N). Ski north along the divide over two small peaks until you can drop off the ridge to the north and into the valley below with a series of small tarns. With some judicious traversing, gain the next ridgeline to the north (504500 E 5486300 N) and coast down to a campsite (504500 E 5486500 N) on a large lake south of Mount Irvine. From camp, ski north and gain the long south ridge of Mount Irvine, which is followed over two subsidiary summits to the top of Mount Irvine (504200 E 5487600 N).

From here, ski north along a narrow ridge around the west side of Irvine Creek for 5 km until the ridge forks. Take the easterly fork and follow it northeast all the way down to the logging road shown on the map as a dashed line (505400 E 5493000 N). From here a downhill cruise for 10 km took the McGuinness–Brown team to a stashed bicycle and a 40 km ride to Nelson to pick up their truck.

NAKUSP RANGE SKI TRAVERSE

Distance 35 km
Total elevation gain 4000 m
Time 4 days

Maps NTS 1:250,000	Lardeau 82 K
NTS 1:50,000	Roseberry 82 K/3
	Nakusp 82 K/4
CanadaMapStore.com	Mount Vingolf 082K003
	Box Mountain 082K012
	Mount Ferrie 082K013
	Mount Jordan 082K022

Avalanche Terrain Rating Challenging Complex

This traverse was first done in 2010 by Sandra McGuinness, Doug Brown, Robin Tivy and Betsy Waddington. It follows the Nakusp Range from Roseberry in the south to Box Lake in the north along the height of land.

Looking north across the Nakusp Range ski traverse toward Summit Peak. Photo Sandra McGuinness

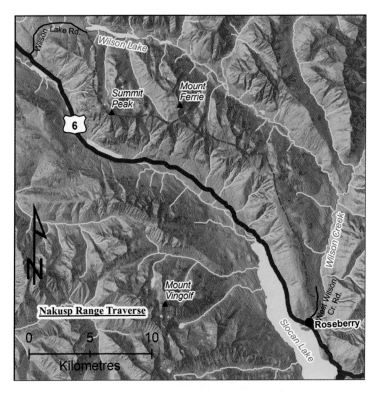

Kilometres

Access and egress is via logging roads and is reported to be quite easy. For more details see "Easy In, Easy Out: Across the Nakusp Range on Skis," by Sandra McGuinness, at www.bivouac.com (subscription required for full report).

From Roseberry take West Wilson Creek FSR for about 4.2 km to Ranch Creek FSR and follow this to the snowline. Leave your car (470600 E 5545400 N) and begin skiing north. Follow the road for a couple of hours to a cutblock, then leave the road and travel north along the ridge, gradually gaining elevation to reach a small highpoint at about 1900 m (468100 E 5555200 N). Camp was established here.

Continue north, climbing steadily to Peak 7243 (465400 E 5555400 N).

Robin Tivy on the Nakusp Range Traverse. Photo Sandra McGuinness

Continue north along the ridge to a col near 464900 E 5556300 N. Ski easily across a large basin to a broad pass (462900 E 5556900 N). A curving traverse leads to a steep slope which is ascended to the ridgeline (461900 E 5558400 N). Camp 2 was established here.

From here, ski west to the col south of Mount Ferrie (460200 E 5558500 N). The next part of the traverse is a delight following the ridgeline west all the way to two small tarns at the base of Summit Peak. Camp 3 was established here (455500 E 5558900 N).

Ski easily to the top of Summit Peak. Continue west down the ridge, then follow a lightly treed ridge north to a 2000 m peak (453100 E 5562000 N). Leave the ridge, heading north, and descend through open trees to a logging road near 1700 m (453400 E 5563900 N) which leads to the main Wilson Lake FSR (454200 E 5564100 N). Descend Wilson Lake FSR to reach your previously placed vehicle.

THE GRAND TRAVERSES

The Columbia Mountains of British Columbia have many magnificent wilderness ski traverses which follow the crests of the Cariboo, Monashee, Selkirk and Purcell mountain ranges. They have been pioneered over the last fifty years and have gradually become more and more popular. Some are now skied by several parties each year.

On the Northern Cariboo Traverse. Photo Dan Clark

A LITTLE HISTORY

The first traverse was the Bugaboos to Rogers Pass skied by four Americans – Bill Briggs, Bob French, Sterling Neale and Barry Corbet – in 1958. It was a visionary expedition and the team took only nine days to complete the traverse. In 1965 Hans Gmoser led a party including Mike Wiegele, Jim and Glenn McConkey, Erwin Tontsch and

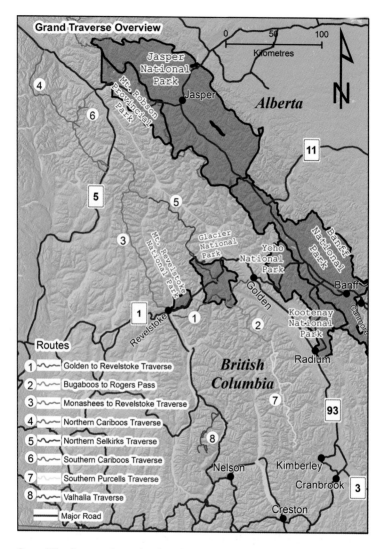

Grand Traverse Overview

0   50   100
Kilometres

N

Jasper National Park

Jasper

Mt. Robson Provincial Park

Alberta

4

6

5

5

3

Mt. Revelstoke National Park

Glacier National Park

Yoho National Park

Golden

Banff National Park

Banff

Canmore

1

1

2

Revelstoke

Kootenay National Park

Radium

British Columbia

7

93

Routes

8

Nelson

Kimberley

Cranbrook

3

Creston

1 〰 Golden to Revelstoke Traverse

2 〰 Bugaboos to Rogers Pass

3 〰 Monashees to Revelstoke Traverse

4 〰 Northern Cariboos Traverse

5 〰 Northern Selkirks Traverse

6 〰 Southern Cariboos Traverse

7 〰 Southern Purcells Traverse

8 〰 Valhalla Traverse

▬ Major Road

Scott Henderson along the Southern Purcells from Toby Creek to the Bugaboos. Heavy metal skis, just being developed at the time, were used on these first two expeditions.

In 1973 Don Gardner, Chic Scott, Dave Smith and Ron Robinson repeated the traverse from Rogers Pass to the Bugaboos. In 1976 the same team added their own line, skiing the Northern Selkirks from Mica Creek to Rogers Pass. On these two traverses wooden Nordic skis and waxes were used.

In the late 1970s and early 1980s a new group of skiers, mainly from Calgary, entered the game. Over two seasons in 1977 and '78, Steve Smith, Bob Saunders, Mel Hines and Errol Smith skied from Rogers Pass to the Bugaboos. The Southern Cariboos traverse was skied for the first time in 1980 by Alf Skrastins, Tony Daffern, Murray Toft and Allan Derbyshire. In 1981 Steve Smith, his brother Phil and Scott Duncan repeated the Northern Selkirks Traverse, and in 1982 the same threesome created the Northern Cariboos Traverse. That same year, Steve Smith went on to ski the Southern Purcells Traverse with Bob Saunders, beginning at the Bugaboos and finishing at St. Mary's Park. Unknown to that group, another party – Errol Smith, Len Potter, Chris Kubinski and Chic Scott – were skiing north from St. Mary's Park to Toby Creek at the same time.

In the early 1980s these traverses gained in popularity and were repeated often. In 1983 a team of women including Lin Heidt, Kathy Calvert, Martha McCallum and Sylvia Forest skied the Rogers Pass to Bugaboos Traverse. That same year saw the first guided traverse when Al Schaffer, Alf Skrastins and Steve Ludwig led a party along the Southern Cariboos Traverse. In 1990 Chic Scott and Rod McGowan guided a group across the Rogers Pass to the Bugaboos.

Until this time these traverses had been an activity reserved for the hard core. Few people knew exactly where they went and how to do them. Then, in 1994, the first edition of *Summits and Icefields* was published and the information became readily available to the general public. Through the 1990s and into the new millennium these traverses have grown in popularity and some are now done by five to ten parties each year.

In 1998 Dan Clark and Chris Gooliaff made the next logical step and connected most of these tours into a gigantic traverse of the Columbia

Mountains. Over a period of 61 days the pair traversed from McBride to Kimberley, a distance of about 700 km, crossing the Cariboos, Selkirks and Purcells. It was an outstanding achievement, considering they had never done one of these traverses before. It was only marred by the fact that they were unable to force a link through the Monashees between the Southern Cariboos and the Northern Selkirks.

The last of the great lines was skied in 2004. Over a period of 21 days Aaron Chance, Greg Hill, Ian Bissonette, Dave Sproule and Jeff Volp traversed the Monashees, bagging 21 summits along the way. Now that the obvious lines have been skied, ski mountaineers are looking for new ways to express themselves. In April of 2005 Troy Jungen, Jon Walsh and Doug Sproule set a new standard for "fast and light" when they skied from Rogers Pass to the Bugaboos in only 80 hours.

In the future these traverses are likely to grow in popularity. They are a great way to have a major adventure with a minimum of expense and hassle. Just place your caches and go.

SKIING THE GRAND TRAVERSES by Mark Klassen

The Grand Traverses take a great deal of time to plan, prepare for and complete. For a general overview of planning a ski tour in the Columbias, see the "Alpine Ski Touring in the Columbia Mountains" chapter at the beginning of this book. If you have not done so already, it is worthwhile to read through that before reading this chapter and starting your plans for a traverse.

Although modern ski touring parties are shattering previously held beliefs about how quickly these trips can be completed, average parties should expect to travel 10–15 km per day. A rough estimate of travel speed would be 3–4 km/h, with an additional hour for every 300–400 m elevation gain.

The terrain

Each traverse involves travel through extensive "Complex" avalanche terrain. This means committing to high-consequence terrain with few options to reduce your risk, so you need stable snow conditions.

You will need to time your trips with care to take advantage of safe conditions.

Some trips may be skied in the direction opposite to how they are described. Depending on the route, conditions and time of year, it may be beneficial to climb up south aspects when they are frozen in the morning and get better skiing down the north aspects. Sometimes the better travel will be up the north slopes and down the corn on the south aspects.

When to go

The combination of serious, complex terrain with a snowpack that often contains persistent weak layers means that timing is one of the most important elements in planning a traverse.

Waiting for the spring melt–freeze cycle to form a relatively stable snowpack is essential to help create certainty in your avalanche risk assessment. This cycle will cause firm crusts on solar aspects and will strengthen the weak layers on northerly slopes. In the late season it is easier to judge whether warm temperatures have weakened a surface crust or penetrated the snowpack to destabilize a lingering PWL; deciding the stability of a winter slab sitting on deeply buried surface hoar is very difficult, even for the most experienced practitioners.

Often the period just before the first spring melt–freeze cycle will be the most dangerous time to deal with a PWL. At that point the layer will have maximum load but is so deep that it will be difficult, but not impossible, for a skier to trigger it. If a slide is initiated it could be a super-sized event that you would not survive.

The spring melt–freeze cycle usually occurs sometime in April. Most traverse parties plan to start their trips in mid to late April and finish in late April to mid May.

Utilizing a good weather window is also important. Good visibility means you can travel faster and gives you more options to reduce your risk. It helps to have flexibility in your start date so you can wait for a clear spell to begin your trip. If I am planning a week-long traverse I usually keep a two-week window of opportunity open. This way we can start up to a week later than originally planned, to take advantage of the best weather and conditions.

Equipment

Rope. Experienced parties usually carry a twin-, half- or single-rated rope that is at least 45 m long. Even for a party of two, that length is required if both members are carrying rescue coils that are double the length of rope that is between them while they are travelling. For parties larger than four a longer rope would be required.

Historically, crevasses probably have been the greatest hazard encountered by skiers on the Grand Traverses. There have been several serious crevasse incidents and at least one crevasse fall fatality. Always carefully consider your reasoning if you do not use the rope on a glacier. Using shorter or thinner ropes significantly increases the risk in a crevasse incident.

A 60 m length of rope is required for the Deville Headwall rappels on the Bugaboos–Rogers Pass Traverse. I often will carry two 30 m lengths instead of one 60 m, to distribute the weight among the group.

Ski crampons. Key for spring conditions, don't leave home without them.

Ice axe and foot crampons. It is recommended the party carry at least one ice axe, and everyone should have foot crampons. Hard melt–freeze crusts on steep slopes should be expected and walking with crampons may be your only option.

Ice hammer and rock pitons. These could be considered if cliffy terrain is expected on the trip. A wrong turn on some trips could lead to a situation where a rappel over a cliff is required.

First aid and repair kits. Make sure these are well stocked and include major binding parts (I carry at least a spare toe piece for my bindings). A small first-aid manual helps, especially if dealing with an injury or illness where quick rescue is not available.

Communications device. Most parties will want some way to communicate with the outside world in the event of a rescue or an early pull-out being required. The go-to system these days seems to be a satellite phone. A vhf radio is able to communicate with local backcountry skiing companies or park authorities in many areas, but a satellite phone may be more versatile in being able to contact a variety of outside resources. Satellite phones are available for rent in major centres. Helicopter companies may also know of local shops that rent satellite phones.

Another alternative is a personal locator beacon. If using a plb that allows for custom emergency messaging (such as the spot units), remember to enter the pertinent mountain rescue contact information in the message.

Helicopter access

Many points along the traverses may be accessed by helicopter, but flights can be long and therefore very expensive. Flights are useful for starting or finishing some traverses, placing food caches, or getting pulled out because of poor weather or conditions or for rescue.

Helicopters are not allowed to land within national parks. The various provincial parks have different regulations on helicopter access; refer to the descriptions of each traverse and/or contact the relevant park for details. Note that in an emergency, evacuation by helicopter is allowed in all parks if organized through the proper authorities.

On some trips, it may be local heli-ski operators that have the machine that is closest to your destination and therefore could offer the cheapest flight. Due to operational requirements, however, not all heli-ski outfits are able to provide flights, and if they are, the availability of their aircraft is entirely dependent on their responsibilities to their clients. Although they will help you out to the best of their ability, expect to be a lower priority than their skiing guests.

Another option is regularly scheduled flights into backcountry lodges in the region, which may be available until mid- to late April. It may be possible to coordinate with these flights to come up with the shortest flying time and significant savings. The helicopter companies may also know of other ski touring parties headed into the same area whom you could coordinate with to reduce costs.

Refer to the Resources section at page 345 for contact information for helicopter companies.

Snowmobile access

Many of the traverses in this book could be accessed and/or food caches placed by snowmobile. Snowmobiles can easily travel up the logging roads in the main valleys as long as there is still snow on them. They may also be able to get to higher elevations in many areas. If you are on a trip and need to get out because of bad weather or conditions, it may be possible to ask snowmobilers already in the area for a ride out, but don't count on it. Carrying a communications device is recommended.

Snowmobiles are not allowed in any of the parks.

Refer to the Resources section at page 345 for contact information for snowmobile companies that may offer backcountry access.

Food caches

Early trips placed food caches on skis prior to the trip. These days, many parties would choose to do so by helicopter, snowmobile or a combination of snowmobile and skis.

Normal food cache locations are outlined in the descriptions. Even if a cache is placed high on an icefield, expect critters such as ravens, wolverines and even grizzly bears to be attracted to it.

If a wolverine or a grizzly really want to get into your cache there is no way to stop them, but you can make it difficult enough to make them decide it is not worth their while. A sturdy wooden box is the best, buried to lessen the smell and make it less noticeable to ravens. Waymark the cache with a GPS and place wands on the surface for reference. Make sure you put a bit of extra fuel in the cache so you can burn the box easily, and once the fire has consumed the wood, carefully pick up the screws that are left.

It's not all skiing.

Ravens

Ravens are smart, hungry and virtually fearless. They will show no hesitation in taking any food that is easily available. I have known them to dig through snow and rip through tents and packs to get at unattended food. Bury food caches well and do not leave food in tents.

THE NORTHERN CARIBOOS TRAVERSE

This traverse, which has been done only a few times, is highly praised by those who have completed it. It stays high most of the way, travels through tremendous mountain wilderness and is truly a major undertaking when completed by linking with the Southern Cariboos Traverse. Many of the peaks and glaciers on this traverse are still unnamed.

The first Northern Cariboos Traverse team (l to r): Phil Smith, Steve Smith and Scott Duncan. Photo Tom Duchastel

The traverse was first completed by Steve Smith, his brother Phil, and Scott Duncan in May of 1982. The trip took 15 days and they battled poor weather much of the time. Most of the information in this description was contributed by Steve. In 2008 a party including Eric Dafoe, Dean Flick and Charlie Delacherois skied the traverse from south to north. The comments in square brackets were contributed by Eric.

Distance 110 km to junction with Southern Cariboos Traverse
    150 km if finishing north through Premier Range
    170 km if finishing south to Miledge Creek
    160 km if finishing via logging roads along N. Thompson River
Total elevation gain 7500 m
Approximate time 14-21 days (depending on finish)

Maps NTS 1:250,000	Canoe River 83 D
	Quesnel Lake 93 A
	McBride 93 H
NTS 1:50,000	McBride 93 H/8
	Eddy 93 H/1
	Mount Winder 93 A/16
	Hobson Lake 93 A/9
	Azure River 83 D/12

Avalanche Terrain Rating Complex

The traverse begins along Highway 16 about 4 km north of the town of McBride, at the point where the highway crosses the Dore River. Ski along logging roads up the river for about 9 km, then turn left up the south fork at 680700 E 5905100 N. Follow the south fork for about 15 km to 674500 E 5891100 N, where you turn left again and climb into a higher valley.

Ski to the end of the valley, then ascend open slopes to reach a pass (672800 E 5885500 N) just south of a small lake. Descend the slope on the west side, angling south, to reach a small lake (671600 E 5884600 N). In the event of bad weather or unstable snow it is possible to descend southeastward to Castle Creek, where logging roads lead along the valley to Niagara Glacier.

Ski south about 1 km toward a larger lake, then begin ascending slopes in a southerly direction to reach the toe of an unnamed glacier.

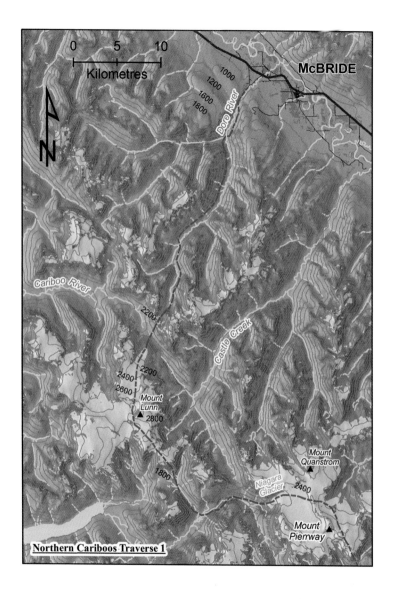

0   5   10
Kilometres

N

McBRIDE

1000
1200
1600
1800

Dore River

Cariboo River

Castle Creek

2200

2200

2400

2600

Mount
Lunn
▲ 2800

1800

Mount
Quanstrom
▲

Niagara
Glacier

2400

Mount
Pierway ▲

Northern Cariboos Traverse 1

217

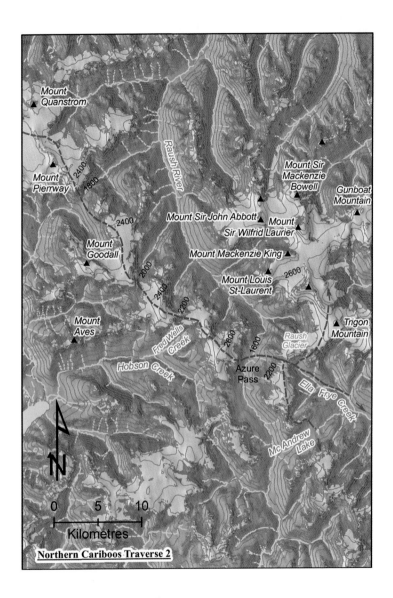

Mount
Quanstrom

Mount
Pierrway

2400
1800

2400

Raush River

Mount Sir
Mackenzie
Bowell

Gunboat
Mountain

Mount Sir John Abbott

Mount
Sir Wilfrid Laurier

Mount
Goodall

2000

Mount Mackenzie King

2400

2600

2200

Mount Louis
St-Laurent

Mount
Aves

Fred Wells
Creek

2600

1600

Raush
Glacier

Trigon
Mountain

Hobson Creek

Azure
Pass

2200

Ella Frye Creek

McAndrew
Lake

N

0   5   10

Kilometres

Northern Cariboos Traverse 2

218

Continue ascending the glacier for about 6 km to reach another col (669500 E 5876500 N), then descend steeply down the south side to another unnamed glacier.

Continue south across the glacier and work your way around the shoulder of Mount Lunn at 670000 E 5873900 N into a basin on the south flank of the mountain. Continue south across this basin, then ascend to the shoulder of an unnamed peak (671100 E 5872100 N). After skiing east across the south face of this peak, descend to the south, avoiding numerous crevasses, to reach a col at 672900 E 5870900 N. Take off your skis and climb on foot up the corniced ridge to the south to reach the top of an unnamed summit (673300 E 5870600 N). [The 2008 party, travelling from south to north, found that this ridge was too narrow and corniced to be traversed safely and were forced to find an alternative way of reaching the col. According to them, this section is a major crux of the trip.] From here a descent to the south takes you to an unnamed creek which is then followed down to the valley of Niagara Creek (678000 E 5863700 N).

The Niagara Valley is a beautiful wilderness area. It is as yet unlogged and the snow is said to be covered in animal tracks. (Castle Creek to the north, however, has a logging road and in an emergency would provide a route of escape.) Follow the valley for about 7 km to the bottom of a very impressive icefall (Niagara Glacier). Climb along the crest of a lateral moraine on the north flank of the icefall until it is possible to traverse out onto the glacier above the worst of the crevasses. Continue ascending, staying on the north flank of the glacier near the edge of the ice. This is very impressive terrain. *[The 2008 party suggested that a better way to reach the upper névé of Niagara Glacier might be to ascend the forested rib to the south of the icefall to reach a crest, then descend north out onto the glacier at 687000 E 5863600 N.]*

When you are up on the névé of the icefield, continue skiing to the east and round some small peaks to the north (690500 E 5866500 N). Descend to the south into the basin of another unnamed glacier, then ascend to the southeast along the east flank of Mount Pierrway to reach a high shoulder (694400 E 5861800 N). From here descend south

Near the top of Niagara Glacier. Photo Scott Duncan

Looking east from the Niagara Valley. Ascending through the trees at right and then going left along the rib to the crest might provide a better alternative route to avoid a Niagara Glacier approach. Photo Eric Dafoe

and slightly east, angling across steep terrain, to reach a pass at the edge of treeline (695900 E 5858200 N). *[The 2008 party rounded Mount Pierrway to the west. They climbed a narrow valley to the southwest of Mount Pierrway from the Clearwater River Valley and crossed a pass at 691800 E 5861500 N.]*

From the pass, climb southeast along a bench on the west flank of the crest. Round a corner beneath an unnamed peak to reach the edge of a glacier (698700 E 5856200 N). Continue ascending the icefield in a southeast direction to cross a ridge (700400 E 5852300 N), then ski out into the bowl above another glacier. After crossing this bowl, round the shoulder of a small peak (700000 E 5849800 N) out onto the south flank of this peak. Descend in a southeast direction to reach the edge of another large glacier (297600 E 5848000 N).

Ascend the glacier in a southeasterly direction, aiming for the peak

Charlie Delacherois, on south to north traverse in 2008, ascends the narrow valley southwest of Mount Pierrway, from the Clearwater River Valley. Photo Eric Dafoe

at the end of the high ridge (299700 E 5845200 N). In this area there are two peaks, not marked on the maps, that may help you navigate to the crest (299100 E 5845100 N and 299500 E 5845100 N). From this summit, christened "Dark Sting Peak" by Chris Gooliaff, there is a difficult descent to the southeast that left one party stranded on a knife-edge ridge in an impending storm. Climb carefully down through steep terrain until it is possible to descend to the east, contouring around the north flank of a small peak to another pass (301100 E 5845200 N). Descend a short distance to the south onto another glacier.

[Coming from the southeast the 2008 party found this section impassable. Wrote Eric Dafoe:

> We did not see a route through the unnamed glacier at 301100 E 5845200 N as indicated in the guidebook. The glacier has receded and presented a steep ice cliff. There may have been a way through but we didn't like the look of it. We descended into a basin to the south on the north side of the main fork of Fred Wells Creek. We then contoured around the ridge at 298700 E 5843700 N and climbed a steep basin to a bench below the pass at 298600 E 5845100 N.]

Contour around the basin at the head of Fred Wells Creek to reach the crest of a ridge descending from an unnamed peak (303900 E 5842600 N). Cross the south flank of the ridge on a bench to gain another glacier. (Note that the crossing of this ridge has proved problematic and one party was forced to descend into Fred Wells Creek and follow the valley bottom to the Azure River.) Ascend this glacier to a col (306400 E 5841200 N), then descend the southeast flank to Azure Pass (309100 5839600 N).

To finish the traverse, ascend eastward to a broad pass (313100 E 5839000 N). From here you have three choices:

- You can end the trip fairly quickly by descending Ella Frye Creek to the North Thompson River and then following logging roads back to Highway 5.

- You can turn north to reach Raush Glacier, then continue through the Premier Range along the Southern Cariboos Traverse as described beginning here at page 223.
- You can turn south, make your way to McAndrew Lake and pick up the southern half of the Southern Cariboos Traverse as described beginning at page 229.

Planning notes

Talk to the Forest Service in Clearwater about the state of the logging roads before you set out. Unless you carry very heavy packs you will likely have to place a cache by helicopter.

THE SOUTHERN CARIBOOS TRAVERSE

This tour was first done in May 1980 by Allan Derbyshire, Alf Skrastins, Tony Daffern and Murray Toft. Since then it has become a real classic and has been repeated many times.

Alan Derbyshire, Murray Toft, Alf Skrastins and Tony Daffern after the first traverse of the Southern Cariboos. Photo Alf Skrastins

Southern Cariboos Traverse 1

Hwy 16
Hwy 5
Kwa Creek
Tête Creek
Mount John Oliver
Mica Mountain
Mount Stanley Baldwin
Tête Glacier
Gilmour Glacier
Helicopter Drop-off
Mount Sir Wilfrid Laurier
Mount Sir John Abbott
Mount Arthur Meighen
Penny Mountain
Mount Lester Pearson
Mount Mackenzie King
North Canoe Glacier
Mount Louis St-Laurent
South Canoe Glacier
Canoe River
Mount Sir John Thompson
Raush Glacier
Trigon Mountain
Northern Cariboo Traverse
Azure Pass
Mount Zillmer
Ella Frye Creek
McAndrew Lake
N
0   5   10
Kilometres
Storm King Creek
North Thompson River

Southern Cariboo Traverse 2

The tour is actually composed of two distinct halves. The first section takes you through the Premier Range and is very rugged and glaciated – big country indeed. The second half of the trip, south of McAndrew Lake, is much gentler and there is less glaciation. Most of the way along this traverse you are far from any highway, so escape in the event of emergency would be problematic. There are no huts on this traverse.

Distance 100 km
Total elevation gain 5000 m
Approximate time 10–14 days
Maps NTS 1:250,000   Canoe River 83 D
       NTS 1:50,000   Valemount 83 D/14

Kiwa Creek 83 D/13
Azure River 83 D/12
Angus Horne Lake 83 D/5
Lempriere 83 D/6

Avalanche Terrain Rating Complex

Northern half

The original party began the traverse by bushwhacking for two days up Tête Creek to Gilmour Glacier. Since then most parties simply fly by helicopter from Valemount to Gilmour Glacier. The drop-off point is about 2 km northwest of Mount Arthur Meighen (326400 E 5854700 N).

If you do the traverse in "pure" style by skiing up Tête Creek, you should begin by following logging roads on the southeast side of the creek. The narrow canyon formed by the lower creek is very difficult and unpleasant. The logging roads lead to the creek bed, which is then followed for about 8 km to the junction with Gilmour Creek. The toe of Gilmour Glacier is heavily crevassed and it is best to follow a lateral moraine on the left. About 4 km farther along, upper Gilmour Glacier is also heavily crevassed and is negotiated by following a ramp to the right of centre which leads to the upper icefield not far from the helicopter drop-off point.

From here the route traverses west toward Gunboat Mountain underneath the south slopes of Mount Stanley Baldwin. From a small pass just south of Gunboat Mountain (322500 E 5854400 N) the route continues southwest through two more passes (322200 E 5853900 N and 321600 E 5853100 N), then descends out onto the head of Tête Glacier just north of Penny Mountain. This section offers some serious avalanche potential and should be treated warily. The climb up to the last of the three passes, called Penny Pass, presents a 100-vertical-metre lee slope of about 35–40°, often overhung with a large cornice.

An alternative that might be less exposed to avalanche hazard is to descend from the col on the shoulder of Gunboat Mountain (322500 E 5854400 N) down a small glacier (crevasses) in a west and slightly north direction, then climb steeply to reach a shoulder at about 320200 E 5854600 N. Ascend south up the shoulder, then traverse out onto the head of Tête Glacier below Penny Mountain. This alternative is only marginally safer.

Alf Skrastins has reported that a much safer alternative exists if you continue skiing down the creek bed for about 1 km to 319600 E 5854900 N and then contour around the end of a ridge for about 400 m to 319500 E 5854600 N. This puts you on unglaciated benches that lead easily to Tête Glacier at 319700 E 5854400 N. From here, relatively crevasse-free ramps lead onto the upper plateau of Tête Glacier. This variation is a few kilometres longer but it offers a safer alternative in the event of unstable snow.

Traverse southwest across the head of Tête Glacier and cross the crest of the ridge to enter the drainage of North Canoe Glacier. It is best not to ski directly through the pass but to take a higher, second notch (319300 E 5852000 N).

The route then traverses around the head of North Canoe Glacier, gradually descending a bench, then climbs to reach a basin below the east face of Mount Sir John Thompson. Continue southward across the basin to reach a broad pass (317600 E 5846700 N) overlooking South Canoe Glacier.

On North Canoe Glacier looking across toward South Canoe Glacier. Photo Al Shaffer

Ascending South Canoe Glacier. Photo Alf Skrastins

The descent for about 200 vertical metres into the basin at the head of South Canoe Glacier can be very tricky and is exposed to icefall. There are numerous large crevasses which make route finding a challenge. It is worth your while to spend some time here scouting the way before heading down.

From the basin (318300 E 5845900 N), continue south, climbing a ramp below a steep mountain wall which leads you to another pass (318400 E 5844300 N). This section is impressive, the route winding amongst giant crevasses and overhung by imposing ice-covered cliffs. From this pass a steep descent is required to reach upper Raush Glacier. Some parties climb a short distance east toward a small peak and then descend steep slopes on foot to reach the glacier below. (A recent party reported that "from the crest of the ridge everything looks like a cliff. We worked down steep gullies and crossed loaded slopes to a bench at 318400 5844000 (NAD 27). This is a crux.")

Traverse south across Raush Glacier beneath Trigon Mountain, then descend along the left flank of the glacier and traverse through a small pass (316200 E 5839900 N). Ski through the pass and descend

Traversing below Trigon Mountain at the head of Raush Glacier. The route crosses the pass in the middle of the photo. Photo Alf Skrastins

about 150 vertical metres to a lake below. From the lake work your way west up open, rolling terrain to reach another pass (313200 E 5838900 N). From here ascend straight south and cross almost directly over a small peak (312600 E 5837800 N). The route then continues for 5 km along the east flank of the Divide, above a tributary of Ella Frye Creek. It crosses briefly onto the west flank of the divide (312700 E 5833200 N), then after only 1 km crosses back onto the east flank (312700 E 5832500 N). The route now turns east and for 2 km traverses the north flank of a small peak to reach a pass at 314700 E 5832600 N. From here a pleasant descent takes you to McAndrew Lake (316400 E 5831100 N).

Southern half

The southern half of the traverse is much less rugged. There is less glaciation and the scale is much less imposing. The tour from this point is very pleasant and enjoyable and is characterized by many small glaciers and passes.

Ascend McAndrew Creek directly south of the lake. At an altitude of about 1970 m, work your way west over an awkward shoulder into another drainage (315400 E 5828700 N). Ascend this drainage, cross a pass (315700 E 5828000 N), then descend to a small lake at the head of St. Julien Creek (315100 E 5826500 N). Continue south for 4 km to another pass, which is crossed on the right shoulder (316200 E 5823000 N). After descending about 300 vertical metres, contour around the head of Knutson Creek at about 1970 m to another lake (319100 E 5821400 N).

From here there are two variations:

1. Climb gently to the south for 2 km, then cross a pass (319900 E 5819500 N) into the head of Stormking Creek. Contour the head of the drainage across east-facing slopes to reach another pass (321400 E 5817500 N).

2. Follow the 1980 route, which ascends to a col at 319400 E 5817700 N and descends southeast to a tributary of Angus Horne Creek. Both routes now continue south to a small glacier and ascend to another pass (322400 E 5814400 N). From here descend steeply to the lake below (323000 E 5813000 N).

Contour south around a treed shoulder and out to a trio of lakes (322700 E 5811200 N). Ascend the glacier above, gradually swinging east, and cross the icefield to the shoulder of an unnamed peak (327200 E 5818300 N). Descend eastward out onto the icefield below. From here climb to the south to a high pass (328900 E 5806000 N). Remaining high, traverse to the southeast, then descend to a small lake at the head of Lempriere Creek (332000 E 5801800 N).

Traverse east across north-facing slopes and round a shoulder into another small drainage (334900 E 5800700 N). The route continues east to a col (336500 E 5800400 N), then descends south to a small lake (336600 E 5799800 N).

From here there have been several different endings, none of them completely satisfactory. The original party continued traversing southeast to the head of a drainage (339700 E 5797200 N) which they descended to reach the Thunder River and which was then followed to the highway. Al Schaffer has descended a small glacier north to reach the head of Miledge Creek (339700 E 5801400 N), which he followed for 7–8 km until he reached logging roads. This route is not recommended, due to the difficult nature of the creek bed. So far, the best finish to the traverse descends north on a small glacier to Miledge Creek (339700 E 5801400 N), then traverses south-facing slopes high above the creek to reach a lake on a high plateau (343000 E 5801300 N). Continue southeast across this plateau to its edge (344300 E 5799800 N) and then descend steeply to the east to a subsidiary creek where logging roads are reached. It has been reported that this descent is made much easier by a large clear-cut. Once the logging roads are reached it is a further 5–10 km on old snowmobile tracks to Highway 5.

Planning notes

One cache of food and fuel is sufficient to do this traverse, and the best place to put it is at McAndrew Lake. The cache can be placed by helicopter or possibly by snowmobile up the North Thompson River (it would be necessary to ski the last few kilometres to McAndrew Lake).

Yellowhead Helicopters in Valemount should be contacted for placing caches and for the initial approach to Gilmour Glacier.

THE MONASHEE TRAVERSE

The Monashee Traverse was the last of the obvious great lines to be skied. It was first done in 2004 by Aaron Chance, Ian Bissonette and Greg Hill. Dave Sproule and Jeff Volp joined them for the first week of the tour. The complete traverse took 21 days and along the way the group bagged 21 summits – quite a tour de force. They had three caches along the way, placed in advance by helicopter. The first part of the tour, as far as Mica Dam, would also make an amazing seven-day tour, car to car.

Distance 210 km
Total elevation gain 30,000 m (without additional summits)
Approximate time 2-3 weeks
Maps NTS 1:250,000   Canoe River 83 D
                                  Seymour Arm 82 M
        NTS 1:50,000   Lempriere 83 D/6
                                  Howard Creek 83 D/7

The Monashee Traverse team (l to r): Jeff Volp, Dave Sproule, Greg Hill, Ian Bissonette and Aaron Chance. Photo Jeff Volp

Nagle Creek 83 D/2
Scrip Creek 82 M/15
Hoskins Creek 82 M/10
Ratchford Creek 82 M/7
Perry River 82 M/2
Mount Revelstoke 82 M/1

Avalanche Terrain Rating Complex

The team began by skiing from Highway 5 up Moonbeam Creek (355300 E 5814400 N) and camped at Moonbeam Lake (363900 E 5808500 N). The next day, they climbed to the broad col between Mount Monashee and Mount Lempriere (366900 E 5806200 N), from where they summited Mount Lempriere and then camped in the col. The following day, they summited Mount Monashee (367900 E 5805700 N), then descended Serpentine Glacier and crossed a pass to the east into the Howard Creek drainage (368700 E 5802400 N). From there they continued to the summit of Oventop Mountain, where they camped (375400 E 5799000 N).

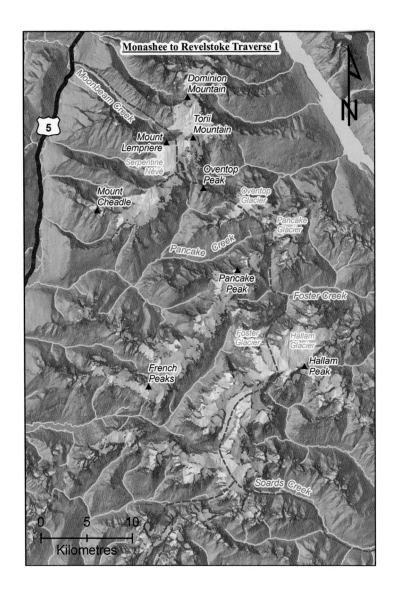

Monashee to Revelstoke Traverse 1

Dominion Mountain

Torii Mountain

Moonbeam Creek

5

Mount Lempriere

Serpentine Névé

Oventop Peak

Oventop Glacier

Mount Cheadle

Pancake Glacier

Pancake Creek

Pancake Peak

Foster Creek

Foster Glacier

Hallam Glacier

Hallam Peak

French Peaks

Soards Creek

N

0   5   10
Kilometres

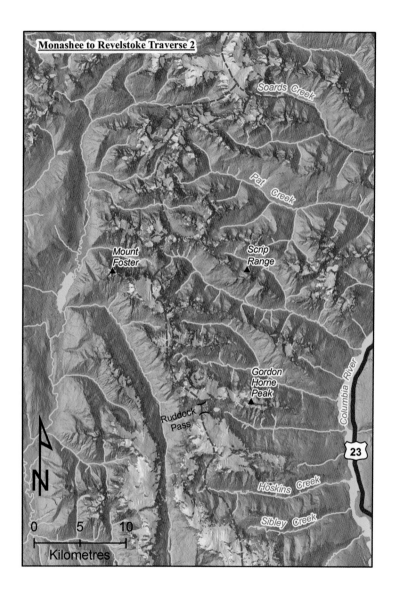

Monashee to Revelstoke Traverse 2

Soards Creek

Pat Creek

Mount Foster

Scrip Range

Gordon Horne Peak

Ruddock Pass

Columbia River

23

Hoskins Creek

Sibley Creek

N

0   5   10
Kilometres

234

Hoskins Creek

Sibley Creek

Columbia

McLennan Peak

Kirbyville Lake

Hwy. 23

River

Fissure Creek

Pettipiece Pass

Bourne Creek

Ratchford Creek

Feline Peak

Bourne Glacier

Cat Peak

N

0   5   10
Kilometres

Monashee to Revelstoke Traverse 3

235

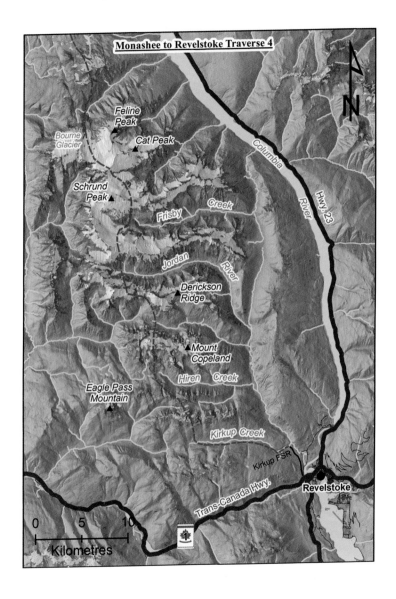

Monashee to Revelstoke Traverse 4

Feline Peak

Bourne Glacier

Cat Peak

Schrund Peak

Creek

Frisby

Jordan River

Derickson Ridge

Mount Copeland

Hiren Creek

Eagle Pass Mountain

Kirkup Creek

Kirkup FSR

Trans-Canada Hwy.

Revelstoke

Columbia River

Hwy. 23

0   5   10
Kilometres

The next day, they descended sketchy southeast-facing slopes and crossed the head of Pancake Creek to Pancake Pass (376800 E 5796000 N). From there they descended Siwash Creek to Foster Creek, then continued up Foster Glacier to a camp at 377200 E 5782500 N. From this camp they bagged several summits: Deception Peak (378500 E 5783200 N), an unnamed peak (379000 E 5782500 N), Hallam Peak (380000 E 5783000 N), another unnamed (377400 E 5785300 N) and a small summit (376900 E 5782200 N).

They then headed west-southwest, crossing a col at 375600 E 5781600 N. Sketchy traversing took them to a shoulder at 374500 E 5780600 N. Camp was set up at 373000 E 5779200 N. From here they headed south down the glacier, then up a headwall to the east at 370800 E 5774400 N. Then they climbed Thunderbolt Peak (369000 E 5772200 N) and camped at Windy Col (372300 E 5771800 N), where they picked up a food cache. Here they parted ways with Jeff and Dave, who skied out Soards Creek, crossing a bridge to reach Highway 23. This is a full-scale industrial bridge located 5 km north of the village of Mica Creek and 4 km south of the dam.

Crossing avalanche debris in Moonbeam Creek. Photo Jeff Volp

The remaining three (Greg, Aaron and Ian) continued to a col at 371700 E 5770200 N, then down the Adams River to 364900 E 5768200 N. They climbed a chute into a hanging valley and climbed to a col. From here they climbed an unnamed peak (366200 E 5764700 N), then waited at the col for the south-facing slopes to cool before heading south to a camp at 362900 E 5761200 N. Here the trio waited two days in storm.

Ascending the glacier at the head of Moonbeam
Creek toward Torii Mountain. Photo Jeff Volp

Below the Foster Icefall. Photo Jeff Volp

On April 16 the team climbed southeast to a high col at 363900 E 5760100 N, then descended south and toured up a creek to Two Lake Pass (365200 E 5755000 N). The route continued down and around a shoulder to camp at 364900 E 5751900 N. From there they followed a direct line to 363600 E 5748200 N, crossed a glacier to a hidden chute (364600 E 5747800 N), then down and across the west side to 364700 E 5743800 N and down a ridge to camp at 365100 E 5741500 N.

Their route continued up to a col at 366200 E 5739900 N, then around a basin to 366700 E 5738300 N and across to Ruddock Pass (369000 E 5737200 N). Here they bagged an unnamed summit (369300 E 5734400 N). They continued east down the shoulder to a camp at Blind Man Lake (370300 E 5731700 N). The route then descended a waterfall and continued down and across Hoskins Creek. From there, an ascending traverse led through a pass (373200 E 5725400 N) to a food cache and camp at the head of Sibley Creek (374200 E 5724600 N).

From here they continued up to lakes and up a gully to a notch at 374300 E 5721200 N, then continued over to McLennan Peak (374100 E 5717000 N). They skied down to a lake and across east to camp at (377800 E 5710900 N). Their route continued southeast up to an unnamed summit (380700 E 5708400 N). They descended, trending east to a lake, then contoured around the headwaters of Fissure Creek and skied up to 383100 E 5702300 N. From here they headed south down a shoulder toward Pettipiece Pass and a camp at 386400 E 5698400 N.

After crossing through Pettipiece Pass they climbed to a notch (388100 E 5694500 N), descended south to a lake, then contoured on the west flank to a large, flat peak (389000 E 5692300 N). They descended to the headwaters of Bourne Creek, then ascended Bourne Glacier to a camp at 389900 E 5685000 N. A short day followed when the trio climbed up to 393000 E 5685000 N, where high winds forced a snow cave day.

After descending a shoulder southwest to 392300 E 5683600 N, they skied east around the shoulder of Schrund Peak, then climbed to a high col at 394500 E 5680000 N. Here a small, unnamed peak (394700 E

5680100 N) was climbed. They then descended to Frisby Creek and a food cache and camp at 395500 E 5677700 N.

The group then skied west up Frisby Creek and ascended the glacier to a col at 392700 E 5675300 N. From here three more peaks were bagged (393100 E 5675400 N, 393600 E 5675800 N and 392000 E 5675100 N).

The group then descended to the Jordan River and climbed a chute to a pass at 395000 E 5670700 N. From here they contoured around south to reach Derickson Peak (397100 E 5670100 N). They descended to Copeland Creek and then climbed to a high unnamed summit (396700 E 5665300 N). They descended a gully to camp at 397600 E 5664200 N, rounded the headwaters of Hiren Creek via a road and then climbed east to a pass at 399000 E 5658900 N. From here they descended to a lake, then climbed up Turtle Mountain (400200 E 5657000 N). A last descent to Kirkup Creek and ski out took them to a vehicle pickup at 411400 E 5654000 N.

THE NORTHERN SELKIRKS TRAVERSE

This ski adventure was first done in 1976 by Don Gardner, Dave Smith, Ron Robinson and Chic Scott. Over a period of 15 days of perfect weather the group traversed from Mica Creek at the northern end of the Selkirks to Rogers Pass. Sections of the route are occasionally repeated but the entire traverse is rarely done, due to its length and committing nature.

The route was repeated in 1999, skiing south to north, by Eric Dafoe, John Kelly, J.P. Kors and Percy Woods. Eric reports that there has been extensive logging in many of the drainages along this traverse. He also says there is now a logging road high into Mica Creek which makes access easier.

The route crosses a number of major and minor icefields, dropping into deep valleys in between. There are only two huts along the way – the very comfortable Bill Putnam (Fairy Meadow) Hut and the delightful Ben Ferris (Great Cairn) Hut. Both of these are located about halfway along the route. For most of the traverse, escape would be difficult and would involve a long, long slog down a side valley to a road.

The Northern Selkirks Traverse team (l to r): Ron Robinson, Chic Scott, Dave Smith and Don Gardner. Photo Don Gardner

(Escape down some side valleys would now be easier due to logging roads)

Distance 200 km
Total elevation gain 11,000 m
Approximate time 15-20 days
Maps NTS 1:250,000   Canoe River 83 D
                                       Seymour Arm 82 M
                                       Golden 82 N
        NTS 1:50,000   Nagle Creek 83 D/2
                                         Kinbasket Lake 82 M/16
                                        Sullivan River 82 N/13
                                        Mount Sir Sandford 82 N/12
                                       Glacier 82 N/5
Avalanche Terrain Rating Complex

Climb the hillside above the town of Mica Creek, then work your way down to reach Mica Creek itself. Follow the creek for about 10 km.

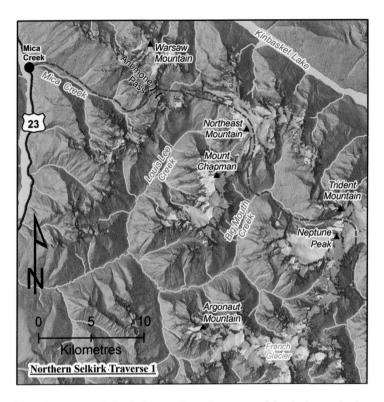

Northern Selkirk·Traverse 1

Travel is not too difficult despite the tight nature of the drainage. At the head of the valley, turn northeast and climb very steeply through the trees along the left flank of a creek to gain a high, open bowl. Ascend this bowl to reach a small col (404400 E 5760900 N).

Descend the other side of this col and ski out into the meadow along Yellow Creek. Contour around the north flank of a small peak and traverse into Anemone Pass. After skiing through the pass, traverse high around the head of Louis Lee Creek to reach a small icefield (411700 E 5759000 N). Climb a steep hill to gain the icefield, then traverse southeast to reach a broad pass (413400 E 5757800 N). From here descend the glacier to the south. Although the descent is relatively steep throughout, it is not too difficult. Once you reach treeline, stay

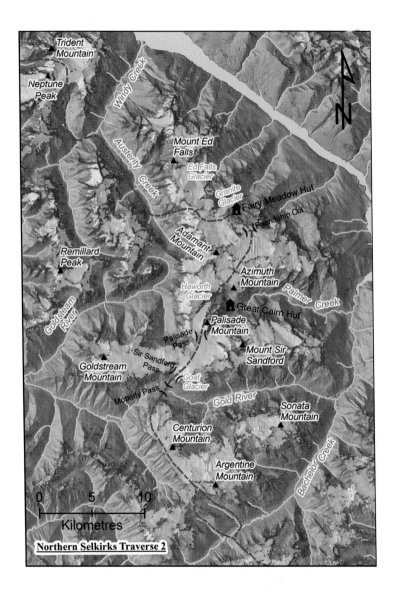

Trident
Mountain

Neptune
Peak

Windy Creek

Austerity Creek

Mount Ed
Falls

Ed Falls
Glacier

Granite
Glacier

Fairy Meadow Hut

Friendship Col

Adamant
Mountain

Remillard
Peak

Azimuth
Mountain

Palmer Creek

Haworth
Glacier

Great Cairn Hut

Goldstream River

Palisade
Mountain

Palisade
Pass

Sir Sandford
Pass

Mount Sir
Sandford

Goldstream
Mountain

Goat
Glacier

Moberly Pass

Gold River

Sonata
Mountain

Centurion
Mountain

Bachelor Creek

Argentine
Mountain

0   5   10
Kilometres

Northern Selkirks Traverse 2

N

243

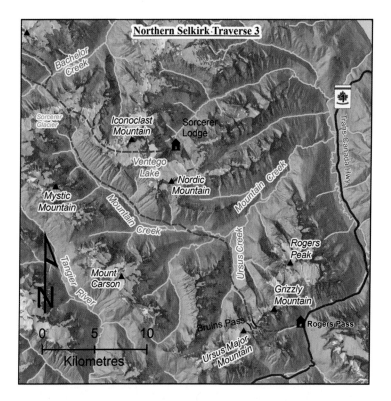

Northern Selkirk Traverse 3

Bachelor Creek

Sorcerer Glacier

Iconoclast Mountain

Sorcerer Lodge

Trans-Canada Hwy

Ventego Lake

Nordic Mountain

Mountain Creek

Mystic Mountain

Mountain Creek

Ursus Creek

Rogers Peak

Mount Carson

Grizzly Mountain

Tangier River

N

Bruins Pass

Rogers Pass

0   5   10

Ursus Major Mountain

Kilometres

on the left bank of the creek and work your way down through the forest to Bigmouth Creek.

Turn east and ski up Bigmouth Creek for about 2 km, then take the right-hand branch of Bigmouth Creek. After about 2 km there is a canyon, which is rounded on the left. Continue for another 2 km up to the head of the valley. From here, climb steeply through the trees straight ahead to reach a lovely hanging valley (418900 E 5748800 N). Ski easily up this valley for several kilometres and then climb a steep slope for about 700 vertical metres to a very small col overlooking a small icefield (422400 E 5748600 N). (Note that one group opted to climb the less steep slopes to the col just south of Rhea Peak (422300 E 5748300 N) but found that the descent on the other side presented some crevasse problems and one section of sérac danger.) Descend steeply to reach the icefield and ski east for about 2 km onto the flats. Descend steeply down the huge slope to the south toward Windy Creek. This slope can offer good skiing but it also offers very serious avalanche potential. Follow the creek down to Windy Creek, avoiding a gorge at the end by staying high on the left above the creek.

Turn left up Windy Creek and follow it along the right bank for about 2 km to the junction with Austerity Creek. Turn right and continue up Austerity Creek for about 10 km until you are directly west of the Adamant Range. Then turn east and climb steeply for almost 1500 vertical metres to a small pass (435800 E 5734900 N) which opens onto the Adamant Icefield. Ski through the pass and descend gently for 200 vertical metres before turning to the right around the end of Colossal Mountain and traversing onto Upper Granite Glacier. Ski down to Bill Putnam (Fairy Meadow) Hut (439300 E 5735400 N). (See page 118.)

From Bill Putnam (Fairy Meadow) Hut the route travels through three passes (Friendship Col, Thor Pass and Azimuth Notch) to Ben Ferris (Great Cairn) Hut. Begin by climbing the hillside to the south of Bill Putnam (Fairy Meadow) Hut and continue up past Echo Glacier and on to Friendship Col (440500 E 5733500 N). From Friendship Col continue south across the icefield to Thor Pass (43970 E 5730900 N). Note that the 150-vertical-metre slope on the northeast side of Thor Pass does not exist – this is a map error. Descend steeply to the Adamant Glacier, then cross the glacier and climb to Azimuth Notch (438400 E 5728800 N, mislabelled on old maps). From the notch, descend, traversing rightward, to reach Silvertip Glacier, which is descended to the toe of the Haworth Glacier. Then continue down to Ben Ferris (Great Cairn) Hut (439100 E 5727000 N) (see page 125). This is a magical spot and the view of Mount Sir Sandford is magnificent.

From Ben Ferris (Great Cairn) Hut ski northwest to reach Haworth Glacier, then turn southwest and ascend the glacier to Palisade Pass between Palisade Mountain and Alpina Dome. From here ski onto the upper reaches of Sir Sandford Glacier and continue southwest to Sir

Looking toward Mount Sir Sandford from Thor Pass. Photo Chic Scott

At Palisade Pass looking across the head of Sir Sandford
Glacier to Sir Sandford Pass. Photo Chic Scott

Sandford Pass. Carefully descend Goat Glacier, avoiding crevasses and icefalls, and continue down to Moberly Pass.

From Moberly Pass head south to reach Bear Glacier. Travel southeast along the slopes of Pyrite Ridge, passing south and west of Centurion Mountain, then climb to a high pass (435000 E 5710600 N). The original party of 1976 descended the drainage direct to the southeast, but the final descent to Bachelor Creek from the hanging valley involved extremely steep tree bashing interspersed with cliffs. A far more pleasant alternative is to descend the bowl south to a shoulder at 434900 E 5708600 N, then descend to the more westerly drainage just south of Bachelor Pass and continue down to Bachelor Creek.

When the 1976 party reached this point the weather had been sunny for almost two weeks, the rivers were raging and the snow was disappearing fast. They opted to take the quickest route to finish the trip. They climbed steeply for 1000 vertical metres from 438300 E 5705200 N to a small pass at 440300 E 5703100 N. From here they descended to the valley of Mountain Creek and followed it for almost 20 km. The

Crossing Mountain Creek in flood. Photo Ron Robinson

valley travel was easy but the big problem was the eventual crossing of Mountain Creek and tributaries which join it from the south. Eventually their route turned south and ascended Ursus Creek for about 5 km. At 456900 E 5686900 N they turned southwest and climbed steeply up a small tributary to reach Bruins Pass (459100 E 5683300 N). From here they descended to Connaught Creek and continued down to Glacier Park Lodge at Rogers Pass.

An alternative finish to this tour via Sorcerer Lodge (451200 E 5699900 N) has been completed. From Bachelor Creek climb south to the col (440300 E 5703100 N), descend southeast for about 400 vertical metres, then climb steeply to the east from 441400 E 5702000 N to 441700 E 5702200 N to reach easier terrain. (It is also possible to turn up left before the col and climb on foot to gain easier ground at about 440700 E 5703600 N). Ski along the east side of the crest above Benedict Creek to a high col southwest of Iconoclast Mountain (445700 E 5699200 N). Contour to the west, cross a ridge at 447200 E 5698900 N and then descend to Ventego Lake. From here you have two choices. You can traverse east across the north slopes of what is called The Wizard to reach Sorcerer Lodge (see page 317) (across what is aptly named The Heinous Traverse, or you can ski north to a col (449200 E 5700900 N), then descend east and south to Ventego Creek, from where you can climb up to Sorcerer Lodge. From Sorcerer Lodge you can fly out to the highway with the regular changeover on Saturday.

Planning notes

One cache is required to do this traverse, which can be placed at the Bill Putnam (Fairy Meadow) Hut (contact the ACC at 403-678-3200).

BUGABOOS TO ROGERS PASS TRAVERSE

The Bugaboos to Rogers Pass Traverse has become very popular in recent years and is now done by multiple parties each season. Consequently this tour has received special attention in this guidebook. Please see page 273 for a detailed route description written by Mark Klassen.

THE SOUTHERN PURCELLS TRAVERSE

This trip has been done in its entirety only twice. It is an excellent ski adventure that takes you through beautiful, unspoiled wilderness. There are no huts on the route and only a handful of logging roads to remind you of civilization. The route begins at Bugaboo Lodge and works its way down the Purcell Mountains to St. Mary's Alpine Provincial Park, where it meets a road not far from Kimberley.

The northern half of the tour was first done in 1965 when Hans Gmoser led a group including Mike Wiegele, Jim and Glenn McConkey, Erwin Tontsch and Scott Henderson from Toby Creek to the Bugaboos. In April 1982 two independent parties attempted the traverse. Len Potter, Chris Kubinski, Errol Smith and Chic Scott headed up Dewar Creek at the south end of the traverse while, at the same time, Bob Saunders and Steve Smith began the traverse from Bugaboo Lodge at the north end. The two parties narrowly missed meeting near Mount Findlay.

The 1965 Purcell Traverse team (l to r): Glenn McConkey, Jim McConkey, Mike Wiegele, Hans Gmoser and Erwin Tontsch. Photo Erwin Tontsch

The Saunders–Smith party completed the route in 13 days. They did the traverse without a cache and started with 35 kg packs containing food for 21 days. The other group skied half the route in eight days, as far as Toby Creek, then skied out to Panorama Ski Resort.

Distance 150 km
Total elevation gain 11,000 m
Approximate time 2-3 weeks

Maps NTS 1:250,000	Lardeau 82 K
	Nelson 82 F
NTS 1:50,000	Bugaboo Creek 82 K/15
	Howser Creek 82 K/10
	Duncan Lake 82 K/7
	Lardeau 82 K/2
	Findlay Creek 82 K/1
	Dewar Creek 82 F/16
	St. Mary Lake 82 F/9

Avalanche Terrain Rating Complex

From Bugaboo Lodge ski back down the road a short distance, then turn right and follow the road up the main branch of Bugaboo Creek. The first objective is Phacelia Pass (522700 E 5613600 N), which is reached by a steep climb from Bugaboo Creek. This climb presents avalanche potential and should be treated with caution. The descent on the south side of Phacelia Pass is straightforward, and after reaching the valley bottom the route turns southwest down Howser Creek for about 5 km.

At 519700 E 5605400 N turn south and ascend an unnamed creek. After 4 km, angle up left and ascend through open forest to reach open slopes which lie on the west flank of the ridge crest dividing the Stockdale and Howser drainages (522900 E 5599600 N). The route then turns south again, out onto the head of Stockdale Glacier. Ski through a pass immediately southeast of Birthday Peak (521600 E 5592600 N) and descend easily onto Starbird Glacier. At the point where this glacier turns to descend to Horsethief Creek (524100 E 5587400 N), begin climbing beneath Mount Monica onto the west shoulder of Glacier Dome. Cross the shoulder (524900 E 5586000 N), then descend to the

0   5   10
Kilometres

N

Bugaboo Creek FSR
Bugaboo Creek

Bugaboo Spire

■Bugaboo Lodge

Bugaboo Glacier

Quintet Peaks

(Bhacella Pass)

Taurus Mountain

Catamount Glacier

Olive Hut ⌂

North Star Peak

Gwendoline Mountain

Howser Creek

Stockdale Creek

Horsethief Creek

Chooser Variation 1965

Eyebrow Peak

Birthday Peak

Lake of the Hanging Glacier

Mount Monica

Southern Purcells Traverse 1

251

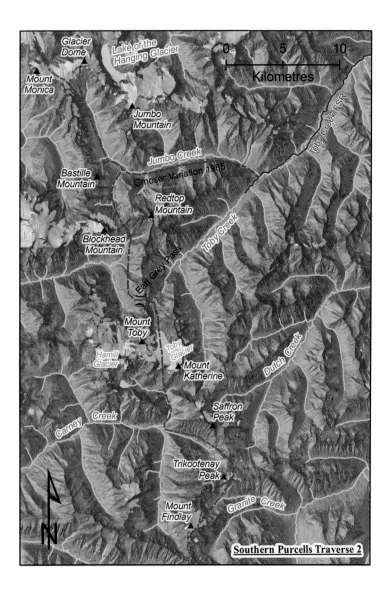

Glacier Dome

Lake of the Hanging Glacier

0   5   10

Kilometres

Mount Monica

Jumbo Mountain

Toby Creek FSR

Jumbo Creek

Bastille Mountain

Gmoser Variation 1965

Redtop Mountain

Blockhead Mountain

Toby Creek

Earl Grey Pass

Mount Toby

Hamill Glacier

Toby Glacier

Mount Katherine

Dutch Creek

Carney Creek

Saffron Peak

Trikootenay Peak

Mount Findlay

Granite Creek

N

Southern Purcells Traverse 2

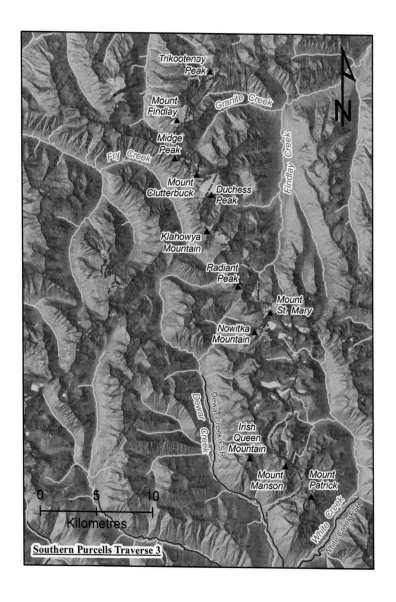

Trikootenay
Peak ▲

Granite Creek

Mount
Findlay ▲

Midge
Peak ▲

Fry Creek

Findlay Creek

Mount
Clutterbuck ▲

Duchess
Peak ▲

Klahowya
Mountain ▲

Radiant
Peak ▲

Mount
St. Mary ▲

Nowitka
Mountain ▲

Dewar Creek

Dewar Creek FSR

Irish
Queen
Mountain ▲

Mount
Manson ▲

Mount
Patrick ▲

White Creek

White Creek FSR

0   5   10
├────┼────┼────┤
Kilometres

Southern Purcells Traverse 3

253

Mount Toby from the Toby Icefield. Photo Chic Scott

Jumbo Creek drainage. Soon, logging roads are encountered, and are followed to a bridge over Jumbo Creek (530300 5578000 N). You should have a cache placed here and spend a luxurious evening around the campfire eating and drinking goodies.

From the Jumbo Creek bridge, ascend a small, unnamed creek south up to a col between Blockhead Mountain and Redtop Mountain (529800 5573100 N). Descend steeply for about 700 vertical metres to the creek below. Then, at about 1820 m elevation, begin a high traverse, contouring above the valley for 6 km to reach Earl Grey Pass. Although this looks difficult, the travel is quite reasonable. From Earl Grey Pass, descend steeply to the east to reach open flats below.

Ascend Toby Glacier to a pass just west of Mount Katherine (534400 E 5561600 N), then descend steeply in a southwest direction to the creek (533000 E 5559300 N). From here the descent down the creek for about 4 km to the junction with Carney Creek is threatened by many avalanche paths. It is best to do this section of the trip early in the morning and as quickly as possible. Turn left (533600 E 5556100 N) and

Looking south toward Mount Findlay. Photo Bob Saunders

ascend Carney Creek for about 4 km, then take the right-hand branch (537700 E 5554300 N) and climb to a pass 1 km north of Trikootenay Peak (539400 E 5552900 N). Traverse around the east flank of this peak to another pass (539400 E 5551600 N).

From this pass remain high and traverse above treeline across the eastern flank of Mount Findlay. High on Findlay (at about 536400 E 5547800 N) is a distinct notch in the ridge that you pass through. From this notch, descend steeply on foot for about 150 vertical metres to reach easier ground, then ski to a frozen lake below. Staying high above the head of Granite Creek, contour around above treeline until below Mount Lees. At about 537500 5544800 N descend about 150 vertical metres to an elevation of 1970 m, then curve around the lower north ridge of Mount Clutterbuck into upper Granite Creek.

Ascend Granite Creek for about 2 km to a small lake (539900 E 5544100 N) below a steep slope. Climb on foot to the pass (540300 E 5543900 N). The descent down the south side of this pass is very steep and technical, requiring a rope and belays (see photo on page 256).

The crux cliff. Photo Chic Scott

The crossing of this pass is the crux of the traverse. It was noted in 1982 that a steep slope farther west which climbs to another col (539300 E 5543500 N) could be investigated if snow stability is good. It could provide an easier alternative.

From here, ascend the glacier south of Mount Clutterbuck to a pass west of Duchess Peak (538500 E 5541300 N). Descend steep, open slopes for about 300 vertical metres to reach an elevation of 2425 m, where you begin contouring around the drainage. Climb to a ridge on the northeast side of Mount Klahowya, then traverse south across a small snowfield to reach another col (540400 E 5537400 N) from where you descend south into the drainage below.

At 543600 E 5535000 N begin climbing toward Mount St. Mary. The drainage itself is very narrow and it is best to follow a draw about 300 m east of the creek. Ascend to a lake (542800 E 5533100 N), then continue climbing to reach a pass on the southwest ridge of

Mount St. Mary. A short, steep descent down the south side of the pass leads to Bleak Lake.

From here the route traverses St. Mary's Alpine Provincial Park in a southerly direction for about 15–20 km to reach a pass about 1 km east of Mount Manson. The route is intricate and meanders up and down and around many small hills and peaks. From Bleak Lake descend to Nowita Lake and continue down to Lyallii Lake. Work your way south over a wooded ridge to Keer Lake and on to Totem Lake. Descend Price Creek and round the corner to reach Huggard Lake. Ascend Spade Creek, then cross another ridge to reach Bird Lakes. Continue south under the slopes of Mount Manson to a pass (546700 E 5518300 N). This pass may be difficult to cross due to a large cornice.

Descend the drainage on the south side of the pass for several kilometres until logging roads are reached. These roads descend, zigzagging back and forth, to reach a major logging road on the east flank of the valley above Dewar Creek. Continue south down this road for about 6 km to reach the St. Mary River Road (544700 E 5508300 N).

Gmoser Variation

Hans Gmoser and his companions were the first to ski from Jumbo Creek north to the Bugaboos. They followed a substantially different route than did the Saunders–Smith party, and here is how Hans described it:

> We drove up Toby Creek as far as we could, which was a few kilometres below the junction with Jumbo Creek. We then skied up Jumbo Creek and onto the high, glaciated saddle (near Mount Monica) that leads over onto Starbird Glacier. From there, up the Starbird to the high col on the east side of Eyebrow Peak and then down the glacier that drains into Stockdale Creek. At the point where Stockdale Creek turns east we went west up a small drainage and onto a high col from where we skied down some quite steep slopes into a broad basin/saddle with several lakes between Stockdale Creek and Howser Creek. We then skied a short way down

Howser Creek, then up Phacelia Pass and into the headwaters of Bugaboo Creek. We camped a few days on the moraine between Anniversary Peak and the main Bugaboo glacier and then came out Bugaboo Creek.

Planning notes

The trip is best done with a cache halfway along the route. Probably the best place for a cache is along Jumbo Creek where the road crosses a bridge over the creek not far from Jumbo Pass (530300 E 5578000 N). This point can be reached by driving up Toby Creek beyond the Panorama ski resort, then following logging roads on a snowmobile. (See Jumbo Pass Cabin on page 141)

To begin the traverse at the Bugaboos it may be necessary to get a snowmobile ride up the Bugaboo Creek road. Leave a car for the end of the traverse where Dewar Creek reaches the St. Mary River road, about 35–40 km from Kimberley (544700 E 5508300 N).

THE VALHALLA TRAVERSE

This great ski adventure offers complicated route finding over intricate terrain. You are continually forced to make critical decisions about snow stability. Escape would be difficult in the event of bad weather or injury. To the east the valleys lead to the uninhabited west bank of Slocan Lake, and to the west it would be a very long trudge along logging roads to reach civilization. In other words, this traverse is not to be taken lightly and should be attempted only by experienced ski mountaineers.

Unfortunately the history of those who pioneered the Valhalla Traverse seems to have become lost in the mists of time.

Distance 55 km to Wragge Lake;
 60 km to Shannon Creek;
 10 km to Hwy. 6 along logging roads
Total elevation gain 4575 m to Wragge Creek
 4965 m to Shannon Creek
Approximate time about a week

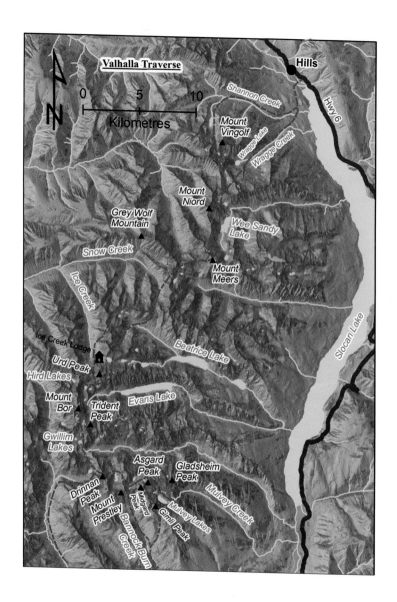

Valhalla Traverse

Hills

Hwy 6

Shannon Creek

Mount Vingolf

Wragge Lake

Wragge Creek

Mount Niord

Grey Wolf Mountain

Wee Sandy Lake

Snow Creek

Ice Creek

Mount Meers

Slocan Lake

Ice Creek Lodge

Beatrice Lake

Urd Peak

Hird Lakes

Mount Bor

Trident Peak

Evans Lake

Gwillim Lakes

Asgard Peak

Gladsheim Peak

Drinnan Peak

Mount Prestley

Midgard Peak

Mulvey Lakes

Mulvey Creek

Gimli Peak

Bannock Burn Creek

0   5   10
Kilometres
N

259

Maps NTS 1:250,000   Nelson 82 F
                               Lardeau 82 K
        NTS 1:50,000   Burton 82 F/13
                               Nakusp 82 K/4

Avalanche Terrain Rating Complex

Historically there have been two approaches to begin this tour. Some parties have followed logging roads up Hoder Creek to reach the high country at Drinnan Pass [some maps read "Drinnon"]. Unfortunately, this approach misses some of the most beautiful terrain on the traverse. A party in the mid-1980s flew by helicopter to Mulvey Basin and began their traverse from there. Do not attempt to ski up Mulvey Creek to begin the trip. The headwall at the end of the valley presents a steep and very dangerous avalanche slope which should not be attempted.

Eric Dafoe has skied the Valhalla Traverse three times and reports that the best way to access this traverse is

> …up the Little Slocan Lakes road to the junction with Bannock Burn Creek. The Little Slocan Lakes road is plowed, as people live up there. It also melts out in March and is the main access to the Slocan Mill tenure. The road up Bannock Burn Creek melts out in early April in the valley bottom at least. Drive as far as possible, then put your skis on.

Follow the Bannock Burn road up into the open upper valley. The summer access road to Mulvey Basin/Gimli S. Ridge climbs sharply back south and climbs to near treeline. If conditions are stable you can climb a couple of switchbacks, then ascend steep west-facing slopes to below the south ridge of Gimli Peak. Then traverse under the south and west faces of Gimli Peak on steep ledges and icy slopes to gain access to upper Mulvey Basin. You can camp on the ridge below the south ridge of Gimli Peak and cross in the morning if you arrive late in the day.

If you continue into the headwaters of Bannock Burn Creek, you can ascend to a pass (451600 E 5513900 N) between Midgard Peak and Mount Prestley. Cross this pass and

Gimli Peak towers above Mulvey Basin. Photo Dave Smith

descend to the lakes below where you will join the route described in the guidebook.

If you chose to fly in to the old hut site (454800 E 5513800 N) in Mulvey Basin, the route ascends west past Mulvey Lakes to Upper Mulvey Lake, then turns north and climbs steeply to a small col on the northeast ridge of Asgard Peak (453300 E 5515000 N). From the col descend steeply down the other side to an elevation of 2300 m. Then contour west and cross a shoulder (452400 E 5515900 N) into the next basin.

Descend to the west about 180 vertical metres to a creek, which is ascended in a southerly direction to the upper of two unnamed lakes below Mount Prestley. From there, climb for about 210 vertical metres to another col (450700 E 5515000 N).

From this col, descend northwest for about 150 vertical metres to a small unnamed lake, then angle down, still heading northwest, to the northern tip of Valhalla Lake. Climb from Valhalla Lake to the southwest for about 60 vertical metres to circumvent a large field of giant boulders. Then descend for about 150 vertical metres to the bowl northwest of Drinnan Peak (near a small sink lake marked on the map at 449300 E 5515900 N). Continue heading north, contouring at the 2000 m level, to the shoulder overlooking Gwillim Creek (448900 E 5516700 N). From here, climb southwest, following a draw, to reach a pass just north of Drinnan Peak (448500 E 5515800 N). Descend to the west for about 240 vertical metres before contouring to the right (north) into Drinnan Pass (447600 E 5516600 N).

Descend north for about half a kilometre to a small, unnamed lake, then turn west-northwest and follow gentle terrain which gradually curves north and descends to Gwillim Lakes. Ascend the headwall north of Gwillim Lakes to the upper lakes (steep), then ascend to the north under the southwest flank of Lucifer Peak to Lucifer Col (446900 E 5519600 N). According to Eric Dafoe, this is a steep climb and must be undertaken early in the day. A moderate descent down the north side for 450 vertical metres takes you to Rocky Lakes, from where easy terrain continues north to Hird Lakes. Climb from Hird lakes up to Urd Col just west of Urd Peak (448000 E 5523800 N). Descend the

Looking south from Lucifer Col. Photo Trevor Holsworth

other side for about 450 vertical metres, contouring to the right over a shoulder to a small unnamed lake (448300 E 5525100 N). Here you will find Ice Creek Lodge, where I am sure you will be welcome for a cup of tea and some pleasant conversation around the fire (see page 335).

The next section of the tour is a tree bash for a short way but safe from avalanches. From the small lake, descend the right flank of the creek to the valley and then follow along the right flank of Ice Creek for a little more than 2 km. Turn right and climb through steep forest into a high basin. Then make your way up to a pass (449100 E 5528000 N). Descend only a short distance down the east side of the pass before heading northeast along a bench. Continue traversing about 120 vertical metres above Avis Lakes, then angle up and climb to a col (450700 E 5529800 N). From here you can traverse along the broad crest of Snow Ridge for a little over 2 km, heading east, before descending to Snow Pass (453300 E 5529500 N).

The entire section between Hird Lakes and Snow Pass has been done a different way. This variation tackles some steep and risky slopes.

From Hird Lakes you can climb east up onto the south shoulder of Urd Peak, then traverse around on very steep terrain into a col on the east side of Urd Peak (448700 E 5523900 N). This ascent is potentially very hazardous and you could be carried over cliffs in the event of a slide. The angle of the terrain is about 35–40 degrees. However, if you do reach this col, you have a great 550-vertical-metre descent to Upper Demers Lake.

From Upper Demers Lake the variation continues climbing north up reasonable slopes to a col overlooking Upper Beatrice Creek. The descent to the north is, however, very steep. It begins by descending an extremely steep chute that takes you into a bowl, then angles over left to descend another steep chute at the edge of the trees. Upper Beatrice Creek is followed easily for 2 km and then the route turns east for a short distance down Beatrice Creek. Begin angling up left through the forest at about 452200 E 5528200 N and work your way over a shoulder and into Snow Pass (453300 E 5529500 N), where the two routes join.

Descend the drainage north from Snow Pass for about 2 km. Then, at an elevation of about 1850 m, begin angling up right, gradually ascending through the trees for about 1 km. Turn east and climb to a pass (454800 E 5532400 N) above Nemo Lakes.

Descend about 120 vertical metres to Lower Nemo Lake. Now climb for about 60 vertical metres to the north and cross a crest (456100 E 5532800 N) into the next drainage. (At this point, escape to the north over a pass into Caribou Creek would take you to logging roads which lead to Shannon Creek and out to Highway 6 at the town of Hills.)

From here a long and serious climb takes you to the summit of Mount Meers. It is best to camp overnight before attempting this ascent, and do the climb in the early morning when the south-facing slopes are frozen. Begin by traversing east across steep slopes on the south flank of two unnamed peaks, then climb steeply for about 300 vertical metres to gain the crest (457200 E 5534000 N). Turn east again and climb gentle slopes to a pass (458200 E 5534300 N) where you turn right and climb southeast to the summit of Mount Meers. From here an excellent descent of about 575 vertical metres takes you down a shoulder to an unnamed lake (459600 E 5534000 N). Turn north here and descend the drainage to Wee Sandy Lake.

Continue north from Wee Sandy Lake for about 1 km to an unnamed lake (459500 E 5538700 N). Continue climbing steeply to the north above the lake to North Boundary Col (458700 E 5539900 N). Descend about 180 vertical metres to the north, then contour into Wragge Pass (459100 E 5541200 N).

If you have had enough at this point, you can descend from Wragge Pass to the

Ascending steep southwest-facing slopes en route to Mount Meers. Photo Dave Smith

east, past two unnamed lakes and down to Wragge Lake (460500 E 5542200 N). Be careful here and do not descend directly to Wragge Lake; instead, traverse to the east to 460900 E 5541700 N before heading down. Descend Wragge Creek to logging roads. The Wragge Creek logging road joins up with the Shannon Creek logging road and leads to Highway 6 at the town of Hills.

If you want to push the route a little farther north, it is said to be possible to continue north from Wragge Pass. You cross the shoulder of an unnamed peak and descend to an unnamed lake (458800 E 5542900 N). From here ascend to a pass west of Mount Vingolf (458600 E 5543700 N). Descend the drainage to the north to Shannon Lake, then continue down Huss Creek to reach logging roads in Shannon Creek. These roads can then be followed for about 10 km to Highway 6 at Hills.

Planning notes

Before heading out, have a good talk with the folks at the Selkirk Resource District office (250-825-1100) about the state of logging roads in the area. In the event of emergency or prolonged bad weather, you may want to abort the trip and follow these logging roads back to civilization. At the end of the traverse you will want to know the location of the logging roads in Wragge Creek and Shannon Creek.

If you abort the trip to the east (down Wee Sandy Creek, for example) you will end up on the west shore of Slocan Lake looking across at civilization on the other side. In the distant past all you could do then was light a fire and hope someone came across the lake to pick you up. Nowadays this has all changed and folks can call in a helicopter anytime they want. It would be a good idea to carry a SPOT locator beacon or a satellite telephone on this trip to call for help in the event of emergency.

GOLDEN TO REVELSTOKE TRAVERSE

The description for this traverse comes from Eric Dafoe. The traverse was completed in April 1998 by John Kelly, J.P. Kors and Dafoe, all from Revelstoke. Much of the terrain is exposed to avalanches, and escape routes would be either very long (Incommapleux River) or as committing as the route itself (Flat Creek or Albert Creek).

Due to unseasonably warm temperatures and isothermal snow conditions later in the trip, the first party adjusted the original route plan. Still, a two-day wait was required at Selkirk Lodge, near the Albert Icefield, to allow for a drop in temperature. The party then finished the route in a two-day dash. It is recommended that three to four days is more appropriate for the leg between the Albert Icefield and Revelstoke. Two food caches were placed, one at Caribou Pass and a second in the Incommapleux River valley in Glacier National Park.

Distance 130 km
Total height gain 9000 m
Approximate time 12 days
Maps NTS 1:250,000   Golden 82 N

NTS 1:50,000

Lardeau 82 K
Vernon 82 L
Blaeberry 82 N/6
Mount Wheeler 82 N/3
Illecillewaet 82 N/4
Cambourne 82 K/13
Revelstoke 82 L/16

Avalanche Terrain Rating Complex

If the Kicking Horse Resort is operating, ride the gondola to the top. The original party were towed to the top of the old ski hill and toured up South Bowl to the ridge. From the ridgetop above South Bowl (493700 E 5680500 N), follow a descending contour right for about

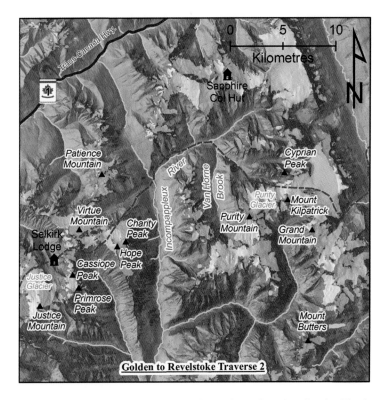

Golden to Revelstoke Traverse 2

2 km, then descend a large avalanche path to Canyon Creek. Climb up Canyon Creek to a point where water is still available and camp (487900 E 5681400 N).

Continue climbing southeast up the main drainage to a junction from the northwest. Follow the drainage leftward out of the forest, then ascend 300 m south to a notch in the ridge (487000 E 5679500 N). Descend Baird Brook to its confluence with the Spillimacheen River (480800 E 5673600 N), then southeast along the Spillimacheen. Camp in meadows along the river (481500 E 5672500 N). From the meadow camp, climb up along the west side of the river, then follow the 1700 m contour around and into Caribou Pass (479700 E 5669100). This section is forested and follows a series of shallow basins. Cross Caribou

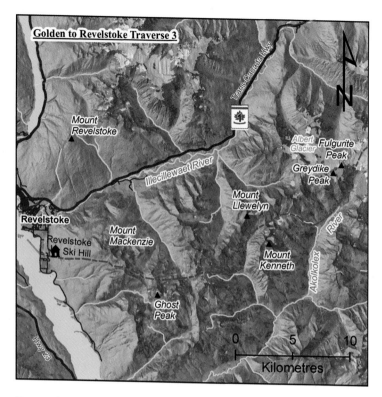

Pass and continue a high contour above the Beaver River. Pick your way through forests and descend slide paths approximately 3 km south of Caribou Pass. Locate a crossing on the Beaver River and follow the west bank below Beaver Overlook. At **479000 E 5663000 N** climb over a low shoulder and drop into the creek draining Grand Glacier. Camp near the creek (**478500 E 5661600 N**).

An early start brings you into the valley of Grand Glacier and a steep climb up south-facing slopes onto Deville Glacier. Stable conditions are required. One should study the slope carefully, as a series of ramps and gullies provide an elegant and surprisingly easy line through what initially appears intimidating terrain. Camp 3 was located on the top of the exit gully on the Deville near Beaver Overlook (**475500 E**

On the Deville Névé on the Golden to Revelstoke Traverse. Photo John Kelly

J.P. Kors in the Incommapleux Valley on the Golden to Revelstoke Traverse. Photo John Kelly

5662600 N). This provides ample time for an ascent of Grand Mountain. From the Deville camp, climb gently west, then contour around Mount Wheeler's northeast shoulder (473700 E 5663400 N) and onto Black Glacier (471100 E 5662900 N). The original plan was to contour Black Glacier to Old Purity Pass (468600 E 5661700 N), then work around Purity Peak on the east and south sides, descend Van Horne Glacier and drop into the Incommapleux Valley. Avalanche concerns and serious crevasses force a switch to a descent into Black Creek via the north edge of Black Glacier. Camp was set up in the Black Creek valley below the access to Purity Pass (Camp 466500 E 5664600 N). An ascent to the east ridge of Purity was made the following day but was aborted due to the crevassed terrain mentioned above. The party descended the narrow, avalanche-prone Mitre Creek valley along its west bank to the confluence with Van Horne Brook, then crossed the creek, climbing up into mature forest. Camp was made where Van Horne Brook meets the Incommapleux River (464000 E 5666400 N).

The ski down the Incommapleux River was forced along the north bank due to a lack of river crossings (deep water). It is best to maintain a consistent contour above the river and not be drawn to the valley floor only to be forced back up as the river meanders. You will be exposed to a large avalanche path complex (Jeopardy Slide) for several kilometres at the end of the day. If it is safe to cross these paths, continue downstream past Bain Brook and camp in the thickest trees available for limited safety (457600 E 5662500 N).

Climb up the shoulder directly above the camp, ascending through gullies and steep open forest to a minor ridge on climber's left. Follow the bench into a burn at 1700 m, then ascend the prominent rib to the base of the glacier. Follow the glacier on easy slopes to a short, steep headwall at 2600 m (454700 E 5659600 N). Climb up onto the plateau and find a camp. In the morning, descend through the Faith–Charity Col (453500 E 5658500 N). The descent is steep and committing from the first turn. This is serious avalanche terrain! Recent avalanche debris forced the original party down slopes on skier's left to the McDougall Creek valley. From the valley bottom, ascend northwest to a notch between Virtue Mountain and Cassiope Peak (449700 E 5656600 N) then along the ridge to the climber's left. You should now see Justice Glacier and the red roof of Selkirk Lodge. Contour around the basin to the south, then drop through steep gullies and undulating terrain into a subalpine basin. Look for a climbing track leading over a low ridge to the lodge at 448500 E 5655500 N. (Any use of the lodge must be prearranged.) BE CAUTIOUS! The original party remotely triggered two large avalanches on the descent from the ridge.

From Selkirk Lodge, ski south and west until the glacier drops toward the Akolkolex Valley (445600 E 5654000 N). The headwall below Justice Mountain is very steep, the avalanche potential large. Ski along a ledge on the east side of the valley to 445100 E 5652100 N, then down a steep rib to the river valley. Slide easily down the Akolkolex River to Llewelyn Creek (441700 E 5648500 N), then turn to skier's right and up a long, steep, forested valley. The terrain eases once the lakes are attained (438900 E 5649200 N). Follow gentle terrain to a low col at 437300 E 5649200 N. Most parties would want to set a camp in this basin. The original party continued over the col and camped in Standfast Creek (436300 E 5642200 N) in a less than perfect camp.

From the low col, the route was planned to continue west to the southwest ridge of Mount Llewelyn, which was to be followed toward Greeley Creek. The alternative is to drop into Standfast Creek and then climb up the west fork of Standfast. From Standfast Camp (436300 E 5642200 N), climb steeply through forest and avalanche path to the 1700 m elevation, then more gently to the lakes (431900 E 5644500 N) and the col at 431400 E 5644200 N. A steep slope drops from the col to Greely Lake and offers excellent skiing under the right conditions. You are now in the City of Revelstoke's water supply, so you should avoid camping. Contour to skier's left and up through forested slopes to the basin below Ghost Peak. Ski through gentle terrain to reach the long ridge extending southeast from Mount Mackenzie. Follow this undulating ridge northwestward until evidence of a snowcat ski operation is encountered. Drop into a west-facing bowl at 424900 E 5644700 N and follow tracks north to a cat track. It is still approximately 3 km of flat walking on the cat track to the descent road. Ski and walk the road to the slopes of the Mount Mackenzie ski hill and you are done.

BUGABOOS TO ROGERS PASS TRAVERSE by Mark Klassen

Distance 130 km

Total elevation gain 10,000 m

The Bugaboos–Rogers Pass Traverse may well be the most sought-after Grand Traverse in Canada, and for good reason. The route has everything, from valley-bottom camps to high alpine cols and airy ridge traverses to multiple, steep rappels. Parts of two different mountain ranges – the Purcells and the Selkirks – are travelled through and you will encounter a variety of snowpack climates. The trip will challenge even the most experienced of ski mountaineers.

The traverse was first done in 1958 by a group of US skiers: Bill Briggs, Bob French, Sterling Neale and Barry Corbet. It was a remarkable nine-day effort, made from south to north.

In 1973 the route was repeated, only this time from north to south. Don Gardner, Ron Robinson, Dave Smith and Chic Scott skied the route over 15 days, which included a five-day storm. Since then the route has gained increasing popularity, and these days several parties a year will attempt it.

Although the trip is quite remote in terms of how far it is from any roads, there is a good chance you will meet other people along the way, especially in the southern section through the Purcells. A few spots are popular with touring parties, snowmobilers play in some valleys, and you will travel through the tenures of three different heli-ski operators. Once you get into Glacier National Park in the Selkirks it usually becomes quieter.

Recommended route Bugaboo Glacier – Bugaboo/Snowpatch Col – Bill's Pass – Conrad Icefield/Malloy Igloo – Crystalline Creek – Climax Col – Hume Pass – Snowman Lake – Syncline Col – Vermont

Creek – Malachite Creek – Carbonate Glacier – Mark Kingsbury Hut – Spillimacheen Glacier – Silent Pass – Beaver/Duncan Divide – Duncan Glacier – Sugarloaf Mountain – Deville Névé – Glacier Circle Cabin – Illecillewaet Névé – Rogers Pass

Cruxes

There are steep slopes, heavily crevassed glaciers and complex terrain along the entire route. No single crux stands out!

Starting point access

You can use helicopter or snowmobile to get to the recommended start at the head of Bugaboo Creek.

Helicopters based in Panorama, Invermere or Golden would be the closest machines that could provide flights. The helicopter based at CMH's Bugaboo Lodge is not available for charter. A flight from Golden would allow food caches to be placed en route with minimal extra expense.

A helicopter landing to access the valley bottom start is outside Bugaboo Provincial Park, so no special permit is required. Higher landings in Bugaboo Provincial Park, such as a drop at Applebee Camp or Vowell Glacier, require the helicopter company to have a Park Use Permit (PUP) and the ski touring party to have a Letter of Permission (LOP). A LOP is reasonably easy to obtain. Contact BC Parks for information about how this permitting system works and for a list of helicopter companies that have a PUP.

A ride by snowmobile up the logging roads to the start of the traverse is about 45 km. The road sees regular snowmobile traffic and the trip would probably take a few hours. Late in the spring the road may plowed partway, which could make access a bit faster.

Refer to the Resources chapter at page 345 for companies offering helicopter and snowmobile rides into this area, and for BC Parks contact info.

The 1958 Bugaboos to Rogers Pass traverse team (l to r): Bill Briggs, Barry Corbet, Sterling Neale and Bob French. Photo Bob French

'This form of mountaineering, the exploration of unknown peaks, glaciers and valleys, the finding and crossing of new passes to connect one area with another, is the most fascinating occupation I know. The variety of experience, the constantly changing scene, the gradual unfolding of the geography of the range are deeply satisfying, for they yield a very real understanding, almost a sense of personal possession of the country explored."

—Eric Shipton

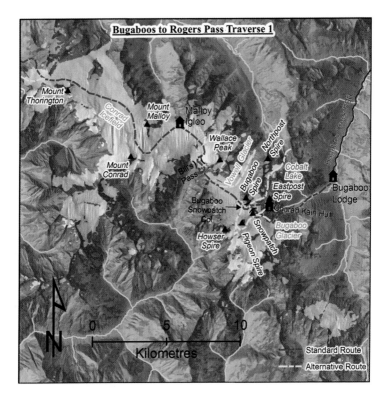

The route

The most popular way to ski this route is from south to north, and this is how the route is described. This way you ascend the hard snow on the south aspects and ski powder down the norths. Also, it is easier to organize transport to Bugaboo Glacier than from it, and the Deville Headwall is rappelled rather than climbed. However, it is also possible to do the traverse in the opposite direction.

The recommended start is from the valley bottom in Bugaboo Creek before ascending Bugaboo Glacier to Conrad Kain Hut. This section will show you exactly what this traverse is capable of. The climb to the hut is quite complex and has some serious hazards. If you can

Bugaboos to Rogers Pass Traverse 2

Glacier National Park

Silent Mountain

McMurdo Hut

Silent Pass

Butters Creek

Bobby Burns Creek

Twin Towers Peak

Carbonate Mountain

Malachite Creek

Mark Kingsbury Hut

Malachite Col

Carbonate Icefield

Battlement Mountain

Malachite Spire

Syphax Col

Vermont Mountain

Duncan River

Mount Syphax

Vermont Creek

Syncline Creek

Lakes Peak

Snowman Pass

Snowman Lake

Crystalline Creek

Snowman Peak

Hume Pass

Climax Col

N

Standard Route
- - - Alternative Route

0   5   10
Kilometres

Mount Thorington

Bugaboos to Rogers Pass Traverse 3

Glacier Park Lodge

Wheeler Hut

Mount Sir Donald

Lookout Mountain

Illecillewaet Névé

The Dome

Asulkan Hut

Glacier Circle Cabin

Mount Dawson

Mount Topham

Glacier National Park

Beaver River

Deville Névé

Mount Wheeler

Grand Mountain

Grand Glacier

Battle Range

Beaver Glacier

Sugarloaf Mountain

Beaver Mountain

Butters Creek

Duncan River

Butters Lake

N

Standard Route
Alternative Route

0   5   10
Kilometres

Marmolata

Alternate route around Pigeon

Howsers

Pigeon

Snowpatch

To Applebee and Bugaboo-Snowpatch Col

Kain Hut

The Bugaboo Glacier approach to the Kain Hut area. Photo Marc Piché

complete this section safely and efficiently you probably have the abilities to finish the trip!

Some parties prefer to start the traverse by flying to Applebee Camp,

2500 m, 515900 E 5621300 N. A LOP for the touring party and a PUP for the helicopter company is required for this landing. This avoids the hazards of the initial climb and the big push it takes to get there. Flying to Applebee puts you in position directly below the climb to Bugaboo–Snowpatch Col.

Flying to a landing in the vicinity of Black Forest Ridge (e.g., 518100 E 5624500 N) may be possible in poorer visibility when landing at Applebee may not be possible. This landing is outside the park, so a LOP and PUP are not required.

From Black Forest Ridge it is about 6 km and 300 m elevation gain to Applebee Camp. The route travels over some steep alpine terrain via the Brenta Spire–Cobalt Lake Spire col (2550 m, 516300 E 5622800 N) and Crescent Tower–Eastpost Spire col (2550 m, 516100 E 5621700 N). This start may still be easier and less hazardous than the Bugaboo Creek approach.

Another alternative helicopter landing could be below the toe of Vowell Glacier at 2050 m, 515600 E 5624700 N. This is at a lower elevation and may have better visibility than the higher landings. The route up onto upper Vowell Glacier will require some crevasse travel but it has fewer hazards and is shorter than the other starts described here. This landing is in the park, so LOP and PUP are required.

For the Bugaboo Creek start, begin in the vicinity of the Bugaboo Provincial Park access road, where you will enter the park. Ski upvalley to the toe of Bugaboo Glacier, which gives a spectacular start to the trip. Glaciers cascade all around you between the peaks of Anniversary, Hound's Tooth and Snowpatch.

Ascend the low-angled glacier to about 2075 m. From here, cut right (north) beneath an icefall and across the crevassed edge of the glacier to the moraines. Continue on an ascending traverse across steep, snow-covered rock slabs and boulderfields, aiming for the bottom of a prominent lateral moraine. Cut around the toe of this to steep trees on the other side and climb through those to the Kain Hut at 2230 m, 516500 E 5620700 N.

The hut is closed until May due to avalanche danger (it has been hit by avalanches in the past), but if you were doing a late spring traverse, this would be a good spot to spend your first night. Contact the

Alpine Club of Canada for reservations. From here, climb to Crescent Glacier, gaining it either on the left beneath the imposing east face of Snowpatch Spire or on the right by the steep lateral moraine above the hut.

BC Parks requests that the only camps in this basin be at Applebee. It is important that care be taken in managing human waste in this area, and the outhouses at Applebee must be dug out and used. Climbers and hikers utilize this area heavily in the summer and thousands of people will drink meltwater from the snow you are camping in. In the past, skiers have defecated right at Applebee, causing a mess and a health hazard for summer campers and park staff to deal with.

From Applebee it is a short hop to the steep snow slopes leading to the Bugaboo–Snowpatch col. You will probably have to bootpack the upper section to get to the col. Gain Vowell Glacier easily to the west.

The Bugaboo–Snowpatch col may be bypassed via a less steep but longer variation. From the edge of Bugaboo Glacier, climb moraines beneath the small satellite peak of Snowpatch (Son of Snowpatch). Gain the Pigeon Fork of Bugaboo Glacier at about 2375 m (crevasses, steep slope) and climb the glacier past the south faces of Snowpatch and Pigeon Spires to the base of the west ridge of Pigeon. The upper Vowell Glacier is accessed from here and a descent can be made to meet up with the regular route near Bugaboo Spire. This variation still contains some steep avalanche terrain, but conditions may be different than the Bugaboo-Snowpatch col slopes. This route can also be accessed by a traverse from the Kain Hut or a descent from Applebee Camp.

Whichever option you choose, once on the upper Vowell a descent is made to the flat glacier below. Passing close by the west side of Bugaboo Spire will avoid the worst of the crevasses in this area, but care must be taken regardless. This is one of the more hazardous spots for crevasses on the entire trip. If you started from a helicopter landing at the toe of Vowell Glacier, you would meet up with the main route on the flats below Bugaboo Spire.

Plod across the glacier to Bill's Pass at 2520 m, 512000 E 5623300 N, admiring the wonderfully sheer towers all around. A steep descent on the other side of the pass down skier's right leads to the flats below.

Eric Harvie and Felix Belczyk on the Conrad Icefield. Photo Mark Klassen

Another very steep ascent to the northeast brings you to about 2400 m on West Glacier.

Turn north at this point, gaining the Conrad Icefield beneath West Peak. If it is getting late you can head for the Malloy Igloo, a small

The Malloy Igloo. Photo Mark Klassen

fibreglass shelter on the edge of Malloy Glacier at 2450 m, 510300 E 5626400 N. The igloo is a bare-bones shelter, nothing more than a shell with a few benches. This is another spot to be careful of human waste. Make sure you do not defecate near summer water sources. No reservation or fee is required for using the igloo.

To get to the western part of the icefield, a high ridge must be crossed. This may be done by traversing over an unnamed

2965 m peak at **508900** E **5624500** N or climbing the glacier to the north of that peak.

Descend the other side of the ridge (leaving Bugaboo Provincial Park). Ski down to the north below Mount Conrad until it is possible to turn northwest. Continue across the icefield past Mount Thorington to a broad pass at 2620 m, **501700** E **5626400** N. This is where it gets spicy again. There are two options, but both involve steep, exposed terrain. In poor light or visibility these would both be difficult routes to follow, and in avalanche conditions this spot could well be a showstopper.

The first option is to ski down the run called Sundance. This is probably the best way to go if you have a food cache in Crystalline Creek. Descend to about 2400 m on the northern edge of the gentle glacier on the other side of the pass. Stay high while trending to the right across steepening morainal features, alternating short traverses and descents amongst ribs and gullies, before making a final steep descent down a large, planar face to the valley below. It is important you don't get pulled

Mt Thorington

The descent into Crystalline Creek. Photo: Mark Klassen

too low too fast, as the terrain is very steep and serious below the toe of the glacier. If in doubt, stay high and traverse right.

Once in the valley, follow it downhill. Soon you will arrive at a point where the stream has carved a canyon. With deep snow it works to ski down it but there are a few potentially exciting little drops! You may also put skins on and make a short ascent to the low ridge on the right (east) and then ski down it to where the main valley flattens out and opens up. The Crystalline is a good place to camp so that you are in position to hit the big ascent to Climax Col early the next day. These will be the first trees you see since starting the trip at the toe of Bugaboo Glacier.

The second option from the Conrad Icefield is probably more hazardous. It involves descending the left side of the glacier below the 2620 m pass, down a run called Sunlight. Below the glacier a planar slope between moraines leads to a pass at 2100 m, 499100 E 562960 0 N. From here a steep gully feature that probably sees a lot of wind effect leads to the valley and the lower part of the route described above. Alternatively, at the pass put your skins on and start a long, contouring traverse and ascent across steep slopes to the northwest, linking bench features as well as you can. This traverse involves exposure to some big slopes and convexities and is the most hazardous route of the Crystalline Creek options. It eventually leads to the bench on the avalanche paths on the route described below. This entire option is probably best attempted from a camp at the end of the Conrad Icefield, where the big slopes you traverse above Crystalline Creek may be gained early in the day before warm temperatures have started to cause instabilities.

From a camp in the Crystalline, get prepared for another crux. Start early to avoid warm temperatures, and switchback up one of the avalanche tracks on the east-facing side of the valley. The paths are all quite steep but the ones up-valley are shorter. A slight bench is reached at about 1950 m on the path directly above the exit to the canyon described earlier. This is the spot the two route options from the Conrad Icefield meet.

Follow this sloping bench on an ascending traverse to the north for over a kilometre, crossing all the avalanche paths. It will feel like the

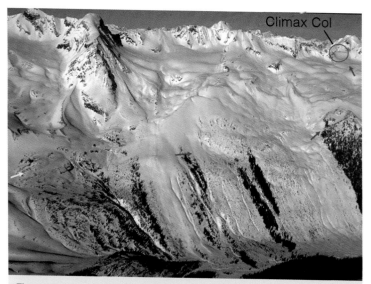
The ascent route to Climax Col. Photo Canadian Mountain Holidays

whole world is above your head, and you will be glad you started early in the morning! You will finally reach the far side of the paths and the terrain starts to get a bit gentler on the edge of a large, thick patch of forest at about 2100 m.

A possible alternative to avoid the traverse across the avalanche paths may be to go downvalley until an ascent can be made directly up through the thick forest all the way. This would meet the route described above at the 2100 m level.

From where the slight bench meets the forest, skin up along the trim line linking steep slopes and small bowl features into the moraines. Get onto the glacier below Climax Col and make the final, steep ascent to the col itself at 2650 m, **496**900 E 5633800 N.

Don't breathe a sigh of relief yet: the other side of the col is steeper and the sun is probably starting to bake it already. Skid down this slope, then across the glacier and into the moraines below before making another steep ascent to Hume Pass, 2450 m, **495**300 E 5633600 N.

A fantastic but committing run straight down the glacier to the north, over a rollover and into a gut between two ridges, brings you to the head of the north fork of Crystalline Creek. This run is called Whiteout. You may also swing farther to the left (northwest) to descend. There is a flat area to camp at about 1800 m if you wish.

It is possible to bypass the entire Climax Col–Hume Pass route via the south and north forks of Crystalline Creek. This would involve about 8 km and 400 m elevation gain via valley bottom travel through forest. It is exposed to the runouts of large avalanche paths. Stay on the east side of the creek or in the creekbed itself.

Felix Belczyk in good form on Whiteout. Photo Mark Klassen

Slap on the skins and climb to Snowman Lake. You may begin to encounter snowmobilers in this area. Continue past the lake, entering a narrow valley between two ridges to the northeast of Snowman Pass. From the 2500 m, **495**100 E **5639**600 N col at the head of this valley, descend a bit before climbing again to a ridge at 2500 m, **495**100 E **5640**100 N. Ski down the other side a short way to a bench and make a hard right to avoid steep slopes with cliffs that are below you. Follow the bench until it is possible to easily ski down to the valley.

To reach this spot more directly, go northeast from Snowman Lake and climb over the ridge via steep slopes on either side. This bypasses the narrow valley between the two ridges and the col at its end, but the terrain is larger and more serious, and a cornice needs to be negotiated on the lee side of the ridge.

You are now in a large basin. Head north toward the col east of Syncline Mountain, which is at 2700 m, **4963**00 E 5642500 N. There are a couple of different options to get across this basin, both having similar terrain of short but steep slopes and rolling moraines.

Cross the col and make a long, gentle run down the glacier as it flows northeast and then east. Once in the moraines, trend slightly left, which will bring you to a steeper section starting at 2250 m.

*This point may also be gained by bypassing Snowman Lake and Syncline Col. From the flat camping area at 1800 m below the Whiteout run, follow the north fork of Crystalline Creek downstream to 1425 m, **4992**00 E **5637**100 N. Climb directly up the unnamed drainage se of Syncline Mountain, bypassing some small cliffs with minor difficulties to reach some flats at 1950 m. Continue upvalley and join the recommended route just before it drops steeply at 2250 m.*

Work through the steep section and then continue to descend to the trees at the head of Vermont Creek.

Go north up the creek, where two options present themselves. You may climb directly to Syphax Col to the northeast of Mount Syphax, at 2620 m, **4978**00 E 5645500 N, and then ascend a ridge northeast to the unnamed 2737 m peak above the col. From there a descent is made down the glacier to the north.

A more direct way to this glacier descent is to climb directly up the run called Arrowhead to reach the col to the east of the 2737 m peak. This col is at 2700 m, **4984**00 E 5645600 N. The ascent of Arrowhead is steeper than the climb to Syphax Col.

Both routes lead to the run Action Direct, an exceptional 700 m descent to Malachite Creek. The upper pitch is large and steep, but lower down, the glacier and the moraines are less serious.

Two other ways to get around Mount Syphax have been used, but both have very steep and committing terrain. Conditions have to be bombproof to go there. One is to descend straight north from Syphax Col into Malachite Creek. Another is by a route around the west side of Mount Syphax and a descent of its north side.

Malachite Creek is a popular place to camp, and by doing so you are

The routes to Syphax Col and up Arrowhead run. Photo Mark Klassen

set up for the next cruxy bit. The climb to Malachite Col and the traverse around the north shoulder of International Mountain have multiple hazards and could constitute one of the more difficult sections of the trip. This would be especially true if visibility is poor.

Malachite Col is located at 2720 m, 495400 E 5647400 N, and is reached via complex moraines and steep slopes. From the col, traverse easily across the low-angled Carbonate Icefield, which clings to the mountainside with the valley far below. The Malachite and Horseman spires directly above you provide a dramatic backdrop.

As you approach the north shoulder of International Mountain you are aiming for a rocky promontory on the shoulder at about 2800 m, 493300 E 5647100 N. However, if you are approaching this promontory directly, the terrain begins to become far more serious. The glacier steepens to slab avalanche angle; there is a dangerous runout below due to large slopes and cliffs; the snowpack begins to thin out because it is more exposed to the wind; and crevasses begin to appear. When I

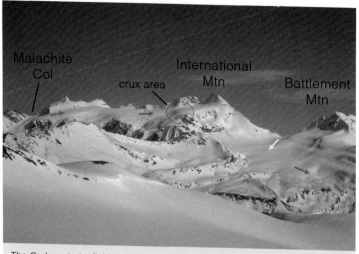

Malachite Col

International Mtn

Battlement Mtn

crux area

The Carbonate Icefield. Photo Chic Scott

passed through here in poor visibility and a brewing storm I fell into a large crevasse. Luckily I had a rope on and my group helped me out but it was a close call.

The simplest way to avoid the worst of these hazards may be to take a high line up the glacier, close beneath the north faces of Richards Peak and International Mountain, at about 2875 m. Then descend the lower-angled north shoulder to the promontory. Crevasses and steep slopes are still at issue no matter which way you take though.

It is not over once you are on the promontory. Another steep snow slope with serious runout potential must be negotiated below, beside the ridge. At about 2650 m you can pop over the ridge, to the west. From here it is yet another descent of a steep slope, but at least this one is often scoured by the wind and the runout is not nearly as dangerous.

Now you are on flattish terrain again. Whew. Traverse west across the glacier and get into the moraines at about 2350 m. Keep contouring west through moraines and short steep sections, slowly losing elevation around the head of the valley and eventually gaining the trees on the north side of the valley at 2150 m. Mark Kingsbury Hut is about a 1 km traverse through trees and glades to the northeast, and it may be a bit hard to find. It is in a meadow at 2190 m, **490**16**0** E 5649**385** N. You can just make out the green roof of the hut on Google Earth. It is an excellent spot to recuperate and get psyched for the rest of the trip. Contact the Columbia Valley Hut Society for reservations.

*Malachite Col may be bypassed by a less serious route over Carbonate Col. This option is highly recommended if there are any doubts about Malachite Col or the Carbonate Icefield. From Malachite Creek ascend moderate-angled south facing slopes to reach the col at 2610 m, **4965**00 5648**4**00. Ski due north down a small glacier to treeline at 2300 m and then follow the drainage to reach an old mining road at 2030 m, **4955**00 565**05**00. Glide down the road to a small creek crossing at 1850 m and then continue down the road to Bobbie Burns Creek. From here follow the creek up to International Basin, crossing the bottoms of several large avalanche paths along the way.*

*A longer bypass through more serious terrain is possible via the pass at 2425 m, **4965**00 E 56**4458**00 N. From there, descend Syncline Creek until it is possible to climb to the Battlement Mountain–International Mountain col,*

Enjoying a nightcap in front of the food box bonfire. Photo Mark Klassen

2600 m, *492*00 E *5646*00 N. *A short, easy descent from here across lower Carbonate Glacier leads to the regular line.*

These options are still subject to complex avalanche terrain, but they are not as high-elevation; visibility would often be better than the normal route; and crevasses will not be as much of an issue.

The next section, from the hut to the Beaver–Duncan Divide, is an outstanding tour that encompasses everything that Canadian ski traverses are known for: complex route finding, a big glacier with good skiing, great views and a final, outstanding 800 m run through the forest.

From the hut, head uphill to a bench at about 2300 m and begin traversing northeast. The terrain is undulating and it is hard to contour without losing and then having to regain elevation. Head for the col at 2450 m, *490*00 E *5651*700 N.

From here the lowest elevation option leads around the SSE ridge of Unnamed 2771 m. Gain the ridge and go up it a short way until you can drop off the other side at about 2500 m. There are steep slopes and cornices to work around to get off this ridge. Climb a shallow, steep draw to gain a ridge and then the edge of Spillimacheen Glacier.

There are two other options to gain the Spillimacheen. Both are more direct but go over higher cols and bigger terrain.

*From the 2450 m, 490*00 E *5651*700 N col described above, the first option continues to the higher col between David Peak and Unnamed 2771 m. This col is at 2680 m, 489*00 E *5652*800 N. Descend the other side, slightly to skier's right to avoid a steep roll, to regain the route across the Spillimacheen Glacier.*

*It is also possible to cross the col between David Peak and Cony Peak, at 2680 m, 489*00 E *5652*600 N. This is steep on the south side and it may require bootpacking. Descent down the north side is less steep than the David–Unnamed col. It looks straightforward to descend fall line from the col (crevasses) to regain the regular route.*

Once on the Spillimacheen, you have a couple of options to get to the Silent Pass area. One is to cross the glacier to the west, making several short descents and ascents across the ridges coming down from the peaks above. On the far side of the glacier, gain Spillimacheen col

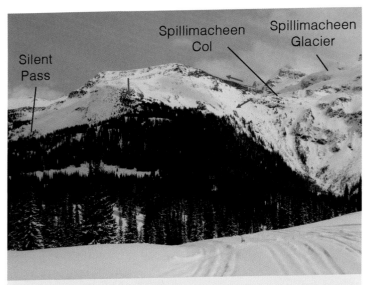

Spillimacheen Col. Photo Mark Klassen

at 2380 m, 488200 E 5653600 N. With low avalanche hazard it is possible to traverse steep, west-facing slopes beneath the small peak that lies to the north of Spillimacheen Col. This brings you to Silent Pass. In less than optimum conditions you can climb over the top of this small peak before descending the lower-angled north end of its west face to Silent Pass.

Alternatively, from the David–Unnamed col, keep descending all the way to the toe of the glacier. Navigate several steep moraine rolls (easier on the far right) to reach a basin at 2100 m, 489000 E, 5655400 N. Traverse north across undulating terrain to reach a ridge at 2225 m, 488200 E 5655400 N, west of a small lake. From here a long glide to the west brings you to Silent Pass.

Spillimacheen Glacier can be bypassed entirely by a descent to McMurdo Hut, which is located at 1750 m, 489600 E 5655600 N. Once the east edge of the glacier is reached via the route described above, descend the creek draining this side of the glacier. The hut is found in a small meadow where the

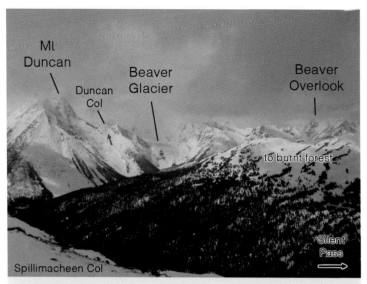

A view to the Selkirks from near Spillimacheen Col. Photo Mark Klassen

main valley opens up, at 1760 m, 489600 E 5655600 N. To gain Silent Pass, go downstream until it is possible to climb to the pass via a logging road, clear-cut and forest. This low route is an alternative for poor visibility or conditions.

At Silent Pass you may run into snowmobilers, so it isn't always that silent but you will soon leave them behind. Do not follow the drainage down from the pass or you will be sorry. Rather, from the pass, head west to a col at treeline, 2290 m, 485500 E 5655400 N. On the other side, make a traverse to the west across a large, low-angled basin. Again it is important to avoid getting sucked into the drainage below. Gain a broad shoulder at about 2150 m, 483800 E 5655900 N. An 800 m fall-line run through an open burnt forest leads to the valley below. If you're lucky, as we were, it will be perfect corn snow and it will feel like a GS race around all the snags! Near the bottom, some short traverses to skier's right (north) will set you up to ski directly down to the Beaver–Duncan Divide.

Erica Roles enjoying the corn snow on the burnt forest run into the Beaver River. Photo Mark Klassen

Time to take a break and recharge your batteries to prepare for the next challenge. The traverse of the Battle Range is one of the Holy Grails of Canadian ski mountaineering! It consists of a high traverse over two 3000 m ridges on continuously steep and crevassed terrain. You will want perfect weather and conditions for this section.

This is the last point that a helicopter pullout is available, as from here on in you are in Glacier National Park. This is also the start of the escape route down the Beaver River.

There is a lake on the Glacier National Park boundary at 1375 m, **481500** E **5656000** N. Ascend the creek above this to the west, which drains Duncan Glacier. Climb straight up, to the right (north) of the glacier, on ever-steepening terrain to reach a small notch in the northeast ridge of Mount Duncan at 2500 m, **478300** E **5655400** N. The terrain on this climb is big, steep and east-facing. There is overhead hazard and the snow may weaken rapidly in the morning sun. Get an early start!

Upper Beaver Glacier is easily gained on the other side of the notch. Head west across it toward Sugarloaf Mountain.

From the Beaver–Duncan divide it is possible to ski up Butters Creek and climb to a col west of Beaver Mountain, which leads to upper Beaver

Glacier. This has significantly more valley bottom travel and is longer and probably more difficult and hazardous than the route described above. However, groups may choose this way because it is the line of the original traverse party.

Past parties have apparently also climbed up Beaver Glacier all the way from the valley bottom. This looks to be a route with difficult travel and significant hazards from steep terrain, huge slopes above and below, terrain traps and lots of crevasses. Not recommended.

This is where it starts getting really wild! From upper Beaver Glacier, climb steep slopes to gain the lower east ridge of Sugarloaf Mountain at about 3050 m, **4759**00 E **5656**00 N. It may be possible to climb more directly up steep slopes to gain the ridge higher and avoid the narrow, corniced ridge described below, but these slopes are big and steep and probably have a cornice above them.

From the 3050 m point on the ridge, probably the best way is to drop steeply off the ridge to the north, crossing a bergschrund to a

Sugarloaf from the south. Photo Jeff Volp

small, hanging glacial basin. Go across the basin to the northwest and climb steeply up (bootpacking may be required) to a broad ridge at about 3130 m, **4755**00 E **5656**200 N. Alternatively, instead of dropping to the north, you can climb along the narrow, heavily corniced ridge (probably on foot). It will probably be too difficult to climb the ridge in its entirety, and a very steep traverse on the northeast side of the ridge, above a bergschrund, is probably necessary to bypass a step in the ridge and gain the 3130 m spot mentioned above.

Both routes end up at the same point. Gentler slopes are encountered after this and they are followed around the north side of the 3242 m peak. Continue traversing around this peak to its northwest side. A final steep traverse is made across a slope, above another bergschrund, until it is possible to descend more easily onto the glacier below, on the north side of Sugarloaf Mountain.

*From the broad ridge at about 3130 m, 4755*00 E 5656*200 N, it may be possible to descend straight to the north down a glacier that leads to Grand Glacier. This glacier is gentle at first but lower down it becomes steep and*

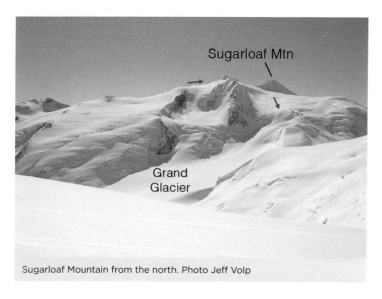

Sugarloaf Mountain from the north. Photo Jeff Volp

crevassed. A traverse right at about 2700 m would be required to avoid a steep section with crevasses. After this descent, more of an ascent would be involved to get to Grand Mountain, but if the weather is deteriorating, this may be the fastest way to get to a descent down the Grand.

From the higher route below the peak of Sugarloaf, ski down the glacier northwest and then the north to reach the broad col-basin at the head of Grand Glacier. This descent is heavily crevassed.

If you encounter bad weather or conditions here, you may consider descending Grand Glacier. Expect steep slopes and complex crevasses on the lower glacier; it would not be an easy escape. On the lower glacier the skier's right side may be the easiest. From the valley below it you may climb up the Beaver Overlook route (see below) or descend farther to the escape down the Beaver River.

From upper Grand Glacier, climb partway up the lower south ridge of Grand Mountain. Traverse below the east side of a small unnamed peak (2963 m) that is a bump on the ridge of Grand. Continue

Grand Mountain from near the summit of Sugarloaf. Photo Jeff Volp

traversing through a crevassed section until beneath the east face of Grand.

From here head for the east shoulder of Grand Mountain A steep climb and bootpack brings you to the crest at about 3020 m, **4737**00 E 56**598**00 N, to the right of a small subsummit on the ridge. A 600 m ski down the other side is your reward, but watch for more crevasses along the way, especially near the bottom. You are finally on the Deville Névé.

A major variation of the traverse manages to avoid the high line through the Battle Range via the Beaver River and Beaver Overlook. Significant avalanche terrain is encountered on this alternative, but it is at a lower elevation and it may be possible to go this way when visibility on the high ridges and peaks is obscured. Many parties end up using this route.

From the Beaver–Duncan Divide, descend the Beaver River a few kilometres until it is possible to ascend the drainage below Grand Glacier. Steep and complex slopes on the southern flanks of Beaver Overlook are climbed to gain the Deville Névé. This route is south-facing and may have a thin

Beaver Overlook. Photo Mark Klassen

Eric Harvie, Felix Belczyk and Erica Roles on a steep uptrack
ascending Beaver Overlook. Photo Mark Klassen

snowpack on the steep, smooth rock slabs. Warm temperatures can significantly affect it, so plan an early start.

For the escape down the Beaver River, see the Escape Routes section at the end of this chapter.

Once on the Deville it is a straightforward shuffle across the icefield to the Deville Headwall. This is the steep rock cliff to the east of the icefall that drains into Glacier Circle.

The descent route down the headwall is located close to the edge of the ice, and descends fall line down steep rock. It involves three 30-metre-long rappels (four if snow levels are extremely low). It is a committing descent requiring comfort and skill in rappelling. All stations were bolted in 2009 and have coloured reflective markers.

Approach the headwall along the eastern side of the glacier. To find the first station, follow the natural terrain depression along the east edge of the glacier, following the line between the ice and rock. There may be a cairn marking the start of the route. The first station is located on the rock outcrop nearest the ice, immediately below the cairn, at 2140 m, **4739**00 E 56**673**00 N.

Traverse between ice and rock

Cairn on top of rock outcrop

The Deville Headwall with the rappels marked. Do not expect the gully pictured at the centre to be full of snow. Photo Parks Canada

- **Rappel One:** Rappel 25 m down the gully, wrapping slightly climber's left (east) to a small exposed rock below a bulging buttress. It is possible to climb back up to the top from this point.
- **Rappel Two:** From the climber's right (west) side of the rock outcrop you are standing on, rappel fall line for 30 m. The station is located below the vertical seam in a small rock corner. This pitch is vertical, committing and long. Make sure there are knots at the end of your rope!
- **Rappel Three:** Rappel fall line 30 m to the steep snow ramp below. From here groups may choose to ski (if conditions allow) or build a T-slot anchor to rappel to lower-angled slopes below. A fourth bolted station is located on the rock face by the ramp but will be visible only in very low snow. During most seasons this anchor will be under several metres of snow.

From the bottom of the headwall, ski toward the large lateral moraine across the valley. Take a slight bench to the right along the middle of this moraine until you can skin up onto its crest. This is an exposed traverse with a relatively thin snowpack, and if it is late in the day you may need to wait until it cools off and the snow stabilizes.

The terrain mellows immediately on the other side of the moraine. Glacier Circle Cabin is only 500 m away but it is famously hard to find in the thick forest that is inconveniently strewn with hut-sized boulders. The cabin is often almost completely buried. (See page 54.)

To find your home for the night, walk across the small lake to the trees on the far side. Follow the edge of the woods along the creek and below the talus slopes on the left for a short way. Where the creekbed begins to narrow, cut rightward into the forest. You may pass by a large boulder; if so, the hut is quite close, at 1820 m, **4724**99 E 5**6691**15 N.

If you decide you want to avoid the technical descent down the Deville Headwall or the avalanche terrain to exit Glacier Circle, it is possible to avoid this section entirely by skiing from the Deville Névé down The Bishops Glacier and Mitre Creek to the Incomappleux River.

From the Incomappleux it is still complex terrain to get out to the road. Perhaps the least hazardous exit would be to ascend toward the Swanzy–Dome col and ski out via Lily Glacier–Loop Brook or Sapphire Col–Asulkan Brook. This route has been done but there is some very steep terrain (including cliff bands) in the forest. However, the alpine terrain is less serious than the exit out of Glacier Circle.

Another option from the Incomappleux is climbing Geikie Glacier to the Illecillewaet Névé. This has also been done but includes some steep terrain through cliff bands and crevasses on the glacier. It is probably not any less hazardous than the Glacier Circle exit.

Unknown possibilities include exits via Asulkan Pass (large, steep slopes); ascending to the col directly north of Slick Mountain and then skiing down into Flat Creek; or descending the Incomappleux to Slick Creek and ascending that drainage before skiing down Flat Creek to the highway.

If you get to Glacier Circle, enjoy your night in the historic cabin. It's probably the last of the trip! If the weather or conditions are poor, though, you may have to wait until it improves. There is some big alpine terrain to travel over yet.

In the worst-case scenario you can descend to the Beaver River from here and ski out to the road that way. If doing that, after getting down the moraine below Glacier Circle Cabin, stay on the right (south) side of the creek while you descend to the Beaver. See the Escape Routes section at the end of this chapter (page 305) for information for the Beaver River.

There are two options for climbing out of Glacier Circle and they both involve steep slopes and overhead hazard. The most common route seems to be to the west, below The Witch Tower. Ascend the crest of a steep moraine, which is discernible on maps, to even steeper slopes up a broad gully. This eventually kicks back as you get onto the glacier above, at 2400 m, **470**700 E 5673000 N. A long, gradual ascent brings you to the Illecillewaet Névé to the northeast.

Another route out of the Circle is to the east, up the huge, steep draw below the west face of Mount Macoun. Start on climber's left

Both exits from Glacier Circle. Photo Parks Canada/Friends of Mount Revelstoke and Glacier National Parks

before cutting to the right into the draw. Climb up it to the icefield at 2500 m, 472500 E 5671200 N. There is perhaps even more real estate over your head on this route, so be sure of the snow stability up there.

An exciting way to finish the trip from the névé is to ski over Youngs Peak. From the névé, ski onto the north ridge of Youngs and follow it to the summit. Then ski steeply down the northeast face of the mountain. Continue down Asulkan Glacier and either ski down the drainage below the glacier or pass by Asulkan Cabin and descend the trees below that. Once in the valley, meet up with the regular line.

If you want to get out relatively quickly and easily, cross the Illecillewaet Névé and descend the skier's left (west) side of Illecillewaet Glacier (watch for crevasses). Get off the west edge of the glacier at about 2000 m and ski down convoluted terrain of ribs and gullies, being careful not to ski over little rock bands (see Lookout Col description page 90 and photo on page 92). Once in the valley you may follow the creek out on its right (northeast) side, although the more common way is to cut left through the forest to Asulkan Brook and follow that.

The 1973 desperados in Glacier Circle Cabin: Ron Robinson, Dave Smith, Don Gardner and Chic Scott. Photo Chic Scott

There will probably be a well-used trail to follow to get to the Asulkan side. Either way brings you to the old railway grade. Turn left on this flat trail and walk a few hundred metres to the parking area beside the highway.

Congratulations! You have just completed the Bugaboos to Rogers Pass Traverse.

Finishing logistics

Vehicles may be left at the Asulkan–Illecillewaet trailhead indefinitely. A National Park permit is required or the vehicle will be towed.

As of the autumn of 2012 Glacier Park Lodge at the summit of Rogers Pass has gone out of business. It is unclear whether it will re-open in the future.

There is cell phone service (Telus and Bell) throughout the highway corridor at Rogers Pass. A call could be made from the Illecillewaet Icefield to arrange for a vehicle pickup on the highway.

The 2009 desperados in Glacier Circle Cabin: Erica Roles, Eric Harvie, Felix Belczyk, Mark Klassen. Photo Mark Klassen

Escape routes

There are not many possibilities for easy or inexpensive escape. The route is a long way from any plowed roads.

A call-out via a satellite-linked device could arrange a helicopter or snowmobile pickup if you are outside Bugaboo Provincial Park or Glacier National Park. Helicopters are able to access most of the route, but in poor visibility you would have to get to treeline or lower to get picked up.

Snowmobiles can easily travel up the logging roads in the main valleys as long as there is still snow on them. They may be able to get to higher elevations in a few areas such as Snowman Lake–Syncline or McMurdo Hut–Silent Pass. There are often snowmobilers already in these areas and someone may be willing to give you a ride out without your having to make a call out.

From the Bugaboos and the Conrad Icefield areas, getting back to Bugaboo Lodge may be an option. Bugaboo Lodge is at 520700 E 5622400 N and has good communications to the outside world. With some sweet-talking and a credit card, flights out may be possible here or arrangements could probably made for someone to come pick you up with a snowmobile.

Bobbie Burns Lodge is in Vowell Creek at 504900 E 5644100 N. Long valley-bottom walks could be made from the Conrad Icefield (Malloy Creek or Conrad Creek), Crystalline Creek or Vermont Creek to get there. These options are 10–20 km of slogging through the forest. Again, flights or snowmobile rides may be arranged from here.

It is possible to ski down the Beaver River to the Trans-Canada Highway from the Beaver–Duncan Divide (40 km), Beaver Overlook (35 km) or Glacier Circle (25 km). There is a summer trail most of the way but it may be difficult to follow in the winter. In the upper section it may be easiest to follow the river, but lower down it is best to stay up on the right (east) bank to avoid a canyon. The park cabins in this valley will be locked.

Food cache logistics and common locations

Food caches are most often placed by helicopter. If you charter a machine from Golden it is easy to place them as you fly to your starting point. Snowmobiles may also access some spots and this would be a less expensive solution. For food caching tips see the "Skiing the Grand Traverses" chapter at page 209.

The following are some common food cache locations for this trip:

Crystalline Creek (helicopter)
Snowman Lake–Syncline area (helicopter or snowmobile)
Malachite Creek (helicopter)
Kingsbury Cabin (helicopter)
McMurdo Hut–Silent Pass area (helicopter or snowmobile)
Beaver–Duncan Divide (helicopter or snowmobile)

Possible ski mountaineering ascents

Crescent Towers, SW Gully–S Ridge
Mt. Conrad, NW Slopes
Mt. Malloy, SW Slopes
Cony Pk., E Ridge
Sugarloaf Mtn., N Ridge
Mt. Wheeler, NW Ridge
Mt. Kilpatrick, NE Ridge
Youngs Pk., N Ridge

Land managers

Bugaboo Provincial Park
BC Crown Lands
Glacier National Park

Huts and hut managers

Conrad Kain Hut – Alpine Club of Canada
Malloy Igloo – BC Parks
Mark Kingsbury Hut – Columbia Valley Hut Society
Glacier Circle Cabin – Alpine Club of Canada

Commercial skiing tenures

Canadian Mountain Holidays – Bugaboos
Canadian Mountain Holidays – Bobbie Burns
Purcell Helicopter Skiing

Helicopter access

Helicopters may land outside Bugaboo Provincial Park and Glacier National Park. Helicopters may land in Bugaboo Provincial Park if the touring party has a Letter of Permission and the helicopter company has a Park Use Permit.

Snowmobile access

Snowmobiles can easily travel up logging roads in the main valleys. They also may be able to access some higher terrain, such as in the Snowman Lake–Syncline and McMurdo Hut–Silent Pass areas. They are not allowed to travel up the Beaver River, as it is in Glacier National Park.

Rescue resources

For emergencies, self-rescue will be faster than calling on outside resources. However, for serious extrications from the backcountry you will probably need to call for help.

Glacier National Park responds to emergencies in that park. The Provincial Emergency Program is responsible for rescue on all provincial lands. See the Alpine Ski Touring in the Columbia Mountains chapter beginning at page 13 for more details on mountain rescue.

The closest rescue resources for much of the route will be the heli-ski companies in the area. However, their first priority is the safety of their guests, so response by them may not be immediate or even possible. You will be asked to pay for expenses incurred in a rescue by private companies unless the rescue has been organized by PEP.

Maps

NTS 1:250,000:	*Lardeau 82 K*
	Golden 82 N
NTS 1:50,000:	*Howser Creek 82 K/10*
	Bugaboo Creek 82 K/15
	Westfall River 82 K/14
	Mt. Wheeler 82 N/3
	Blaeberry 82 N/6
	Glacier 82 N/5
Canadamapstore.com:	*Cobalt Lake 082K077*
	Mt. Stone 082K076
	Conrad Creek 082K086
	Mt. Hatteras 082K085
	Syncline Mtn. 082K095
	Spillimacheen Glacier 082N005
	Mt. Duncan 082N004
	Mt. Topham 082N014
	Mt. Donkin 082N013
	Mt. Afton 082N023

Other maps

Summit Series – Bugaboos (covers the same area as Canada Map Store map Cobalt Lake 082K077)

The Adventure Map – Rogers Pass (covers the same area as Canada Map Store map Mt. Afton 082N023)

Backroad Mapbooks – Kootenay Rockies BC (logging roads)

THE BACKCOUNTRY SKI LODGES

Mountain hospitality goes back a long way in the Columbias. It all began in the late 19th century when the Canadian Pacific Railway began importing Swiss guides to lead its clientele from historic Glacier House near Rogers Pass to the summits of the Selkirk Range. For over 100 years this tradition has grown and today adventure tourism is a major component of the economy of British Columbia. In the late 1970s the first of the modern backcountry lodges was established in the Purcell Range near Kimberley. Since then, interest in backcountry skiing has blossomed and today there are about twenty of these lodges, offering a variety of experience. All of the lodges are warm and cozy and offer great skiing.

These backcountry lodges offer a professional guiding service, the majority employing guides certified by the Association of Canadian Mountain Guides. All ski guides are trained in first aid, avalanche safety, emergency response, snow stability evaluation, client care and a host of other skills. They can fix your broken binding in a snowstorm or show you how to get your skins to stick on a cold winter day. They can also help you with your ski technique if you are new to backcountry skiing. By employing a professional guide who knows the terrain intimately you can find the best skiing. And their knowledge of the year's snowpack will allow you to ski steeper and deeper than you would dare on your own.

Most lodges offer a guided and catered experience several weeks of the year, but many lodges now offer the self-guided alternative. If you and your group are experienced backcountry skiers, familiar with all aspects of safe travel in avalanche terrain, you can just rent the lodge and lead your own tours. However, if you are new to the area it will take you a while to be able to find the best runs, so for your first trip to a lodge it might be best to ski with a guide. You also have the choice of doing

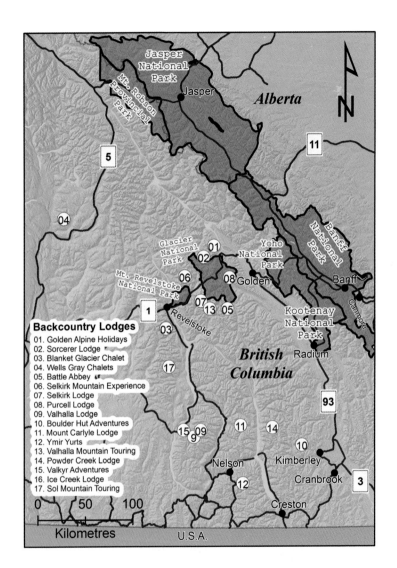

Backcountry Lodges

01. Golden Alpine Holidays
02. Sorcerer Lodge
03. Blanket Glacier Chalet
04. Wells Gray Chalets
05. Battle Abbey
06. Selkirk Mountain Experience
07. Selkirk Lodge
08. Purcell Lodge
09. Valhalla Lodge
10. Boulder Hut Adventures
11. Mount Carlyle Lodge
12. Ymir Yurts
13. Valhalla Mountain Touring
14. Powder Creek Lodge
15. Valkyr Adventures
16. Ice Creek Lodge
17. Sol Mountain Touring

Nighttime at Powder Creek Lodge. Photo David R. Gluns

Russ Lybarger on Dessert at Golden Alpine Holidays. Photo Chic Scott

your own catering at many lodges, so if you like to cook, this is a good alternative.

The terrain varies from lodge to lodge and they all have their own special attractions. You have a choice of glacier skiing in the bigger mountains, long fall-line powder runs or mellow Nordic touring across alpine meadows. All the lodges have tree skiing for those snowy, overcast days. The snowpack is deep in the Columbia Mountains, usually 3–5 metres by the end of the season.

There is a tremendous variety of lodge construction, from deluxe hotel-like structures with all the modern conveniences to Asian yurts. Over the years, many of the lodges have improved their facilities and some now offer hot and cold running water, showers, flush toilets, electricity and wireless Internet. Most lodges still have a wood stove to sit around and they all have hot saunas to refresh you after a day of skiing.

All lodges, with one exception, are accessed by helicopter. Canada is a huge country that bush pilots had a big part in building, and these men and women are among the best trained and most experienced in the world. A short flight lifts you from the valley to the lodge at the edge of treeline where the best skiing is found. Then the machine leaves for the week and you are alone with your friends and the silence of the hills.

If you decide to visit one of these lodges, here are a few things you should bear in mind.

Pack light for the helicopter ride to the hut. Your luggage may be weighed and you may be charged for overweight items. If the trip is catered and guided you do not need to bring much – just a change of clothes, hut shoes, a toilet kit, a book and a bottle of your favourite beverage (in addition to your ski equipment). The lodge will send you a detailed list of what you need to bring.

In the event of bad weather the helicopter may not be able to pick you up on the appointed day and return you to civilization. You may have to wait an extra day or two until the pilot can fly safely.

If you are taking medication, be sure you have extra for several days. It always is a good idea to leave a few buffer days after your stay at the lodge before you catch your flight home. If you do get out on time you can always ski for a day or two at the local resort.

Earplugs are a necessity at some of the lodges where you may be sharing a room with several others. If you snore, bring earplugs for your roommates.

If you are self-guided and self-catered you must be able to ski safely and competently in a wilderness setting. You must be able to do your own avalanche hazard evaluation and route finding and be able to deal with any emergencies. As well, you must know how to cook on propane stoves and heat with wood stoves. You should be sure you are familiar with the operation of all aspects of the lodge before you depart.

Note: All prices in this book are for the winter season 2011/12 and will change with time.

GOLDEN ALPINE HOLIDAYS

Golden Alpine Holidays is one of the best-established ski operations in the Columbia Mountains, going back about thirty years. A great ski week can be had here.

Location Golden Alpine Holidays has four lodges located in the Esplanade Range of the Selkirk Mountains about 50 km northwest of Golden. All lodges are at the edge of treeline, above 2100 m: Sunrise Chalet is located at the head of Wisted Creek, on the edge of a small lake (**4618**00 E **5711**00 N). Meadow Chalet is at the head of Carrol Creek (**4595**00 E **5713**00 N). Vista Chalet is at the head of Schlichting Creek (**4587**00 E **5715**00 N).

Meadow Chalet. Photo Chic Scott

High in the Selkirk Mountains, near the Golden
Alpine Holidays lodges. Photo Chic Scott

Russ Lybarger skis Paradise Ridge near the Golden Alpine
Holidays Meadow Chalet. Photo Chic Scott

Sentry Lodge is at the north end of the Esplanade Range (**4572**00 E 57**2080**0 N).

Map Mount Sir Sandford 82 N/12

Access By helicopter from a staging area 50 km west of Golden, adjacent to the Trans-Canada Highway.

Facilities Three buildings (Sunrise/Meadow/Vista) are identical and offer six double-occupancy bedrooms. Wood and propane stoves heat the chalets, while propane is used for lighting and cooking. Outdoor toilets, with a chemical toilet for night use. Each chalet has an outstanding rustic sauna. All three lodges were completely renovated in the autumn of 2010. Sentry Lodge is much more deluxe, built in 2011. It is an elegant and simple timber frame building that sleeps 12. It has hot and cold running water, 120-volt AC current, high speed Internet and Skype and there are two indoor waterless urinals and two outhouses. Wood heating.

Host There is a custodian present at the lodge.

Contact information
Box 1050, Golden, BC V0A 1H0
info@gah.ca.
www.gah.ca
250-344-7273, fax 250-344-7274

Cost For fully guided and catered ski weeks, prices ranges from $1890 to $2350. You can also rent Sunrise, Meadow or Vista Lodges for $4500 to $5000 per week. Sentry Lodge can be rented for $6900 to $7900 per week. Helicopter costs are included in the catered and guided weeks, but are about $350/person for self-guided and self-catered weeks.

Skiing The ski terrain is superb at Golden Alpine Holidays. The runs are located on ridges and peaks just above treeline and are generally 500 to 700 vertical metres. There are no glaciers at GAH. There is lots of tree skiing for those snowy, overcast days. A week-long ski tour of all four lodges is also offered.

SORCERER LODGE

Sorcerer Lodge has been offering ski touring holidays for 24 years and has many dedicated admirers. The terrain is varied – there is glaciated and non-glaciated terrain and there is good tree skiing. This is a good destination for more experienced skiers.

Location In the Selkirk Mountains about 25 km north of Rogers Pass, beneath the north flank of Nordic Mountain. The hut is at the edge of a small lake at an elevation of 2050 m (**451**200 E 56**999**00 N).

Map Glacier 82 N/5

Access By helicopter from Heather Mountain Lodge, 55 km west of Golden

Sorcerer Lodge. Photo Alf Skrastins

Facilities Sorcerer Lodge is a three-storey building with rooms for up to 18 people. There is a separate dining area and sitting room and a fully equipped kitchen with propane stove. A wood stove heats the main area of the lodge, with a propane heater for the drying room. Solar-powered electric lights, with a generator for darker days. Large wet sauna. Outdoor toilets.

Host Tannis Dakin

Contact information
Box 161, Golden, BC V0A 1H0
info@sorcererlodge.com
www.sorcererlodge.com
250-344-2804, fax 250-344-2805

Cost Fully catered and guided weeks cost about $2000/person. Self-guided and self-catered groups can rent the lodge for $6000/week plus $375/person for the helicopter.

Skiing The terrain near Sorcerer Lodge is serious and alpine. There are outstanding glaciated runs of up to 1000 vertical metres and it is possible to reach the summit of several big peaks. For poor visibility days there is tree skiing just below the hut, with chutes and jumps, but it is not for the faint of heart.

Dave Fullerton ripping it at Sorcerer Lodge. Photo Mark Klassen

Sorcerer Lodge. Photo Mark Klassen

BLANKET GLACIER CHALET

This unique chalet specializes in self-catered and self-guided weeks, although Al and a handful of other ACMG guides offer at least one guided week per month. The area is noted for its deep snowpack and it is not unusual to see over 100 feet of total snowfall in a winter.

Location In the Monashee Mountains about 20 km south of Revelstoke (4**121**00 E 56**2790**0 N).

Map Revelstoke 82 L/16

Access By helicopter from Revelstoke

Facilities The three-storey A-frame sleeps 16 guests. It has a separate large sauna building with change room and shower. The main chalet is equipped with both wood and propane heating stoves, propane cooking stove and a fully equipped kitchen. Solar-powered lights. There are foam mattresses and pillows but guests bring their own sleeping bags. Outdoor toilets.

Hosts Al and Marion Schaffer with help from their son Marty

Contact information

Box 8150, Canmore, AB T1W 2T9

info@blanketglacierchalet.com

Blanket Glacier Chalet. Photo Al Schaffer

www.blanketglacierchalet.com
403-678-4102

Cost Self guided and self-catered, $1040 per week

Skiing There is more than ample tree skiing for all levels of ability. A large glacier system offers great skiing late into the season, with runs of up to 1000 vertical metres. The highlight of the week is the ascent of Blanket Peak, which yields a descent of 1000 vertical metres back to the chalet.

WELLS GRAY CHALETS

Wells Gray Chalets has many devoted fans, some of who come back year after year. Ian Eakins is the host and a great storyteller. Their prices are one of the best values in the business.

Location In Wells Gray Provincial Park in the Trophy Range of the Cariboo Mountains north of Clearwater. There are three chalets:
Trophy Mountain (3**048**00 E 57**388**00 N),
Fight Meadow (3**000**00 E 57**562**00 N)
Discovery (3**045**00 E 57**454**00 N).

Trophy Chalet.

Map West Raft River 82 M/13

Access By helicopter, snowcat or skis

Facilities The Trophy Mountain and Fight Meadow chalets are identical and sleep 12. The Discovery Cabin sleeps 10. All three cabins have propane heat and kitchen, solar lights, electric plug-ins, cedar saunas and new composting toilet systems.

Hosts Ian Eakins and Tay Briggs

Contact information
Box 188, Clearwater, BC V0E 1N0

info@skihike.com
www.skihike.com
250-587-6444, fax 250-587-6446, toll free 1-888-754-8735

Cost Guided and catered, $185/person/day. The cabin can be rented for $500/night (10 per cent less in low season). A guide can be hired for $325/day.

Skiing The runs at Well Gray Chalets are shortish, about 300 to 400 vertical metres, but there is plenty of terrain to choose from. There are no glaciers and most of the skiing is near treeline, so it is excellent for those snowy and cloudy days.

BATTLE ABBEY LODGE

Battle Abbey Lodge. Photo Alf Skrastins

This unique and comfortable lodge is the creation of American mountaineer and historian Bill Putnam. Over the years, it has gradually evolved into one of the most interesting and complex structures around, with power production, running water and a stereophonic sound system. A ski holiday at Battle Abbey is highly recommended.

Guide Marc Piché takes a little air on Blue Danube
near Battle Abbey. Photo Chic Scott

Location In the Battle Range of the Selkirk Mountains about 35 km south of Rogers Pass. The lodge is at an elevation of 2200 m, high above the head of Butters Creek (4**760**00 E 56**478**00 N).

Map Westfall River 82 K/14

Access By helicopter from Golden

Facilities The lodge consists of a kitchen/dining area, living room and four sleeping lofts which can accommodate 14 guests. There is hot and cold running water and a shower. Electricity is supplied by a wind generator and solar panels. Outdoor plumbing but indoor toilets for nighttime use.

Hosts Roger Laurilla and Robson Gmoser

Contact information

Box 1854, Golden, BC VOA 1H0

info@battleabbey.ca

www.battleabbey.ca

250-344-5292

Cost fully guided and catered, $2100/week

Skiing The ski experience is excellent at Battle Abbey. Much of the terrain is above treeline, some of it on glaciers. There is a mix of mellow and steep to suit all tastes. Most runs are quite long and the descent from the summit of Typee Mountain is over 1000 vertical metres. There is plenty of tree skiing for overcast days.

SELKIRK MOUNTAIN EXPERIENCE

Selkirk Mountain Experience is for serious, fit, backcountry skiers.

Durrand Glacier Chalet. Photo Chic Scott

Location Selkirk Mountain Experience operates in the Selkirk Mountains about 50 km northeast of Revelstoke. The main lodge, Durrand Glacier Chalet (4**316**00 E 56**802**00 N), is located on a knoll at 1950 m, not far from Durrand Glacier. A smaller lodge, the Mount Moloch Chalet

(4**363**00 E 56**841**00 N), sits on bedrock not far from Dismal Glacier.

Maps Glacier 82 N/5, Illecillewaet 82 N/4, Downie Creek 82 M/8, Revelstoke 82 M/1

Access By helicopter from Revelstoke

Facilities Durrand Glacier Chalet is a pine and cedar Swiss-style alpine chalet offering accommodation for 17 guests in single and two-person bedrooms. Meals are served family style. Indoor toilets, hot and cold running water, electric lights, sauna, Internet, satellite telephone. The Mount Moloch Chalet is smaller and more rustic and can accommodate eight guests.

Hosts Ruedi and Nicoline Beglinger

Contact information
Box 2998, Revelstoke, BC V0E 2S0
info@selkirkexperience.com
www.selkirkexperience.com
250-837-2381

Cost All ski weeks at SME are fully guided and catered. The cost is $2200/week.

Skiing There is excellent skiing at Selkirk Mountain Experience. Most of the terrain is above treeline, often on glaciers, and many summits can be reached. In poor visibility, groups often ski this terrain led by guides who know the area. There is some tree skiing.

SELKIRK LODGE

Location At the Albert Icefield in the Selkirk Mountains east of Revelstoke at an elevation of 2200 m (4**489**00 E 56**550**00 N).

Map Illecillewaet 82 N/4

Access By helicopter from Revelstoke

Facilities A two-storey lodge that accommodates 12 guests in four bedrooms. Wood

Selkirk Lodge. Photo Michael Morris

heating and propane cooking. Sauna, shower, indoor toilet, solar-powered lighting.

Host Grania Devine

Contact information

Box 911, Golden, BC V0A 1H0

Selkirk@hughes.net

www.selkirklodge.ca

250-344-5129, fax 250-344-5177

Cost The lodge is rented to groups for a week at a time. All groups must be guided. Usually guides book the lodge and come up with their own guests. The average cost is $2125/person/week.

Skiing Selkirk Lodge offers high-end skiing suitable for strong intermediate and advanced skiers.

PURCELL LODGE

Location At an elevation of 2180 m in the Bald Mountains in the Northern Purcells, 25 km west of Golden (**478**00 E 56**790**00 N).

Maps Mount Wheeler 82 N/3, Blaeberry 82 N/6

Access By helicopter from Golden

Facilities This is truly a deluxe lodge – a hotel high in the mountains,

Purcell Lodge.

in fact. It boasts hot and cold running water, showers, flush toilets, and electricity, as well as forced-air central heating. There are beds for 24 guests in ten private rooms. There is also a luxurious honeymoon apartment. A conference room is available with all audiovisual amenities. Fireplace, licensed dining room and sauna. Casual gourmet dining.

Hosts Sunny Chen (owner) and Doug Latimer (guide)

Contact information

Box 1829, Golden, BC V0A 1H0

info@purcellmountainlodge.com

www.purcellmountainlodge.com

250-344-2639 or 1-888-767-8989

Cost Purcell Lodge offers 3-, 4- and 7-day fully guided and catered packages in a variety of accommodation. Prices vary from $415/night to $615/night, including helicopter.

Skiing The skiing at Purcell Lodge is mellower than at most of the other lodges. There are rolling meadows with incredible views and plenty of terrain nearby to make turns. There is also tree skiing for overcast days.

VALHALLA LODGE

Valhalla Lodge is a very comfortable lodge set in excellent ski country. It is a great destination for skiers of all abilities who want a safe environment with lots of ski possibilities.

Location In the Valhalla Range northwest of Nelson at an elevation of 2130 m (4**411**00 E 55**186**00 N).

Map Burton 82 F/13

Access By helicopter from a staging area near Burton

Facilities A two-storey post-and-beam building providing accommodation for 12 in four double rooms and one dorm-style room. Wood heating, propane cooking, propane and solar lighting, stereo system, VHF radios, satellite phone, Internet, cedar sauna and shower. Outdoor toilets.

Hosts Leo Jansma and Brian Cross

Contact information

Box 1206, Nelson, BC V1L 6H3

info@valhallamountainlodge.com

Valhalla Lodge. Photo Chic Scott

The McKean Lakes Basin below Woden Peak offers
excellent ski terrain for all abilities. Photo Chic Scott

www.valhallamountainlodge.com
250-229-4661

Cost Guided and catered, $2035/week; guided and self-catered, $1575/week; self-guided and self-catered, $1150/week.

Skiing The skiing is excellent at Valhalla Lodge. There is a great variety of terrain for all skill levels near the lodge and in ten surrounding bowls, with runs up to 1000 m and numerous circuits over high passes. There are mellow runs for beginners, lots of tree skiing for those stormy days and steep chutes for the more advanced skiers.

BOULDER HUT ADVENTURES

Boulder Hut was the first of the backcountry lodges to be developed and has been in operation for over 30 years. They offer an authentic old–school experience with down–home hospitality.

Location In the Southern Purcell Mountains about 30 km northwest of Kimberley on the boundary of the Purcell Wilderness Conservancy. Boulder Hut (5**542**00 E 55**105**00 N), at an elevation of 1980 m at the foot of Mount Higgins, is the main lodge. Seven kilometres down the valley is Ptarmigan Hut (5**542**00 E 55**152**00 N) at an elevation of 1550 m.

Maps Dewar Creek 82 F/16, St. Mary Lake 82 F/9

Access By helicopter from Kimberley

Facilities The main lodge, Boulder Hut, offers accommodation for 12 guests in a mix of single and double partitioned beds. There is a propane kitchen, hydro-powered electric lights, drying room and an outdoor wood-fired hot tub. Outdoor toilets. Historic Ptarmigan Hut has a ten-person bunkhouse, main lodge and wood-fired sauna.

Hosts Mark and Sarah Yancey

Contact information
Box 11, Kimberley, BC V1A 2Y5
info@boulderhutadventures.com
www.boulderhutadventures.com
1-888-204-6525

Cost Guided and catered, $2150/week; self-guided and self-catered, $9750/week for the lodge (maximum 12 people).

Skiing There is excellent terrain for skiers of all abilities. Alpine bowls

Some of the outstanding ski terrain near Boulder Hut.

with runs up to 600 vertical metres and lots of tree skiing for stormy days.

MOUNT CARLYLE LODGE

Mount Carlyle lodge is under new ownership.

Location In the Northern Kokanee Range 50 km north of Nelson at an elevation of 2100 m, beneath Mount Carlyle (4**900**0 E 55**301**00 N).

Map Slocan 82 F/14

Access By helicopter from the Kaslo airport

Facilities The lodge accommodates 14 people in four bedrooms. There is running water, solar power, lights, a sound system, indoor bathroom and nighttime pee toilet. Propane-equipped kitchen. Dining and relaxation area with fabulous view. Sauna. Outdoor toilets.

Host Brian Cross

Contact information

Brian Cross, the new owner, in front of Mount
Carlyle Lodge. Photo Dave Waag

GR-9, C-9, RR 1, Winlaw, BC V0G 2J0
info@kmhbc.com
www.skihikebc.com
250-355-2269

Cost The lodge rents for $1150/person/week self-guided and self-catered. Self-guided and catered is $1650/person/week; guided and catered is $2100 person/week.

Skiing There is great skiing on all aspects – open alpine bowls, chutes and tree skiing. The main Mount Carlyle Basin is just outside the door. Many ridge walks and a circumnavigation of Mount Carlyle, accessing five basins, is possible

YMIR YURTS

Location In the Nelson Range of the Selkirk Mountains about 15 km southeast of Nelson. There are three locations:
Qua Yurt (4**9240**0 E 54**7160**0 N),
Yurtopia (4**9460**0 E 54**7440**0 N) and
Wildhorse Cabin (4**9440**0 E 54**7030**0 N).
Map Nelson 82 F/6

Access By helicopter, snowcat or skis

Facilities There are three cabins, some with accommodation for up to 8. Heating by kerosene. Propane lights and cooking. New for 2012 is Ark Lodge in the vicinity of Qua Yurt with accommodation for 12 skiers.

Cost $700/person/week including snowcat transportation.

Host Trevor Holsworth

Contact information
Box 406, New Denver, BC V0G 1Y0
yurts@kootenayexperience.com
www.ymiryurts.com
250-358-7277

Cost Trips of 2 to 5 days are available to the yurt camps at $25 to $50/person/night. You can ski guided or self-guided, catered or self-catered.

Skiing Tree skiing, bowls, glades, chutes and peaks. Runs of up to 600 vertical metres.

VALHALLA MOUNTAIN TOURING

Location In the Ruby Range about 20 km northwest of New Denver, near the head of Shannon Creek (4**576**00 E 56**490**00 N) at an elevation of about 1800 m.

Map Nakusp 82 K/4

Access By snowcat

Facilities This is a deluxe timber-frame lodge built in 1998. There are six 2- to 3-person bedrooms. Spacious living area and dining room. Electric lights. Wireless Internet. Hot and cold running water. Wood fired sauna. Indoor toilets.

Hosts Dale Caton

Contact information
Box 3407, Garibaldi Highlands, BC V0N 1T0
info@vmt.ca

Valhalla Mountain Touring's Ruby Creek Lodge.

www.vmt.ca

250-412-5319 (lodge) or 604-848-1462 (cell)

Cost Guided and catered, $1850/person/week; guided and self catered, $1450/person/week; self-guided and catered, $1450/person/week; self-guided and self-catered, $1050/person/week.

Skiing Runs of up to 600 vertical metres in alpine terrain; summits and ridges with great views and lots of tree skiing.

POWDER CREEK LODGE

Location In the Southern Purcells at the head of the Powder Creek drainage, 17 km east of Kaslo (5**233**00 E 55**280**00 N) at an elevation of 2150 m.

Map Kaslo 82 F/15

Access By helicopter from Kaslo

Facilities Two-and-a-half-storey lodge with six 2- to 3-person bedrooms that sleep up to 15 guests. Fully equipped kitchen. Large sauna and bathhouse. Hydro power. Propane and wood heat. Indoor and outdoor toilets.

Hosts Guus Diks and Heather Smith

Contact information
Box 832, Nelson, BC V1L 5S9
info@powdercreeklodge.com
www.powdercreeklodge.com
250-359-5916

Cost Guided and catered, $2250/week; self-guided and catered, $1800/week; guided and self-catered, $1900/week; self-guided and self-catered, $1200/week. There is a $200/person discount for shoulder-season weeks.

Skiing There is a variety of treed and open terrain for

Powder Creek Lodge.
Photo David R. Gluns

333

all levels of ability. The five big alpine basins that surround the lodge comprise 7000 hectares of terrain with everything from gentle treed and gladed slopes to steep 900-metre descents.

VALKYR ADVENTURES

Location In the Valkyr Range about 60 km northwest of Nelson (4**305**00 E 55**254**00 N) at an elevation of 2280 m.

Map Burton 82 F/13

Access By helicopter from staging area near Burton

Facilities Valkyr Lodge has five bedrooms (double-bed/twin-bed combination) and one bedroom with two bunks. There is a comfortable living room with large windows. Deluxe sauna with hot shower. Indoor toilets and hot and cold running water. Hydroelectric power. Wireless Internet. Hilda Hut is a three-storey building with room for 12 guests in five private bedrooms. Hot and cold running water, showers, wood-fired hot tub, indoor toilets and hydro power.

Hosts Martin and Shelly Glasheen

Valkyr Lodge.

Contact information
    Box 20, Fauquier, BC V0G 1K0
    info@valkyradventures.com
    www.valkyradventures.com
    phone/fax 250-269-7237 or 1-888-482-5597

Cost Guided and catered, $2100/week; self-guided and catered, $1550/week; self-guided and self-catered, $1150/week.

Skiing There is a variety of terrain, with plenty of tree skiing, ridges and peaks.

ICE CREEK LODGE

Location At the head of Ice Creek, just northwest of Urd Peak in the Valhalla Range, 50 km northwest of Nelson (4**483**00 E 55**254**00 N). The lodge is in the middle of the Valhalla Traverse, at an elevation of 1900 m.

Map Burton 82 F/13

Access By helicopter

Facilities A post-and-beam two-storey lodge with loft-style communal bunks for 10. Wood heat. Newly renovated, propane-equipped kitchen. Sauna. Outdoor toilets.

Ice Creek Lodge. Photo Chris Ankeny

Hosts Russell and Courtney Hulbert
Contact information
S8, C13, RR 1, Winlaw, BC V0G 2J0
info@icecreeklodge.com
www.icecreeklodge.com
250-355-2647
Cost Guided and catered, $1900/week; guided and self-catered, $1400/week. The lodge can be rented for $8400/week.
Skiing Steep tree lines and long alpine bowls. Descents up to 1100 vertical metres.

SOL MOUNTAIN TOURING

Location In the Monashee Mountains south of Revelstoke at the south border of Monashee Provincial Park at an elevation of 1900 m (**415**199 E 55**892**78 N).
Map Mount Fosthall 82 L/8
Access By helicopter from Cherryville
Facilities This is a three-storey timber-frame lodge. There are 10

Sol Mountain Lodge.

rooms, each sleeping 2–4 guests. Wood-fired sauna with extra "honeymoon" suite above. Large living room and large drying room in the main lodge and a full commercial kitchen. Hot and cold running water, three showers and five bathrooms. WiFi and electricity in the lodge. Children friendly.

Hosts Aaron Cooperman and Dave Flear

Contact information

Box 3, Clearwater, BC V0E 1N0
info@solmountain.com
www.solmountain.com
250-674-3707

Cost Guided and catered, $2225/week; self-guided and self-catered, $1200/week.

Skiing There is a large variety of terrain, including ridges, several peaks and lots of tree skiing close to the lodge.

"The picture that unfolded itself about me surpassed anything else that could be presented to man on earth. I felt as if I were standing on the edge of immeasurable space where mysterious worlds revolve forever and ever. Only a step separated me from the stars. I could touch the moon with my hand; and under my feet I felt the globe of the earth, a slave to the unyielding laws of gravitation, continuing to revolve in its orbit, through the night of universal space."

— *Sven Hedin*

RESOURCES

North American Public Avalanche Danger Scale
Avalanche danger is determined by the likelihood, size and distribution of avalanches.

Danger Level		Travel Advice	Likelihood of Avalanches	Avalanche Size and Distribution
5 Extreme	4 5 ✖	Avoid all avalanche terrain.	Natural and human-triggered avalanches certain.	Large to very large avalanches in many areas.
4 High	4 5 ✖	Very dangerous avalanche conditions. Travel in avalanche terrain <u>not</u> recommended.	Natural avalanches likely; human-triggered avalanches very likely.	Large avalanches in many areas; or very large avalanches in specific areas.
3 Considerable	3	Dangerous avalanche conditions. Careful snowpack evaluation, cautious route-finding and conservative decision-making essential.	Natural avalanches possible; human-triggered avalanches likely.	Small avalanches in many areas; or large avalanches in specific areas; or very large avalanches in isolated areas.
2 Moderate	2	Heightened avalanche conditions on specific terrain features. Evaluate snow and terrain carefully; identify features of concern.	Natural avalanches unlikely; human-triggered avalanches possible.	Small avalanches in specific areas; or large avalanches in isolated areas.
1 Low	1	Generally safe avalanche conditions. Watch for unstable snow on isolated terrain features.	Natural and human-triggered avalanches unlikely.	Small avalanches in isolated areas or extreme terrain.

Safe backcountry travel requires training and experience. You control your own risk by choosing where, when and how you travel.

North American
Public Avalanche Danger Scale

Danger Level		Current Conditions	Know Before You Go
5 Extreme		**Canadian Avalanche Bulletins** www.avalanche.ca	☑ Does your group have the skills, knowledge and training to travel in avalanche terrain?
4 High		**American Avalanche Advisories** www.avalanche.org	☑ Are you carrying transceivers, shovels and probes?
3 Considerable			☑ Can you self-rescue? Do you have a plan?
2 Moderate		Parks Canada Parcs Canada canadianavalanchecentre	☑ Do you know the emergency number?
		caic UAS	☑ Have you checked the current avalanche bulletin and weather forecast ?
1 Low			☑ Have you checked out with someone?
			☑ Do you have any other route options?

You control your own risk.

AVALANCHE TERRAIN EXPOSURE SCALE

Simple (Class 1)
>   Exposure to low-angle or primarily forested terrain. Some forest openings may involve the runout zones of infrequent avalanches. Many options to reduce or eliminate exposure. No glacier travel.

Challenging (Class 2)
>   Exposure to well-defined avalanche paths, starting zones or terrain traps; options exist to reduce or eliminate exposure with careful route finding. Glacier travel is straightforward but crevasse hazards may exist.

Complex (Class 3)
>   Exposure to multiple overlapping avalanche paths or large expanses of steep, open terrain; multiple avalanche starting zones and terrain traps below; minimal options to reduce exposure. Complicated glacier travel with extensive crevasse bands or icefalls.

ATES TECHNICAL MODEL

	Simple	**Challenging**	**Complex**
Slope angle	Generally < 30°	*Mostly low-angle, isolated slopes > 35°*	*Variable with large percentage > 35°*
Slope shape	Uniform	Some convexities	Convoluted
Forest density	Primarily treed; some forest openings	Mixed trees and open terrain	Large expanses of open terrain; isolated tree bands
Terrain traps	Minimal; some creek slopes or cutbanks	Some depressions, gullies and/or overhead avalanche terrain	*Many depressions, gullies, cliffs, hidden slopes above gullies, cornices*
Avalanche frequency (events:years)	1:30 ≥ size 2	1:1 for < size 2 *1:3 for ≥ size 2*	1:1 < size 3 *1:1 ≥ size 3*

	Simple	Challenging	Complex
Start zone density	Limited open terrain	Some open terrain; isolated avalanche paths leading to valley bottom	Large expanses of open terrain; multiple avalanche paths leading to valley bottom
Runout zone characteristics	Solitary, well-defined areas; smooth transitions; spread deposits	Abrupt transitions or depressions with deep deposits	Multiple converging runout zones; confined deposition area; steep tracks overhead
Interaction with avalanche paths	Runout zones only	Single path or paths with separation	*Numerous and overlapping paths*
Route options	Numerous; terrain allows multiple choices	A selection of choices of various exposures; options to avoid avalanche paths	*Limited chances to reduce exposure; avoidance not possible*
Exposure time	No exposure or limited exposure when crossing runouts only	*Isolated exposure to start zones and tracks*	*Frequent exposure to start zones and tracks*
Glaciation	None	Generally smooth with isolated bands of crevasses	Broken or steep sections of crevasses, icefalls or sérac exposure

Using the technical model

Any given piece of mountain terrain may have elements that will fit into several classes. Applying a terrain exposure rating involves considering all of the variables described above, with some default priorities.

Terrain that qualifies under an *italicized* descriptor automatically defaults into that terrain class or a higher one. Non-italicized descriptors carry less weight and will not trigger a default, but must be considered in combination with the other factors.

Calling for assistance

If calling for assistance, indicate that you need a mountain rescue and be ready to relay the following information:

- your exact location (both the name of the tour and a GPS coordinate are best)
- what type of emergency it is and the number of victims
- your name and phone number including area code
- the time the accident occurred

Emergency phone numbers
Glacier National Park 1-877-852-3100 or 911
All other areas 911 and ask for the RCMP detachment nearest to your location.

HELICOPTER SIGNALLING

If a helicopter flies by you, use the signals shown here to indicate whether you need a rescue or not.

CANADIAN AVALANCHE CENTRE COMPANION RESCUE PLAN

See page 350

GEAR

Ski equipment and backcountry gear can be purchased at:

Calgary
Mountain Equipment Co-op 403-269-2420

Canmore
Gear Up Sports 403-678-1636
Valhalla Pure Outfitters 403-678-5610
Vertical Addiction 403-609-8226

Banff

Mountain Magic 403-762-2591

Monod Sports 403-762-4571

Lake Louise

Wilson's Sports 403-522-3636

Fernie

The Guides Hut 250-423-3650

Golden

Dark Side Snow and Skate 250-344-4546

Selkirk Source for Sports 250-344-2966

Summit Cycle 250-344-6600

180 Mountain Sports 250-344-4699

Revelstoke

Valhalla Pure 250-837-5517

Free Spirit Sports and Leisure 250-837-9453

Revelstoke Outdoor Sports 250-837-2525

Nelson

Valhalla Pure 250-354-1006

Snowpack 250-352-6411

Rivers, Oceans and Mountains (ROAM) 250-354-2056

MAPS

Many of the shops listed above will have maps. In addition, here are some online sources:

Canada Map Store Maps

Available only at www.canadamapstore.com

Map Town

Probably the best online resource for NTS and Gem Trek maps

www.maptown.com

Natural Resources Canada, Mapping Services Branch

General information on NTS maps:

www.maps.nrcan.gc.ca/topo_e.php.

Free downloads of NTS maps:

http://ftp2.cits.nrcan.gc.ca/pub/toporama

Selkirk College – Selkirk Geospatial Research Centre

www.selkirk.ca/research/sgrc

Click on the links that lead you to Web Mapping Services and then Kootenay Spatial Data Partnership.

iMap BC
   http://ilmbwww.gov.bc.ca/content/e-services/geobc/imapbc
Backroad Mapbooks
   Available at gas stations, grocery stores etc.
   www.backroadmapbooks.com
Adventure Map Series
   www.chrismar.com

TRIP PLANNING

Weather
www.avalanche.ca/cac Click Pre-trip Planning. This site has links to
   forecasts, satellite imagery, radar, mountain cams, model outputs
   and real-time weather dataloggers.
www.weatheroffice.gc.ca Links to weather warnings, current conditions and forecasts, radar, aviation weather, analyses and model-
   ling, historical weather and more.
www.snow-forecast.com Ski area specific forecasts, including many
   backcountry zones.

Avalanche Bulletins
www.avalanche.ca/cac Click on Bulletins. Links to all public avalanche bulletins in the Columbia Mountains.
Toll-free bulletins, all regions 1-800-667-1105

Discussion Forums
www.avalanche.ca/cac Click Pre-trip Planning.
www.facebook.com/ParksMountainsafety

Mountain Conditions Reports
www.acmg.ca/mcr Conditions reports from the Association of
   Canadian Mountain Guides.

Miscellaneous Planning Resources
Canadian Avalanche Centre
   www.avalanche.ca/cac Click Pre-trip Planning.
   250-837-2435
Highway Conditions www.drivebc.ca

Parks Canada

Glacier National Park
  www.pc.gc.ca/eng/pn-np/bc/glacier/index.aspx
To contact Glacier National Park
  revglacier.reception@pc.gc.ca or phone 250-837-7500
Glacier National Park avalanche and weather information
  250-837-6867
Follow these links for Rogers Pass restricted-area permit information:
  Glacier National Park Home Page>Visitor Information>Winter Permit System Information
Follow these links for Rogers Pass daily restricted-area status:
  Glacier National Park Home Page>Winter Restricted Area Status
www.parksmountainsafety.ca and
  www.twitter.com/ParksMtnSafety

Helicopter Companies

Airspan Helicopters (Invermere) 250-341-3409
Alpine Helicopters (Golden) 250-344-7444
Canadian Mountain Holidays (Banff) 403-762-7100
Coldstream Helicopters (Golden, Panorama) 778-475-6224
RK Heli-ski (Panorama) 250-342-3889, 1-800-661-6060
Yellowhead Helicopters (Valemount) 250-566-4401

Snowmobile Companies

Alpine Country Rentals (Valemount) 250-566-9774
Boulder Mountain Sled Shed (Revelstoke) 250-814-0018
Golden Snowmobile Rentals and Tours (Golden) 250-344-6100
Golden Snowmobile Trail Society (Golden)
  www.snowmobilegolden.com
Great Canadian Snowmobile Tours (Revelstoke) 1-877-837-9594
Kimberley Snowmobile Adventures (Kimberley) 250-427-5501
Revelstoke Snowmobile Tours (Revelstoke) 250-837-5200
Snowmobile Revelstoke www.sledrevelstoke.com
Snowpeak Rentals (Golden) 1-888-512-4222
Toby Creek Adventures (Invermere) 1-888-357-4449

Tourism information

Banff Lake Louise Tourism Bureau
403-762-8421

Travel Alberta
www.travelalberta.com
1-800-252-3782 (within North America)
1-780-427-4321 (outside North America)

Tourism British Columbia
www.hellobc.com
1-800-435-5622

The Alpine Club of Canada
Box 8040
Canmore, AB T1W 2T8
403-678-3200
www.alpineclubofcanada.ca
info@alpineclubofcanada.ca

Glacier Park Lodge [please see note at page 51 re lodge closure]
www.glacierparklodge.ca
1-888-567-4477

Mountain Guides

Guiding and instruction can be obtained through:

The Association of Canadian Mountain Guides
www.acmg.ca

Mark Klassen ACMG/IFMGA Mountain Guide
www.alpinism.com
403-762-3540

INDEX

SOURCES/READINGS

French, R. "Bugaboos Ski Mountaineering." *CAJ* 43 (1960): 76.

———. "Skiers Travel 110 Miles across Mountain Ranges." *Summit* 5 (January 1959): 6.

Scott, C., "High Level Ski Tours." *Polar Circus* 1 (1986): 15.

———. "The Great Canadian High Level Ski Tours." *CAJ* 61 (1978): 1.

———. "Odyssey in the Canadian Icefields." *Nordic World* 7, no. 6 (February 1979): 36.

Smith, Phillip, Ski Traversing in the Northern Cariboos, *CAJ* 66 (1983): 85.

Toft, M. "Two (More) High Level Ski Tours." *CAJ* 65 (1982): 27.

Wagon, S. "The Haute Route." *CAJ* 74 (1991): 52.

"Why should we be in such desperate haste to succeed, and in such desperate enterprises? If a man does not keep pace with his companions, perhaps it is because he hears a different drummer. Let him step to the music which he hears, however measured or far away."

—Henry David Thoreau

SPONSORED BY

COMPANION RESCUE

NEVER STOP EXPLORING™

---

1 **Choose a leader to organize and direct the rescue**
- Be in charge – delegate tasks

---

2 **Assess safety**
- Avoid travel on adjacent slopes or above the avalanche site if this could trigger additional avalanches

---

3 **Head count:** how many are missing?
- Identify the last-seen point; mark if possible and question witnesses

---

4 **Turn all transceivers to Search:** do a physical check

---

5 **Determine the search area:** look for signs of victims on the surface, then start searching below the last-seen point in areas of deposition
Priority search areas:
- Fall line below last-seen point
- In line with clues such as lost gear
- In terrain traps

LAST SEEN POINT

---

6 **Signal search**
- Send one or two searchers ahead
- Use 40 m search strips
- Look/listen to transceiver
- Investigate visual clues
  (pull out of snow; mark if possible)
- Prepare probes, shovels, first aid kit

40m
40m

20m/40m/40m/20m

SINGLE SEARCHER | MULTIPLE SEARCHERS